How to Love
Your Marriage

About the Author

EVE ESCHNER HOGAN, M.A., is an inspirational speaker and educator. She serves as a relationship advisor for several websites, which have included iVillage.com, Dreammates.com, AmericanSingles.com, and JDate.com. She has appeared as a relationship expert on Lifetime Television network, *The Other Half, Iyanla,* and BBC Worldwide radio, and she has been quoted in *Cosmopolitan, Men's Health,* and *Bride.* Her relationship Q-and-A column, "With Aloha," appears in the *Maui Weekly,* as well as online.

In addition to *How to Love Your Marriage,* Eve is the author of *Intellectual Foreplay: Questions for Lovers and Lovers-to-Be, Virtual Foreplay: Making Your Online Relationship a Real-Life Success,* and *Way of the Winding Path: A Map for the Labyrinth of Life,* as well as coauthor of *Rings of Truth.* She is also the senior editor for *Chicken Soup for the African American Soul* and *Chicken Soup for the African American Woman's Soul.*

Eve is the founder of Wings to Wisdom, which offers self-mastery seminars helping people to discover their inner resources, expand their awareness and strengthen their life skills. Eve's specialty is relationship enhancement, whether the relationship is with yourself, your sweetheart, your family, or with God. She also serves as a labyrinth facilitator and wedding officiant, lives on the island of Maui with her husband, Steve, and together she and Steve run Makena Coast Dive Charters.

DEDICATED TO CAPTAIN STEVE HOGAN,
THE CAPTAIN OF MY HEART

You've been persistent, when I would have given up.

You've taken risks, when I would have played it safe.

You've been patient and kind, when I needed it the most.

You've earned my eternal gratitude and undying love,
while simply honoring me with yours.

Thank you for showing me the way.

HOW TO LOVE YOUR MARRIAGE

Making Your Closest Relationship Work

Eve Eschner Hogan, M.A.

Hunter House PUBLISHERS

Hunter House Inc., Publishers
PO Box 2914
Alameda CA 94501-0914

Library of Congress Cataloging-in-Publication Data

Hogan, Eve Eschner, 1961-
How to love your marriage : making your closest relationship work / Eve Eschner Hogan.— 1st ed.
p. cm.
Includes bibliographical references and index.
ISBN-13: 978-0-89793-457-2 (pbk.)
ISBN-10: 0-89793-457-1 (pbk.)
1. Marriage. I. Title.
HQ734.H73 2006
646.7'8—dc22   2006003256

Project Credits

Cover Design Brian Dittmar Graphic Design
Book Production Stefanie Gold/Brian Dittmar
Developmental and Copy Editor Kelley Blewster
Proofreader John David Marion
Indexer Nancy D. Peterson
Acquisitions Editor Jeanne Brondino
Editor Alexandra Mummery
Publicist Jillian Steinberger
Customer Service Manager Christina Sverdrup
Order Fulfillment Washul Lakdhon
Administrator Theresa Nelson
Computer Support Peter Eichelberger
Publisher Kiran S. Rana

Printed and Bound by Bang Printing, Brainerd, Minnesota

Manufactured in the United States of America

9 8 7 6 5 4 3 2 1   First Edition   06 07 08 09 10

contents

Part IV: The Bigger Picture

Foreword

I've known Eve Eschner Hogan for almost twenty years, having first met her when she attended my Self-Esteem in the Classroom workshop. During the day, I led an exercise designed to help the participants gain clarity on their life purpose—who they are and what they are here to do. After the workshop Eve walked up to me and said with great newfound conviction, "I discovered today that facilitating self-esteem workshops is what I am supposed to do with my life; this is my life purpose. How do I do it?" After we talked, she immediately signed up for my Facilitating Skills Seminar and has been conducting life-changing seminars ever since.

One of the most gratifying things as a teacher is to see your students grasp a concept in the classroom and then successfully apply it to other areas in their lives. Eve has been one of those students for me. I have watched her over the years as she has taken to heart the self-esteem and success principles I teach, applied them in her own life, and adapted them to her work with students, teens, parents, entrepreneurs, and now to people wanting to create healthy, fulfilling relationships. She has mastered them, added to them, and expanded upon them from her own experience. She has taken many of the principles and strategies that I have written about in my latest book, *The Success Principles,* and applied them here as successful *relationship* principles. Just to name a few, they are:

- Take 100% Responsibility for Your Life.
- Decide What You Want.
- Feel the Fear and Do It Anyway.
- Ask! Ask! Ask!
- Keep Your Eye on the Prize.

- Embrace Change.

- Transform your Inner Critic into an Inner Coach.

- Practice Uncommon Appreciation.

- Keep Your Agreements.

- Start Now... Just Do It!

Much of my life's work has been dedicated to teaching people about the importance of self-esteem as a necessary foundation for success in every aspect of their lives. *How to Love Your Marriage* emphasizes the reality that in order to love, honor, and cherish someone else, you must first love, honor, and cherish yourself. Working on building your self-esteem is a necessary ingredient for building healthy relationships. Eve has wisely included several steps you can take to raise your self-esteem. One of the powerful tools that I teach is the "Rule of Five." This means that every day you do five things to raise your self-esteem. Every day you acknowledge your strengths, talents, and skills. Every day you practice the mirror exercise to re-affirm your self-love. Every day you work to become more aware of your self-talk and use empowering words and thoughts, instead of disempowering and destructive language. Every day you need to take responsibility for what you are creating and what you are experiencing.

The same "Rule of Five" applies to your marriage. Every day, find a way to serve your partner. Every day, thank your partner for the role they play in your life and the ways that they serve you. Every day, tell or physically demonstrate to your spouse that you love him or her. Every day, engage in a "meaningful moment" filled with either loving touch, loving words, or loving eye contact. Every day, make the choice to love your marriage and choose behaviors that support that goal. If your relationship is truly important to you, make the "Rule of Five Commitment." *How to Love Your Marriage* provides you with a myriad of options for doing so.

One of the other concepts that I teach is "Awareness + Risk-Taking = Growth." We, as teachers and trainers, can share information that will expand your awareness, but you have to take the risks to apply your new knowledge if you want to achieve true growth. *How to Love Your Marriage* offers a wealth of information and steps that can expand your awareness. This book also supplies several exercises—action steps—that invite you to take the risk to love more openly, to communicate more fully, and to tell the truth faster. Eve worked hard to write a wonderful and powerful book full of compassion and encouragement. Now, it's your turn to do the work. Read the book, do the exercises, apply the skills in your relationship—in *all* of your relationships. Start now... just do it! The results are well worth the effort. And remember, be gentle with yourself and your partner, and enjoy the journey.

— Jack Canfield
Cocreator of the *Chicken Soup for the Soul* series
Author of *The Success Principles: How to Get from Where You Are to Where You Want to Be*

preface

Aloha,

I'm Eve's husband, Steve Hogan. I volunteered to write a Preface for *How to Love Your Marriage* because I thought a book with this title and addressing this subject would be incomplete without some kind of statement from the spouse about how our relationship has continued for nearly fifteen years.

When I helped with Eve's other books by doing research, I interviewed many couples who had been married for over ten years. I would talk to them aboard my scuba charter boat while they were visiting Maui, Hawaii. The common thread running through each happy relationship was that both people stated, "We are still friends." I can say the same for Eve's and my relationship. It's not that we always agree or that we do everything together, but we do a lot of things together and we care about what happens with the other's life goals. We also keep reasonably fit so that we stay attractive to each other, even with age creeping in. I have to admit, speaking only for myself, it helps a lot that Eve is intelligent, kind, and always considerate, and it helps that she's cute, too.

We have gone through richer and poorer, sickness and health, and we have managed to stay by each other's side. It is definitely harder in the poorer and sicker times; however, I feel that those times are the proof of unconditional love. I must say also that my wife is one of the strongest people I know when it comes to having unconditional love and reaching a place of understanding—not only for me but also for others whom she loves, that is, her family and her friends. This does not mean she puts up with everything I or others do or say, or that we never argue, but we always manage to find some middle ground and to let go of anger after a short time. We laugh, get silly, travel, and have managed to live where we love to be. I can say that I will always love her, and I know she will always love me, too.

Here's my advice: When you're angry, pause for a while, then discuss what is bothering you. People seem to treat strangers better than the ones they love. Be sure to turn that around and treat the ones you love even better than you treat strangers.

Hope this helps. God Bless.

— Capt. Steve Hogan

Acknowledgments

To my beloved husband, "Captain" Steve Hogan: In addition to all else—and there are so many things to thank you for—thank you for putting up with my sitting in front of the computer for hours and hours a day writing about marriage instead of actively engaging in our time together. I deeply appreciate your support of my work and of me. I love you *and* our marriage.

Special thanks to my mom and dad, Meg and Al Eschner, for showing me what unconditional love and continuous spiritual growth—together—look like. I am humbled to have been raised by such devoted, beautiful souls. I have learned so much from you. This is my attempt to put my observations into words.

Lauralyn Eschner, you are not just my sister, but also my best friend. I don't know what I'd do without you.

Eddy, Wendy, Amy, and Emily Eschner—thank you for your awesome love and inspiration. My prayer for you is that when all the challenges have cleared, simply love will remain. You are my heroes.

Unending appreciation to Ocean Love for your continuous love, compassion, guidance, and clarity. Thank you for showing me truth and love and allowing me to bask in it.

Thank you to Karlene McCowan (and her husband) for allowing us to reprint her inspiring story.

Thank you to Bob Berkowitz for the generous permission to use his sex tips.

Thanks to Jack and Inga Canfield, Lucia Capacchione, Lisa Nichols, Berny and Lynn Dohrmann, Joel and Heidi Roberts, Jim Britt, Jane and Mike Foley, Maryanne Comaroto and David Raynal, Gail Swanson, Suzie and Jonathan Livingston, Kristin and Dan, Cindy and Paul Levy, Julie and Paul Signore, Marji Knowles and

Michael Tibbott, Barbara Smith, Herchel and Lonnie Newman, Bob and Becky Hall, Rik Fitch and Heather Mueller Fitch, Bobbi and Ron Newman, Bruce Moffatt, Laurie and Tim Thompson, Debra Lordan, Keith and Joy Heidbreder, John Thompson, Marvin and Narrye Cohen, Patricia Frostholm and Woody, Sheryl Jai, Janet Kira Lessin, Alf Luechow, Richard and Lee Kaye, Roger and Phyllis Munn, Mace and Sue Perona, Sharon Owens, Sue Peterson, Winnie Brinney, Eddie and Helena Avina, Rabindra Danks, Freidemann Bender, Buck Joiner, Nancy Gilliam, the *Chicken Soup for the African American Soul* volunteer team, and any others who helped with surveys, interviews, endorsements, and spreading the word. Some of you helped directly with the book; some helped me while I was writing the book. Thank you! I apologize if I left anyone out of the acknowledgments in print; you remain acknowledged in my heart!

To the team at Hunter House—Kiran and Jeanne, Kelley, Alex, Christina, Jillian, and the rest—thank you for your continued love and support, and on this one, thanks for your extra patience! I love working with you!

To my gurus, with eternal devotion, love, and gratitude.

Important Note

The material in this book is a review of information on creating and maintaining healthy marriages. Every effort has been made to provide accurate and dependable information. The contents of this book have been compiled through professional research and in consultation with professionals.

The skills, tools, and exercises provided in this book are meant to educate the reader and should not be considered a substitute for professional help when warranted. The publisher, authors, and editors, as well as the professionals quoted in the book, cannot be held responsible for any error, omission, or dated material. If you have questions about the application of the information described in this book, consult a qualified professional.

All names have been changed to protect the identity of the people who participated in the research for this book. Any similarities to real people with the same names is coincidental.

introduction

We waste time looking for the perfect lover,
instead of creating the perfect love.

TOM ROBBINS

Many people think that the secret to marriage is *finding* the love of your life. While important, that is only one step. Of equal if not greater importance is *creating* or maintaining the love of your life from that moment on. Whether you just got married or have been married for fifty years, there are things you can do to grow closer to your mate, to love more deeply, and to have a healthier relationship. As the title implies, *How to Love Your Marriage* offers tools, skills, information, and exercises for doing so.

Virtually every marriage—even the best of them—hits a "wall" when things get tough. Over the years a marriage may encounter several of these challenging times. When the moments of truth occur you have to either do something to mend the marriage or suffer—in the marriage or out of it. In my own experience and based on what I've gathered from interviewing couples who have achieved loving, lasting marriages, when two people manage to see their way through the wall of difficulty—for better or for worse—what awaits them on the other side is a beauty, a depth, a trust, a friendship, and an intimacy that are well worth the effort. In fact, without the difficult times it is unlikely that we would experience the personal growth necessary to achieve the same depth of connection and understanding. So in a strange sort of way, it is a good thing that bad moments come along.

The core of my training has been in enhancing self-esteem. I have found that the secrets to loving oneself and the steps to loving one's marriage are very closely aligned. Throughout this book you will be shown the connection between loving yourself and loving your partner, and by the end of the book you will be empowered to do both more fully. The more your relationship with yourself improves, the more your relationship with your partner will improve, or at least change. Thus, the book focuses heavily on you, on what you are doing (or *not* doing), and on what you can do to improve yourself, your marriage, and your life.

The Courage to Love

We are taught at a very early age to start thinking about "when we grow up and get married," and yet we are not taught how to find the mate of our dreams, how to determine what is important and what is not, or how to keep that love alive and thriving.

They didn't teach us in school what we need to know about how to create joyful and lasting love. Relationships permeate every aspect of our lives—school, work, home, romance, and family—and they consume a huge amount of our time and energy, whether the energy is spent trying to get into one, trying to get out of one, or trying to maintain one. The quality of our relationships is critical to our livelihood, our success, our happiness, and our sense of joy. Yet they left "relationships" out of the three R's (reading, writing, and 'rithmetic) that were identified as the critical building blocks of our education. Unless a successful marriage was modeled for us, we were pretty much left on our own to figure out how to build one. Consequently, marriages are often a roller-coaster ride more akin to a soap opera than to the fairytale "happily ever after" scenario for which we thought we were signing up.

> **Did you know?** In a National Institute of Education study, one thousand thirty-year-olds were asked if they felt their high-school education had equipped them with the "skills they needed in the real world." More than 80 percent answered, "Absolutely not." The number-one skill they wished they had been taught was relationship skills.

If the 21.3 million viewers who were drawn to the premiere episode of the hit television show *Desperate Housewives* are any indication, things are pretty desperate. Oprah did a show on the *Desperate Housewives* phenomenon in which participants in the audience confessed that they were "just like" various characters on the show and it wasn't until they saw the show that they were able to see themselves—and what they were doing to their marriages—clearly. Men and women are tuning in and seeing dramatized variations of themselves portrayed on television. We haven't been taught to look at ourselves. We haven't been taught to look at our marriages. We are far more skilled at judging others than evaluating, and improving, ourselves. Not only have we never been taught these skills, but we have also become lazy about learning them. We want love to work all by itself, but unfortunately love is not enough.

When you stop to realize that statistically the odds of making a marriage work are slim, that most of us have friends and family whose marriages have fallen apart, and that many of the images of marriage we have been subjected to are negative, it is impressive that we keep saying the vows, holding the hope, and aiming for everlasting love. In fact, in light of the odds, getting married is a courageous act. Courage is not the absence of fear; to do something you are not afraid to do requires no courage at all! Courage is to move forward *in the face of fear*. Marriage is courageous because we get married regardless of our skills and regardless of the images, statistics, and role models we have been exposed to. We go forth holding an expectation that we can create something better, that our marriage will be satisfying and fulfilling; we go forth believing that we can make our closest relationship work. And indeed, we can. However, to be able to do what we haven't yet done, we need to gain some new skills and tools. We have to make the quality of our marriages a priority. *How to Love Your Marriage* will expand your repertoire of options to draw from for making your marriage work—and joyfully at that!

Since we are constantly growing and changing, our skills need to continuously expand as well. This book will activate your creativity, allowing you to respond constructively to the different stages of your relationship. Just like a garden needs maintenance as it grows, love needs our attention in order to thrive and stay strong. When you feel as though the grass is greener on the other side, you need to water your lawn. This book provides the necessary tools for keeping your marriage nourished and growing, and for making it more beautiful.

A Matter of Choice

I come from a line of marriage "lifers." My parents were married for over fifty years, my great-grandparents for over sixty, my grandparents for fifty-five, and my aunt and uncle for fifty. Growing up with these role models of loving and lasting marriages has caused me to ponder—and practice—the ingredients that make relationships work.

In their seventies, my parents were one of those couples you'd see walking down the street holding hands. You could tell they were still in love. They met on a blind date and had a long-distance relationship before they married. They were together for over five decades, until my mother got A.L.S. (Lou Gehrig's disease), which rendered her unable to walk, talk, eat, or move her arms. Yet in her last days her eyes still said, "I love you," and my father still took her for daily walks in her wheelchair, holding her hand at every opportunity. He even moved her hospital bed next to his bed so he could hold her hand as they slept.

They passed a lot of their relationship sense along to their children; just growing up with parents who weathered the storms, solved problems, and celebrated life together was inspiring. But when I was graced with the opportunity to help my dad take care of my mom during the last months of her life, what I observed was invaluable. My parents constantly focused on what really mattered, even in the midst of grief, stress, ill health, and exhaustion. They managed to create a sense of joy, and they honored their devotion to God and to each other right up to the last minute. Dad didn't take care of Mom out of duty or because he'd said he would more than fifty years earlier in his marriage vows. He took care of her by choice.

The relationship between husband and wife is an exceptional one in that it is a relationship of choice. Unlike other family relationships, getting married is a choice, staying married is a choice, and loving your marriage—your mate and yourself—is also a choice. Honoring, protecting, and committing to your union is not a choice you make only once; it is a choice you make consciously and repeatedly over time, perhaps every day or even several times a day.

However, it seems to be a choice that we as a society aren't making very well. In the United States, marriages have only a 40 to 50 percent success rate (which translates to a 50 to 60 percent *divorce* rate). Although several factors impact relationships—such as improved women's rights, financial independence for women, social acceptance of divorce, increased awareness and intolerance of domestic abuse—it is also true that we used to rely much more heavily on parents, matchmakers, spiritual leaders, and community members in helping us choose our partners; as a team we and those close to us put a lot more thought into what makes a match. Now we typically pick our partners based on "looks good" and "feels good," without taking the time to see if the match really *is* good. We tend to rely on the mysterious and elusive elements of attraction and chemistry rather than taking into consideration values, religion, family, and practical matters such as finances and raising children. While it is seemingly unromantic to take such a practical approach to love, there is absolutely nothing romantic about divorce. We would be well served to put a bit more thought—intellectual foreplay—into our choices, to ask more questions, and to pay more attention.

Interestingly, in arranged marriages (in which parents pick their son's or daughter's marriage partner) there is the expectation that the marriage *will* work. Rather than entering into a marriage as two people who are already in love and hoping that love doesn't die (as Western couples typically do), couples entering arranged marriages are generally not yet in love. They work from that moment forward *to create love* between them. We can learn from this concept.

How would our marriages be different if we entered them with the intention of *continuously growing the love we share with our spouse*—rather than just honoring a love that already exists or once existed? How would our marriages be different if we entered them without considering divorce an option? The powerful element here is the sense of responsibility it gives us; the implication is that there are things *we can do* that will *cause* us to love our marriages. Indeed there are!

I am treating this topic as if divorce is not an option that you want to pursue, and thus the entire focus of the book is about how to improve what you have. Divorce, however, is an option. Divorce is a choice, just like marriage is. It is also the result of choices, whether made consciously or unconsciously. This book will take a careful look at the choices you can make prior to and instead of divorce in a concerted effort to avoid that harsh reality.

My Personal Experience

I began my work in the arena of personal growth when I was teaching school in the late 1980s. I took a class on how to raise self-esteem in schoolchildren from Jack Canfield, cocreator of the Chicken Soup for the Soul series and author of *The Success Principles.* Prior to Jack's class, I thought that my job was to teach *subjects,* like math, English, social studies, and science; after Jack's class, I realized that my job was to teach *children.* With that momentous shift in understanding, I began teaching my students empowering concepts, such as positive thinking, communication, responsibility, and relationship skills. In class I would often hear the kids talk about what their other teachers were saying and doing. So while I tried to teach the children how to protect their self-esteem from the impact of other people's words and actions, I began teaching workshops for educators to help teachers understand esteeming and empowering principles, so that we could work together as a team. In a sort of domino effect, I also realized that to truly help my students I had to teach their parents as well, so I started offering self-esteem workshops at night for the parents. Relationship issues emerged in those classes, and I began applying the principles to marriages so the parents could work better together in creating a harmonious home. I also offered self-esteem workshops for entire families to assist them in creating a common vision and recognizing each person's contribution to the family.

> **Consider this:** If you were told you only had a 40 to 50 percent chance of surviving the next five years, you'd likely do everything in your power to save your life. You would read books, seek professional help, change your diet and exercise routines, seek out support groups, and very likely revitalize your spiritual life. If you were told the same about your marriage's survival chances, would you just sit back and watch to see what happens?

At about this time, I met a wonderful man while I was on vacation on Maui. We spent a week becoming acquainted and then spent the next five months on the phone between Hawaii (where he lived) and California (where I lived) getting to know each other better. Wanting to make sure we were deciding wisely since one of us would have to relocate if we chose to be together, we asked each other a lot of questions about values, interests, goals, spirituality—everything! We coined the term "intellectual foreplay" for this process and began writing a book by the same name. The book is full of questions for people to ask each other—both prospective partners, so they can make wiser decisions about whom they get involved with, and people who are already in a relationship, to help deepen the communication and intimacy between them.

Although the process of intellectual foreplay helped my husband and me make a great choice in each other, there were still some challenges ahead. After we got married, things went really well for the first few years. I had a lot of adjusting to do since I was in a new place; had a new job, husband, and friends; and lived nearly three thousand miles away from my family. Although I had been teaching personal growth, self-esteem, and self-mastery to people for several years, about three or four years into our marriage I needed a serious dose of my own medicine. I suddenly found that I was resisting being married. I started feeling controlled, as if I were no longer in charge of my own life, and as if I had few, if any, choices. I didn't like the feeling. I began resisting everything my husband did and said, and I started thinking about getting out. Of course, at the time, I thought it was my husband's fault. After all, it was what he was saying and doing that was making me angry; therefore (I reasoned), it was his fault that our marriage was strained. I felt like I had fallen out of love, and I didn't believe I could get it back. In my mind the marriage was going downhill fast, and I had no hope for saving it (because I couldn't imagine that he was going to change).

My husband, on the other hand, probably didn't even know what hit him. We'd been getting along well. We'd each done our homework in picking a partner we were compatible with. We'd waited until we were in our thirties to get married (both for the first time). We had everything going for us, so he undoubtedly couldn't figure out why the honeymoon was suddenly over. When I thought about leaving the marriage, I felt trapped. We owned a house together, we had a dog and a cat and a business together. We weren't *supposed* to get divorced! Our lives were entwined, and I angrily believed I was stuck.

One night, after hours of tossing and turning, I jumped out of bed and walked through the house to look at all that was keeping me "trapped." As I looked at my home and the things that filled it, I realized that I could leave the house and everything in it to him. There was nothing important enough to keep me in an unhappy situation. I could leave the business to him. I could even leave the dog and cat with him. I could walk away from it all just to be done with it; none of these things were reason enough for me to stay. Then, in the wee hours of the morning, as I stood looking at all I was willing to walk away from, I realized that I was still standing there. I could have walked out the door right then because all my excuses for staying had just been resolved. But something was keeping me there. Something else—not the house, business, pets, or any other thing—was stopping me from leaving my marriage.

Suddenly, I didn't *want* to leave. This was a whole new feeling. Until then I had been blaming all the outer reasons for why I *had* to stay and thus was missing the inner reasons for why I *wanted* to stay. I believed in marriage. I believed in love. I knew my husband was a good man and that we had common values. Just a few years earlier I had loved him so much that I'd moved away from all the other people I loved. Maybe, just maybe, I was still there because I still loved him. Maybe love hadn't really gone away; it was just being blocked. Maybe I hadn't given him or my marriage my best shot. All I had taught others about taking responsibility for the quality of their lives loomed over me, and I knew I had not been holding up my end of the bargain.

I deeply believed, and taught, that the people and circumstances in our lives are not what creates our experiences or our feelings. Rather, our *response* to the people and situations we encounter is what creates the way we feel and experience our lives. I had learned this principle many years earlier, in my studies with Jack Canfield. He taught the equation "Event + Response = Outcome," or E + R = O. People and circumstances fall into the "event" category. (This concept is discussed in depth in Chapter 2, where I have added "solutions" to the end of the formula to make it the EROS equation, a prescription for restoring love.) As I pondered my marriage early that morning, I realized that I was blaming the "event," blaming my husband, for all I was experiencing in our relationship rather than taking responsibility for how *I* was *responding* to him, how I was responding to being married, how I was showing up as a partner. I was blaming the event for the outcome instead of transforming the outcome by changing my responses.

Although it should have been obvious to me much sooner, I felt like I had been slugged in the stomach with this awareness. I didn't immediately want to embrace the thought that perhaps everything I had been blaming him (and blaming our house, business, pets, vows, etc.) for was really my responsibility. At the same time, I felt an amazing sense of power in the recognition that if the problem was actually *my* doing, then the solution was in my hands as well. Of course, there were things my husband could have done differently, and some of the issues I raised were certainly valid, but I had the powerful realization that I needed to *respond* to him differently and to *handle* those issues differently. It occurred to me, based on the material I had been teaching for years, that if I responded to him differently, he would automatically respond to me differently, and thus we would *both* be changing the way we were showing up in the relationship just because *I* was showing up differently. I didn't have to enroll him in saving our marriage; I just had to make it my own personal goal.

I sat on my living room couch as my husband continued to sleep in the bedroom, unaware that our lives had been teetering on the edge of major change all night—first negative and now positive. I began to feel like there was hope after all. Maybe I could take this little spark of love hidden deep in my heart that I believed was the real reason I remained in the marriage and fan it once again into a full flame. Was it really possible? How long would it take? How long was I willing to give it? As I pondered these questions, I decided I would give myself six months to transform my relationship, to fall back in love. If

I couldn't do it in six months, I would again open the door to the possibility of leaving, but until then divorce would not be an option. I had six months to find another way. This could not be six more months of unhappiness and resistance; it would be dedicated to bringing out the elation in my *relation*ship.

I used the equation Event + Response = Outcome & Solutions as a guiding principle, and the "outcome and solution" I wanted were clear. I wanted to fall back in love with my husband and to make our marriage into a healthy and thriving partnership. I wanted to love my marriage again. The "event" (my husband) was not in my control to change, so I set about taking a deep look at my "responses." I realized that all my responses to him—all my thoughts, words, and actions—needed to be aligned with the goal I was seeking: love. Anything that failed to move us in the direction of love was not the response I wanted because it didn't lead toward a positive solution.

Once again my husband probably didn't know what hit him—only this time it was a good thing. I didn't tell him what I'd decided. I didn't tell him that I was trying to save our marriage or even how close to ending it I had come. I felt that if I told him or expected him to overtly participate in the six-month transformation, then it would mean I was still hoping the "event" (my husband) would change. I truly wanted to test this principle by seeing if I really held the power to change the outcome—to change my marriage—by only changing my responses. I wanted to know if this stuff really worked.

So I began to be self-observant, paying attention to what I was saying, doing, and thinking. I began to choose words, thoughts, and actions that were in alignment with my goal. I began to practice what I preached. The funny part was how different my husband looked when I looked at him differently! Lo and behold, the honeymoon began to return. The love began to flow between us again. The elation in our relationship returned and our partnership was restored. It didn't even take six months, and he didn't have to actively participate. He did participate, though, because it was also his goal to make our marriage work. In fact, I don't think he ever lost sight of that goal. He participated by responding positively to the new and improved situation.

Whenever we hit a rough moment, I reset my intention on the goal and made the choice again to align my thoughts, words, and actions with loving my marriage and accepting my partner. As I said earlier, this is not a choice that is made only when we first agree to marry or when we say, "I do," but a choice that we make continually, thousands of times throughout the marriage. It is a choice I continue to make every time I find myself annoyed or frustrated.

Many years have passed since that challenging time, and our relationship continues to strengthen. What I have found on the other side of the "wall" is a depth, a trust, and a respect in both my husband and our marriage that I am not sure I ever would have encountered if the marriage hadn't been put to the test. When I talk with other couples who are making their closest relationships work, they recount similar experiences. Surviving challenging times makes the relationship stronger—and makes surviving the next challenges easier. A healthy marriage is always a work in progress.

Love doesn't go away. It just gets blocked with negative experiences, comments, thoughts, and beliefs. When we learn how to remove those obstacles, to let go of the past, to move beyond our egos to the heart of the matter, and to align our actions with our goals, we can reawaken the love or keep it alive and thriving.

Now, Let's Get Real about Who Should Use This Book and Why

If you just got married and want to learn how to keep your love alive, or if your marriage is just not quite what you want it to be, or if you've hit a bump in the road and you want a little tune-up or a jump start, great! This book is for you. Or maybe someone gave you this book as a wedding or engagement gift or you came across it on a list of suggested reading, and you are wondering why you should bother since everything is fine in your marriage. Perhaps you are in the planning stages of getting married or are in a long term, serious relationship. Let me assure you, learning these skills now can save you a lot of heartache, make your relationship thrive, and empower you to continue to create the love of your life.

If you are a "desperate housewife" (or husband) or are dealing with bigger issues of deep discontent, lack of trust, or fear, then, no joke, you have some work to do—first on yourself, then on your marriage. The task ahead is not necessarily going to be easy. For you, doing the necessary work may be "tough love," but it will be the best thing you have ever done for yourself—and for your marriage. Learning this material is what you are here to do; your relationship is difficult so that it can provide you with extra motivation to learn and grow. It is not an accident that this book has found its way into your hands. Until you learn and master this work, you will likely see the same patterns repeat themselves in your relationships.

I don't want to gloss things over as if working through this material is going to be a piece of cake. This book will confront your beliefs about yourself, your spouse, and your marriage. It will ask you to stretch your personality to try new things. Most of all, it will ask you to take total responsibility for what you are experiencing. That, guaranteed, is the hard part. It is also the good part. When you take responsibility, you realize your personal power. When you know your power, you hold the ability to experience love, joy, and happiness—either because of your marriage or in spite of it.

Love Tip: If we needed to know math, we would take a class and study. If we needed help typing, we would buy software and practice. When our love life or interpersonal skills need improvement, we need to utilize the resources and tools available to us, learn new skills, and practice them. The reward is more love—a worthy goal indeed!

Although this book is full of information that will assist you, simply reading it will not be enough. Exercises and questions are presented throughout the book that you will need to take the time to answer—whether through silent contemplation, by writing in a journal, or in discussion with your spouse. Don't be lazy when it comes to love! If all you do is read the words contained within these pages but do not practice what you learn, you will simply be someone who "knows better." If you truly want to love your marriage, you will need to put what you learn to use—again and again and again. By doing so you will not simply "know better"; you will *be* better, and so will your marriage.

Making the assumption that only one partner is reading this book, I will primarily be speaking to you about what you can do *on your own* to love and restore your marriage. Although working on a marriage is always preferable when both partners are interested and willing to do what it takes, you can make major improvements all by yourself. Included thoughout the book are opportunities to share exercises and information with your spouse. If he or she is not willing or interested, or if you are not ready to do the work with your spouse, do the work alone anyhow. Your partner's inability or lack of desire to participate need not stop you from taking action to improve the relationship.

Love Tip: Everyone is at a different stage of evolution, readiness, and understanding. What you gain from an experience may be totally different from what your partner gains. Trust that although your path and your partner's may be different, you can be in different lanes on the same highway, see totally different things, and still enjoy the journey together.

What You Will Find
Within These Pages

Whether you are reading this book as *prevention* (happily in love with your marriage and wanting to keep it that way) or as *cure* (wanting to save a marriage that is teetering on the edge), it will give you not only hope but also concrete, practical steps you can take immediately to bring out the elation in your *relation*ship. You'll discover tools for creating the relationship you desire, and you'll gain insight into how to love your marriage, yourself, and your mate. The principles, skills, and tools contained in these pages are applicable to every aspect of your life. As you master them in your marriage, you will find the effects rippling outward to enhance other areas of your life. You will be empowered through the "how to" steps you can take—even if your partner is unwilling to take them with you—and you will learn skills for removing the obstacles that block love from flowing.

How to Love Your Marriage is divided into four parts. In Part I, "It's All about You," you will be given skills, tools, and concepts to help strengthen, educate, and prepare you for either restoring the love in your marriage or maintaining it. The skills provided in this section are essential in helping you to better handle any situation you may face. Chapter 1 outlines ten primary relationship principles that are the underlying foundation of this work. In Chapter 2, you will discover the EROS formula for making powerful decisions that lead to loving, lasting relationships. Chapter 3 will help you to identify your values and goals, both as individuals and as a couple. As you gain clarity and insight into these, you can use them to guide your actions for years to come. In Chapter 4, you will gain an eye-opening understanding of the impact of self-esteem on your relationship and the impact of your relationship on your self-esteem, and you will learn what to do to improve these interdependent connections. Having this understanding can deeply shift the way you look at yourself, and it can also assist you in seeing your spouse and children in a different light, allowing you to better guide them. Chapter 5 provides you with a tool for assessing your self-esteem and your marriage. As you become more aware of the specific areas that need attention, you will be able to set goals and take action toward improvement. Chapter 6 shares essential life skills for applying all the information you've gained to issues that may come up in your marriage.

When we are in a relationship, all of our skills and everything we know get put into practice—and put to the test—especially when it comes to emotions. Emotions are tricky because they may have nothing to do with the current moment, but rather can be triggered by a past memory or a fear about the future. Personalities, past experiences, emotions, fears, and egos are all dancing around in our conversations and interactions, often making it challenging to sort out what the real issues are and how to handle them. Part II, "Working as Two," will guide you though the mire of emotions that get triggered in relationships and will provide tools for managing your, and your spouse's, emotions. Chapter 7 focuses primarily on handling the fear of events that *may* happen and the changes arising from specific events that *have* happened or which happen naturally over time. Chapter 8 looks at the integrity agreements we have with each other and at how to express and manage the guilt and anger we feel when these agreements are broken. The chapter speaks to the critical importance of communication—especially in the midst of difficulties—and will assist both spouses in becoming more "emotionally available" and better able to hear and receive each other's emotions when either is hurt or upset. The art of "intellectual foreplay"—asking questions, showing interest, developing curiosity, and sharing yourself—will be introduced to help you deepen your conversations and make them more intimate.

Part III, "Playing Together," is all about the fun parts of a relationship: romance, love, and physical intimacy. So often in marriages the very thing that brought the couple together in the first place begins to disappear over time. Chapters 9 and 10 will help you to reignite the love and passion between you and your partner or keep it burning eternally. Suggestions for romantic and sexual encounters are provided. When it comes to making your spouse feel loved, cherished, sexy, and desirable, the littlest things can often make the biggest difference.

In Part IV, "The Bigger Picture," we take a step back and look beyond the marriage at the larger issues of family and spirituality. Chapter 11 serves two functions. If you have children, grandchildren, nieces, or nephews, it will show you how to apply all of the concepts in the book to raising healthier, happier children. The earlier they learn these skills and become familiar with these concepts, the better equipped they will be for creating loving relationships with their friends, families, future sweethearts, and, most importantly, with themselves in the form of self-esteem. This chapter also serves as an excellent review of the book and offers a different application of the material, so even if you don't have children or don't plan to have children, it will still provide a deeper understanding of the concepts you have been studying. Chapter 12 looks at marriage as a spiritual journey and explains that beyond the goal of creating a healthy, loving relationship is the recognition that mastering relationship skills and mastering spiritual skills are one and the same. Learning these skills is critical to our life purpose and our sense of well-being, joy, and happiness. Doing so also improves our relationship with God (If the term "God," which is used periodically throughout this book, is not fitting for you, feel free to substitute wording that better suits your experience: Goddess, Spirit, the Universe, the All That Is—whatever term you prefer for a higher power. Please don't let the words get in the way of the message.) Our marriages provide us with the perfect workplace and playground for developing as individuals and deepening and strengthening our spiritual lives.

As you have already seen, strewn throughout the book are "Love Tips." You can use them immediately, both in the context of the information surrounding them and as a daily inspiration for loving your marriage, by simply thumbing through the book and reading the Love Tip you land upon. To make them even easier to find, they are accompanied by the marker shown below:

You will also find question-and-answer letters from my advice column, "With Aloha," which runs in the *Maui Weekly* newspaper as well as on several websites. Not all of these are about marriage, but they are all about relationships and interpersonal skills. They are located where they will support the surrounding text while illustrating how to apply the concepts to real-life situations. I've also included advice from other people who love their marriages. They share perspectives of what works—and what doesn't.

Throughout the text you will also find exercises, activities, or sets of questions for you to answer. These are the practical steps that will help you put all of this information to use in your own marriage.

Recognizing that this journey might not be easy for you, it is with compassion that I invite you to venture into the pages of this book and into the depths of your soul. You will discover new things about yourself, develop new skills, gain new tools, explore a new intimacy with your spouse, and find a new depth to your ability to love, honor, and cherish.

About to be wed and wondering

Dear Eve,

I'm about to get married, and I'm wondering what it takes to make a marriage not only last but also thrive. I don't want to be another divorce statistic.

Aloha,

Congratulations! I had a conversation on this very topic with my parents right after they celebrated their fiftieth anniverary, so I'll share with you both my perspective and theirs. Making a good choice in a partner and being a good choice as a partner are always excellent starting points. This requires using both your head and your heart in the process of courtship. It is also why I recommend practicing "intellectual foreplay": asking and answering questions, and exploring each other more deeply than "looks good" and "feels good." Intellectual foreplay is the preparation for an intimate relationship that includes communication focused on discovering each other's values, interests, and goals.

Here are a few of the things that are required for making a marriage/relationship work:

1. Remember that love is not jealousy, envy, sabotage, belittling, or hurting the other person. Those emotions and actions are based in ego. Rather, love is communication, support, honoring, and concern for the other person — and doing these things unconditionally. Whenever you find yourself reacting to your partner in a way that is not based in love, you need to take a deep breath, regroup, and make a new choice.

2. Remember that your goal is a lasting, thriving, growing love. Love is a "process goal," not a "product goal." By this, I mean it is a state we aim to maintain rather than one we aim to reach. When we lose sight of this goal, we unconsciously choose behaviors that lead us toward resentment, anger, hurt, and pain, instead of love.

3. Recognize that what you say, think, and do results in the quality of your relationship. Make sure that all your actions, words, and thoughts are in alignment with your

goal of a healthy, happy relationship. Too often we resort
to blaming someone or something else for our problems
rather than taking responsibility for how we respond to
that person or that situation. How you feel is a direct
result of what you are thinking. Rather than looking
outside for the source of your problems, look inside for
the source of your solutions.

4. Look for ways to grow together rather than ways to
escape. My parents explained that, for them, getting a
divorce was never even a thought. Just as most of us do
not ever consider murder or suicide as a solution to a
problem, they never considered divorce. Instead, they
turned within and to each other to find mutually agreeable
solutions, all the while holding the other person's happiness to be as important as their own.

5. Look at everything that happens as an opportunity for
your growth. Your challenge is not to "live through it,"
but rather to find ways to "love through it"!

I wish you the best in the next phase of your adventure
through life.

With aloha,

Eve

PART I

IT'S ALL
ABOUT YOU

For one human being to love another:
that is perhaps the most difficult of our tasks;
the ultimate, the last test and proof,
the work for which all other work is
but preparation.

RAINER MARIA RILKE

CHAPTER 1

The Relationship principles

Love one another and you will be happy.
It's as simple and as difficult as that.

MICHAEL LEUNIG

My goal in writing this book is to help you achieve *your* goals as they relate to living joyfully and lovingly. In this case, I'm making the assumption that you are reading this book because you think (or at least hope) that your marriage has a chance of being loving and joyful. This book is about taking a realistic look at where your marriage is now and where you want it to be, and about doing everything you can to bring out the elation, or joy, at the heart of your relationship. This book is *not* titled *Why to Stay in a Marriage That Makes You Miserable* or *How to Leave an Abusive Spouse*. Those are different topics. Rather, loving your marriage involves loving yourself, loving your mate, and treating your marriage as an entity (almost like a child) that needs protection, attention, and nurturing in order to grow strong and thrive.

To love your marriage you are going to have to *want* to love your marriage. You have to want to love it enough to read this book, do the exercises, practice the principles, and apply the skills. When things are going reasonably well and the marriage just needs some extra oomph, the task is not so tough. However, some of you are dealing with recovery from infidelity in your marriage. Some of you are managing with limited time, little or no money, children who demand your energy, or ill health—challenges that make everything difficult. Some of you are dealing with partners or children who have terminal or chronic illnesses, or with other circumstances that test your strength and all you believe in at every turn. Some of you are dealing with spouses who are abusive or who are totally "emotionally unavailable." Some of you are dealing with low self-esteem and are abusive or emotionally unavailable yourselves. Some of you feel trapped. Some of you are jealous and possessive or have partners who are control freaks. Some of you have relatives or friends who are meddling in your marriage. Some of you are abusing mind-altering substances that interfere with your perspective or have a spouse who is doing so. Some of you are at your wits' end, reading this book as a last-ditch effort with only a glimmer of hope in your heart. If any of these scenarios are true for you, you definitely have some work to do and some hard decisions to make. And yet, here you are reading this book, which means to me that you *want* to make your marriage work.

If you are in a marriage that you are honestly not sure you want to stay in (or are sure you *don't* want to stay in) or that your partner doesn't want to stay in, this book will *still* help you. As I discovered in my own marriage and as I shared in the Introduction, one partner has the power to save a marriage. However, one partner can also end it, so this work may not save your marriage. But it will save *you* by strengthening you, teaching you skills, and providing you with tools that you will be able to apply during the upcoming changes in your marriage and beyond. If the relationship does stand a chance, this material will definitely give it that chance. If getting out of the marriage is what is next for you, this material will help you gain clarity and will fortify you for that next step.

If you are in an abusive marriage or one in which your (or your children's) safety and well-being are in jeopardy, immediately seek support, safety, and shelter, and *then* read this book. Please do not think that this material is implying that if only you did more, or if only you were better, the marriage would be okay. Abusive partners— whether men or women—need help. There is simply no excuse for inflicting physical or emotional pain on one's family. However, deciding what to do about the situation you are in (and then doing it) *is* your responsibility. Making sure you protect yourself and your family and fortifying yourself so that you don't allow yourself to get into a situation like this again is also your responsibility. Even though your partner may be or may have a problem, you are the one *with* the problem since you are the one married to your spouse. Thus, you are the one who needs to do something.

As you read on, you may think that I am implying that everything is your fault because I am telling you that everything you experience is your responsibility. Here is the difference between "fault" and "responsibility." Fault is about who is to blame for the past. Finding fault is useless because there is nothing that can be done about the past. Responsibility is about having the power to change your present moment and your future. Responsibility (response + ability) is about having the *ability to respond* to life's circumstances in such a way that you are able to transform your life and your marriage. However, if your spouse were the one reading this, I would be telling him or her that everything he or she experiences in the marriage is *his or her* responsibility and that he or she has the power to change it. Whoever is the one wanting change is the one with the responsibility to change—oneself or the situation.

Responsibility is a beautiful thing because it gives you power; so, yes, I am saying that everything you experience is your responsibility. I am saying that you are powerful, and I want you to know it and feel it, and to use that power to bring more love and joy into your life and your marriage.

The scenarios of what goes on—and what goes wrong—within marriages are too numerous to address individually. Rather than being a manual on "when this happens, do this . . . ; when that happens, do that . . . ," *How to Love Your Marriage* offers principles, tools, and skills that will help you handle *any* situation, regardless of what it is, in a way that is in alignment with your values, and that leads you toward the goals you desire. That is a big, bold statement about the power of this work, but the truth is that we aren't working on your *marriage;* we are working on *you.* As you gain strength, insight, and the ability to respond more effectively to life's circumstances, you will be empowered to tackle any of the myriad variables that come up in a marriage. Let's start with some new principles and a common understanding.

The Ten Relationship Principles

The following relationship principles are the foundation of this material and are recurring themes throughout the book. They are introduced here and are explained more fully in the coming chapters. Whether you want to love your marriage, yourself, your children, your job, your body, or your life, these relationship principles will come into play. However, if this is your first exposure to them, they may be a little daunting. This is usually true whenever you begin to wrap your brain around new concepts.

Since your marriage is in the domain of your heart, it would serve you and your goal of loving your marriage to "listen" with something other than your ego. I encourage you to read through these principles not only with your head but also with your heart and soul. When we read with our intellect alone, we compare what we are reading with what we already know and either agree or disagree based on whether or not there is a match with our existing knowledge. When we do this, we don't learn anything new; we just reinforce what we already believe. We inadvertently block new wisdom from coming in when the new information challenges previous beliefs that may have been ingrained in us since childhood. Since these principles may challenge your ego, it is in your ego's best interest to try to dispute them. However, if your old beliefs and behaviors were adequately serving you, you probably wouldn't be reading this book. In order to learn something new and create something different, you may be called upon to let go of, or challenge, old beliefs—as well as your ego.

Read the principles slowly, hold the possibility that they are true, and try them on to see how they feel. Let the meaning of each one sink in before moving to the next. Hopefully you will begin to adopt them as a foundation for everything you do.

Principle number one:
Relationships are a process, not a product

Life is a great big classroom and relationships are our teachers. We are here (in human form) to learn, love, laugh, and serve. Every experience we have is geared to present us with an opportunity to gain more compassion, practice acceptance, transcend our egos, maintain our sense of humor, and expand our wisdom. The goal of marriage is not just about achieving the end result, or "product," of "forevermore," but rather is about improving the "process" of how we are showing up, what we are learning, and how we are growing. It is about the quality, not the quantity. Although we certainly want our marriage to last, more importantly we want it to serve each partner's personal and spiritual growth.

Principle number two:
Every effort you make will benefit you

If you practice and master the skills presented here, you may save your marriage and make it healthier, stronger, and more enjoyable. It is also possible that you or your spouse will decide to get out. *You need to do the work either way.* The benefit of gaining these essential life skills is that you will achieve greater self-mastery and will be healthier and happier—even if your relationship doesn't continue. These skills will follow you into every situation and will serve you in every relationship throughout your life.

Principle number three:
Your values act as guideposts for your decisions

Every problem can be solved by more than one solution. However, not all solutions will be in alignment with your authentic self. For example, if your goal is to have lots of money, you could take up robbing banks. However, for most people this is not an option because it is out of alignment with their values. To be in integrity with who you really are and what you really want to create, you will need to consciously make choices that are guided by your values. To allow your values to guide you, you will need to determine exactly what they are. In a relationship it is not necessary that your values be exactly the same as your partner's, but it is important that your values be complementary and supportive of one another's and that you respect each other's priorities. If your goal is to love your marriage, identifying and operating within your values will guide you with integrity.

Principle number four: Ego is *always* what blocks love and joy

True love does not go away—ever. It just gets blocked from flowing (by ego). An active ego shows up in the need to control and in the need for approval. It materializes in relationships through nagging, sarcasm, judgment, disappointment, jealousy, possessiveness, hurt, and fear. When you dislike what you are experiencing in yourself, in your marriage, or in your life, this state of mind blocks the flow of love and joy. As you learn to transcend your ego, you can restore the flow of love in all of your relationships. Your job, if you want to restore a loving marriage, is to remove the obstacles that dam the flow of love between you and your partner.

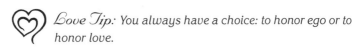 *Love Tip:* You always have a choice: to honor ego or to honor love.

Principle number five: You are the common denominator in all of your relationships

You are a primary ingredient in every relationship you're in. How you handle things—what you say and what you do—enhances or destroys the quality of those relationships. If you lack a strong sense of your worth, you will find ways to sabotage your relationships. So if you want to have healthy, loving relationships with others, including your spouse, you need to start by building a healthy, loving relationship with yourself.

A big part of building a strong relationship with yourself is the discovery (or rediscovery) of your authentic self, what I refer to as your soul essence. Our souls *are* love; they are loving, lovable, and joyful. At the soul level we are creative, funny, honest, wise, intuitive, and spiritual. These are critical qualities for successful relationships. The more in touch you are with your soul essence, the healthier your relationships will be. The more you know yourself and love yourself, the more authentic you will be in your self-expression. The more authentically you show up, the more authentically someone can love you (because they will actually know who you are).

Principle number six: You can only change yourself, but doing so influences others

You cannot change your spouse (or your kids, boss, parents...). You can, however, change the way you *relate* to your spouse, which will in turn trigger a new response from him or her. *Your spouse will change in relationship to how you treat him or her.* Whenever you are faced with a difficult situation, instead of pondering how your partner needs to change, ask yourself what *you* can do differently to change the situation.

Principle number seven: You are responsible for your experience in your relationships

It is our natural inclination—especially in relationships—to blame the other person when we are not feeling loving, loved, or joyful. However, as I've mentioned, ego is always what blocks love, and transcending the ego to restore the flow of love and joy is our personal responsibility. In fact, it is not something our partners can do for us. We have to do the work ourselves. The work may come in the form of negotiation, communication, acceptance, or forgiveness, but the job is our own. Although you cannot directly change your partner, you can change your relationship by changing the way you show up in it.

Principle number eight: Self-observation is the key to change

By observing yourself (noticing what you are doing, thinking, saying, and feeling in any given moment), you will become aware. When you are aware, you are given the golden opportunity to determine whether or not you like what you are aware of, and whether it is serving you. If you do not like what you are thinking, doing, or feeling, your awareness allows you to make a new choice—one that is in alignment with your goals and values. Choice makes you powerful. When you are powerful, you can transform your relationships rather than being a victim of them.

Part of the self-observation process is self-inquiry. When you observe an emotion that is impacting you, taking yourself through a series of questions to better understand what is triggering the emotion will help lead you to the limiting or even false belief that is causing you pain. Self-observation and self-inquiry are essential skills for understanding yourself and relating more effectively with others.

Principle number nine:
Change can (only) happen in a moment

When you want to change something—your fitness level, your organizational skills, the quality of your relationship—it is overwhelming and self-defeating to try to change the entirety of the situation at once. You cannot improve your fitness from this day forward, but you can, in any given moment, change how you care for your fitness *in that moment*. While you cannot change the entire quality of your marriage from this day forward, you can change how you care for and handle any given moment in your marriage. Each transformed moment connects to the next moment and the next. By simply paying attention to how you are handling each individual moment, you can change the quality of the whole relationship.

Principle number ten:
Relationships are a spiritual journey

Regardless of your religion, or even if you don't subscribe to any particular set of religious beliefs, the qualities generally called upon to live a spiritual life—honesty, compassion, forgiveness, service, devotion, dedication, intention, trust, unconditional love—are the very same qualities needed to have a healthy relationship. At the same time, relationships are the perfect place to develop these qualities. In fact, relationships are the only way we can practice and master these qualities, because by their very nature they are applied and experienced *with* someone else—whether that be God, your spouse, your friends, your family, or strangers.

The larger point is that there is a greater purpose to gaining these skills than simply keeping your marriage together—which is, of course, a wonderful and worthy goal. Our "spiritual job" as humans is to master these skills for the ultimate relationship: our relationship with the Divine. Again, this requires surrender of the ego. Although this book is not a "spiritual" book per se, the skills required for loving your marriage are, indeed, spiritual skills.

Why Do the Work?

There are many reasons to do this work, even without your spouse's participation. The first and foremost is because *you want* your marriage to work; *you want* to love your marriage. How do I know? Because you are reading this book. That is a good enough reason to get started, but that is just the little picture. Again, the big-picture reason is because relationships—marriages in particular—are the perfect "classroom" for mastering what you are here to learn. They provide the ideal way to learn how to—

- increase your capacity to love

- resolve problems

- achieve self-mastery and the ability to enjoy your life

- accept others for who they are

- love yourself enough to know where to draw the line

- gain wisdom

- honor integrity agreements

- enhance compassion

- transcend your ego and align your actions, thoughts, and words with your true essence, your authentic self

- experience your relationship as a spiritual journey

These reasons are critically important because even if you are unable to make your marriage work (after all, it does take two to tango), by attaining these skills you will be learning to make your *life* work. These skills will go with you into any situation and any relationship—work, family, or romance—and will allow you to know your own power and strength. Relationships are the ultimate spiritual path; they grant you the means to transcend your ego, open your heart, awaken your spirit, and meet another person heart to heart.

A "working" marriage is not defined simply by how long it lasts. The future is tough to predict or control. Rather, "a relationship that works" is one in which you are able to transform any given moment into a healthy one. A "healthy relationship" is one in which the partners are aware of their own behavior and can self-adjust when what they are doing, saying, or thinking is building an obstacle to love. The goal is to clear the path of ego obstacles so that love, compassion, forgiveness, kindness, honesty, respect, and acceptance can grow and thrive in the environment of the relationship.

When you have done all you can to support, nurture, and nourish your marriage or partnership, you will feel inner peace and love, regardless of the result. And, chances are, when you have done all you can to love yourself and your mate, he or she will feel that power and will respond in kind. If you have children, not only will every ounce of effort you put into self-mastery be rewarded through your relationships with them, but you will also see the benefit reflected in their enhanced self-esteem. You will be modeling skills that will serve them throughout their lives.

Love Tip: We commonly think it takes two to love, but it really only takes one. It takes two people to have a relationship. When you "get" the distinction between these concepts, you will realize that the love you seek is already yours. To have the relationship you desire, you must then share that love with another.

So Why *Wouldn't* You Do the Work?

One word can describe why you wouldn't choose to do the work involved in learning to love your marriage, yourself, and your mate: Fear. Fear of loss. Fear that you can't do it. Fear that you will rock the boat. Fear that your partner won't show up for you. Fear that it is too hard. Fear that it is too late. Fear that it will take too long. Fear that you will do it wrong. Fear of being alone. Fear of spending your life with the same person. Fear of starting over. Fear of failure.

Fear is often viewed as a weakness or something to be embarrassed about—as an admission that we can't "handle it." If fear is allowed to rule your life, perhaps that concern would be true. However, fear also serves a beautiful purpose that is rarely if ever recognized. *The beauty of fear is that it reveals that which you most value and treasure.* Just behind fear is something you want to preserve and protect, something you honor and appreciate.

When you are afraid to do something that could endanger your life, fear reveals the value you place on living. When you are afraid you are going to lose someone, fear reveals how much you value that person, or that relationship, or companionship in general. When you are afraid you can't do something, fear reveals the importance you place on competence, doing a good job, and doing what you say you'll do.

When you are afraid to love and to share your heart and soul with someone, the fear may be revealing the value you place on feeling balanced and free of pain and drama (although your method of achieving that result may be *causing* pain and drama). Fear of rejection reveals how much you value being appreciated and accepted. It also reveals the importance you place on holding onto hope—hope for lasting love.

 Love Tip: When trying to avoid pain, be sure that what you are choosing instead isn't even more painful.

Once you look beyond your fear to what is really important to you, you are given the opportunity to choose what to honor: fear, or that which fear protects—love, peace of mind, safety, friendships, and relationships. When you realize what you really treasure, your approach to a situation can be entirely different. Rather than facing a relationship filled with fear, you'll face it full of appreciation for love and well-being, two totally different perspectives from which to move forward. When you recognize what it is you are trying to protect, you can use that information to go toward your goals with a conscious plan for how to protect what you value, rather than letting fear paralyze you. When you shift from honoring your fear to honoring what you value, you shift from internal weakness to personal power.

A Matter of Honor

Fear stands for *"fantasized experiences appearing real."* What you fear isn't happening to you now, so if fear is stopping you, realize that you are imagining the worst and are allowing your imagination to stop you. If fear is stopping you from doing what it takes to love your marriage, yourself, and your mate, you have some choices to make:

Are you going to honor fear or love?

Are you going to honor despair or hope?

Are you going to honor doubt or faith?

Are you going to honor stagnancy or growth?

Are you going to honor unhappiness or joy?

Are you going to honor deception or honesty?

Are you going to honor anger or compassion?

Are you going to honor resistance or acceptance?

Are you going to honor ego or spirit?

Are you going to honor complacency or commitment?

Are you going to honor resentment or forgiveness?

Are you going to honor your relationship as a spiritual journey?

Are you going to honor your marriage?

Are you going to honor yourself?

The choice is yours.

 Love Tip: Learning to *"love like you've never been hurt"* is a preferable task to dealing with the hurt of

never being loved or, worse yet, never truly loving. Discover
ways to approach each new opportunity with an open heart and
an open mind, ready and willing to expand, learn, grow, and ex-
plore.

Fear is the number-one thing that stops us from opening our
hearts fully to another human being. If you choose to honor fear, remember that fear will stay with you. It will stay in your life whether
your partner does or not. If you want success, if you want to shake the
fear loose, you are going to have to take some risks: the risk to love
completely, the risk to forgive and to ask for forgiveness, the risk to
accept your partner as he or she is, the risk to tell the truth, the risk to
do the work. Make a conscious choice to honor that which is hiding
behind your fear: love!

Wife wonders why she should change for him

Dear Eve,

I think my husband is bored with me. We have been together
for ten years and have a two-year-old daughter, and I love
him very much. But he goes out with his friends, cheats
on me (three times that I know of), and says he feels
trapped. I don't understand why I should "transform" for
him. He is the one who is messing around and who refuses
to talk. Please help me.

Aloha,

If you look at your relationship from the viewpoint of
your ego, the answer to the question "Why should I change
for him?" is, "You shouldn't! He's the one screwing up.
He's the one damaging the relationship." From this viewpoint you will be very justified in blaming him and expecting him to do the changing. However, you will also be
very disappointed in the results because you have no control over making him change. The only result will be the
death of the love in your marriage.

If, instead, you look at your relationship as your very
own personal/spiritual growth class, then the answer to

that question becomes something very different. If your
goal is keeping him and staying married, the question
becomes, "In what ways do I need to transform in order to
meet my goals?" It may seem as though you are doing it for
him, but you are really doing it for you. Or maybe your
personal goals have to do with establishing and protecting
your boundaries. If this is the case, you need to determine the kind of treatment you are willing to accept, and
you need to take action in alignment with that goal. It
may be that your goal is to practice unconditional love
and forgiveness, in which case you are smack dab in the
middle of the perfect situation. If your goals don't
involve keeping him, you still have to transform yourself,
but the transformation will likely lead to your leaving
the marriage. Ultimately, what you need to do is decide
what you want. Then, do a careful self-analysis to see if
your actions, words, and thoughts are in alignment with
those goals.

I encourage you to consider what you want from several
different viewpoints. Ask, "What does my ego want?" Egos
tend to want to "put people in their place," "teach him a
thing or two," or prove that we are "right." Egos are also
the number-one obstacle to love, so exploring your ego's
thoughts will be very helpful in recognizing what may be
damaging your relationship. Also ask, "What does my heart
want?" Then explore, "What do I want as the mother of my
child?" Then, "What do I want (or need) in the way of my
spirit's well-being or from my self-esteem's perspective?"
From this viewpoint you may find a part of yourself that
is begging you to make a stand for yourself or make some
sort of life change, like going back to school or joining
the gym or taking up a hobby or becoming more dynamic (for
yourself, and, as a by-product, for your husband). It may
be that although your spouse's method is unkind, his mission is to give you a jump start toward putting some spark
back in you life.

If you pretend that you are the only one in the marriage
capable of making changes and that the entire marriage can
transform if you figure out what needs transformation in
yourself, you may find all kinds of empowering opportunities that you weren't aware of before. For instance, you
may discover an attitude that you want to alter, a tone
of voice that you want to stop using, a negative or blaming mindset that you want to eliminate, a lackadaisical

approach to your physical being or fitness that could use improvement, or a possessive or mistrusting quality that doesn't serve you or your marriage. Although making these changes for yourself may or may not transform your marriage, doing so will definitely transform you into a more powerful, joyful, masterful, purposeful being. There is very little chance that your marriage would not be affected by such a shift in you. After all, you are a primary ingredient in your marriage!

Ultimately, an unhappy relationship often reveals that which we need to take care of in terms of our personal growth. As we do the work on ourselves, the relationship will either improve or it will end. In other words, as long as we do our part in improving ourselves, we almost don't have to fret over the decision about whether to leave or stay; the situation will take care of itself. The moral of the story is: Do the work on yourself and the relationship will change.

I wish you the best.

With aloha,

Eve

♡ *Love Tip:* When what we are doing isn't working, we have to do something different. Remain open to the possibility that the "something different" is something you've never tried before, or that it won't make sense until you do!

The EROS Equation

Circumstances don't make the man, they reveal him.

JAMES ALLEN

E ros was the god of love in ancient Greece; thus it is fitting that the EROS equation is the formula that can lead you back to love in your marriage—and in all other areas of your life. The EROS equation is definitely a tool you will use over and over again to restore, revitalize, and maintain the love in your marriage, so I heartily recommend adding it to your relationship tool belt. In fact, I've included it near the beginning of the book because it serves as a foundation for all the material yet to come. By understanding the EROS equation, you will be empowered to transform your marriage and your life.

You've Got the Power

Typically, and perhaps naturally, people think that events, circumstances, and other people are responsible for their experiences. We blame our kids when we blow up. We blame our husband or wife for our unhappiness. We blame our job for our lack of income. We blame our parents for the way we turned out. We generally look outside of ourselves to find a source of blame for our problems and thus expect something outside of ourselves to generate the solution.

We think we would be happy if only.... *If only I were married. If only my spouse listened to me. If only I had a bigger house. If only the kids would behave. If only my spouse were more open and communicative. If only I were single. If only I had another child. If only the children would move out. If only I had more money.* There are a million things we think would make us more joyful, if only the world and other people would cooperate with our desires!

The truth is, however, that events and other people alone are not what create our experience. As long as we are giving other people that power, we feel like victims. As long as you think that your husband or wife is responsible for what you are experiencing in your marriage, you will feel powerless. This is where the EROS equation comes in.

The EROS equation is
Event + Response = Outcomes and Solutions.

What E + R = O & S means is that events (people and circumstances) alone do not create the outcomes you experience. Events *plus* your responses to the events are what create the outcomes and solutions you experience.

An event is simply *what is;* we have very little—if any—control over the events of our lives. We are generally powerless to change events because the minute they happen they are in the past, no longer changeable, and they are often a result of other people's behavior, over which we have no control. As long as we are trying to change the event, we are powerless. Where we do have power is in our ability to respond to that event. By choosing a response that is in alignment with the outcome we want to bring about, we make ourselves very powerful.

> ♡ *Love Tip:* Bring your creativity into all aspects of your life. Your life is your canvas, and you are the artist. If you don't like the painting you've created, use creative license and change it. Make your life—and your love life—a masterful work of art!

The Choice Is Yours

Let me give you an example of how this works. A few years ago on my birthday, my husband was taking me out to dinner, so we got all dressed up. Since we live on Maui, I was wearing several beautiful flower leis that friends had given me. On the way to the restaurant, he wanted to stop at the hardware store to pick up something. When we left the store, we walked past a hotdog kiosk as the worker was closing up shop. Just as we were passing, she unplugged the water hose that connected her cart to the spigot. Apparently she hadn't turned the faucet off, because a surge of water gushed out of the wall and onto my husband and me. It was like she'd aimed a fire hose in our direction. Being ever so quick, my husband ran away from the wall of water, while I, not realizing what was happening, hesitated for a moment before moving. So of course I got drenched. The girl turned off the water, and he and I stood there, stunned. Since it all happened so quickly, we went into a strange sort of altered state in which we slowed down and were able to make a conscious decision about how we wanted to respond instead of just reacting the way people normally do. Getting sprayed by water was the event, and what we were trying to determine (without realizing it) was the response we were going to choose, which would make or break the quality of our experience: the outcome and solution.

One of us suggested that we should be indignant and demand something from the hotdog stand, but the other pointed out that a lifetime supply of hotdogs wasn't going to serve us very well since I didn't eat red meat and my husband ate few hotdogs. Then we considered yelling at the girl for being so stupid, but she was really young, and if we'd had a teenage daughter who'd made such a mistake we wouldn't want people treating her poorly. Then we discussed how we "should" be really angry, but it was my birthday and I didn't want to be angry. Coming up with no other suitable ideas that would create an outcome we wanted, we decided to respond by laughing about it and going home to change clothes before setting out for the restaurant again. That is exactly what we did, and we ended up having a wonderful evening—and a funny story to tell.

The event was getting sprayed by water. The response was to laugh and change clothes. The outcome and solution were an enjoyable evening.

I am sure you can imagine how that evening could have gone in a very different direction if we had chosen a different response. We could have chosen to become angry, and the result would have been to get in a really bad mood. We could have insulted the girl and made her feel horrible. I could have responded by blaming my husband, since it was his "fault" we were at the hardware store in the first place. He could have criticized me for not moving out of the water faster. In short, we could have escalated the whole event into a series of horrible outcomes. The point here is that the event was the same either way; it would not have changed. The only thing that changed the outcome we experienced was how we chose to respond to the event.

Although our experieince had a surreal quality to it due to our momentary shock, the truth is that we all have the option to choose how to respond to every situation presented to us by life (or by our partners, friends, family, etc.).

This recognition of choice is the very quality that allows someone to take a really challenging circumstance like rape, illness, or a physical handicap, overcome it, and end up making huge contributions to society with the wisdom he or she has gained. Someone who does not understand the power of choice ends up feeling like a victim of life's circumstances. Powerlessness takes over and depression sets in. The result is *not* caused by the event; it is caused by the individual's *response* to that event. We are responsible for the outcome we create and for the solutions we shape.

In relationships, this equation, Event + Response = Outcome and Solution, is particularly powerful. The "event" can be looked at as your partner's beliefs and behaviors. Thus, the Other Person + Your Response to the Other Person = Your Experience. We have no control over another person and his or her behavior. *Our power lies entirely in our ability to choose our responses to the other person or to the event.*

Let's take some time to apply the EROS equation to your life. As mentioned in the Introduction, when you come across a heart like the one below, it is a signal that an exercise is being offered, or a question is being posed, that will help you gain deeper mastery of the topic. Although merely contemplating the topic or the activity will certainly hold some value for you, taking the time to write in a journal about your thoughts and/or taking the time to do the activities, either alone or with your spouse, will give you an even greater understanding of yourself and your spouse, and will offer greater insight into your marriage.

EXERCISE ∼ *Think about any situation that has happened in your life. How did you respond to it? What other responses could you have chosen that would have created different results?*

What about in your marriage? Think of any situation between you and your spouse in which you could have chosen a different response and created an entirely different outcome. ∼

When you look back at previous relationships and at situations within your current relationship with the EROS equation in mind, you start to see things you might have responded to differently, thereby creating a different outcome. This process can be a bit uncomfortable at first, possibly even upsetting. You may find yourself getting a little irritated with the EROS concept because you start to see that you are responsible for all the things you have been complaining about—even if it is just a matter of being in the situation in the first place. Also, the word "responsible" reeks of "fault," and that doesn't feel good. As I discussed in Chapter 1, I encourage you to look at responsibility differently. This isn't about finding fault; this is about finding power—not power over other people but power over yourself, your choices, your experiences, and your future. When you let the idea settle in a little, it is actually exciting! Using the EROS equation, you have the power to bring love back into your marriage.

Love Tip: In order to take a "new approach" you have to know what your "old approach" was. Practice self-observation to identify what you are doing and what you aren't doing so that you can make adjustments.

Putting EROS into Practice

We really have only four response options when an event happens or when we encounter a behavior we don't like in another person:

1. We can **negotiate** to change the other person's behavior or the event.

2. We can **resist** the other person or the event and stay in the relationship.

3. We can **accept** the other person's behavior or the event and stay in the relationship.

4. We can **get out** of the relationship (or change the nature of the relationship).

Each of these response options leads to a predictable outcome, as illustrated in the chart on page 41.

While it may be easy to see multiple choices when the situation is as simple as getting sprayed with water, let's look at the what the response options mean and how they work in the case of a more difficult event than getting sprayed by water—one that might affect you on a daily basis. Let's use as the event the example that my husband doesn't do dishes.

EVENT: Husband doesn't do dishes.

Negotiation

Negotiation is an effort to change future events or the other person and is a valid place to start. In this case, I can certainly start by asking my husband to help with the dishes. However, he doesn't enjoy doing dishes and doesn't want to do them; therefore, it is very possible that my request will not be honored—but it is still worth a try.

How you approach negotiation makes a great deal of difference in its chances for success. Be sure to be specific about the problem and how it affects you, and offer alternatives or solutions. Remember, the idea here is to *solve* the problem, not complain about it. This means no passive-aggressive behavior, nagging, or attempts at manipulation, but rather an honest and open negotiation for change. Although we have no control over what another person chooses to do and people do not change easily, sometimes people do change their behavior upon request. Depending on what you want changed,

RESPONSE OPTIONS AND OUTCOMES

EVENT	+ RESPONSE	= OUTCOME/SOLUTIONS
What is	Your thoughts, words, and actions	The result: Your experience and your feelings
What happens or What your partner (or another person) says and does	1. Negotiate. Attempt to change the "event" or the other person's behavior.	A. A change of behavior for future events B. No change of behavior (Either result leads you to response option 2, 3, or 4)
or Circumstances life presents	2. Resist "what is" and stay in the relationship. This often looks like nagging, sarcasm, judgment, and criticism, but it can also be much more subtle: rolling the eyes or casting them downward, heavy sighs, a total lack of expression, or even silence.	Blocks the love in the relationship Fighting, arguing, discontentment, resentment, hurt feelings, lowered self-esteem, depression, apathy, or passive-aggressive behavior. Little chance of living "happily ever after"
	3. Accept "what is" and stay in the relationship.	Compatibility, contentment, love Potential for living "happily ever after"
	4. Get out. Remove yourself from either the relationship or the situation.	No relationship with current partner (or a change in the nature of the relationship)

negotiation may work if you are explicit about what you are trying to accomplish.

Negotiation can be as easy as saying, "I get upset when I climb into a bed that's damp and cold from the wet towel left on it all day.

Could you please put the towel on the rack in the bathroom when you're done with it, or leave it on *your* side of the bed instead of mine?" You presented the problem and a statement about how it made you feel, along with a possible solution. Your partner may not even realize that he or she was leaving the towel on the bed, and this simple request could raise his or her awareness and bring about change. If, instead, you say, "You are really making me angry by leaving your wet towel on the bed; knock it off," you will likely cause your partner to be defensive, which will create little desire to cooperate. In any case, this kind of response on your part will not lead to a greater experience of love (the goal, remember?). Your response makes all the difference in the outcome and the solution. Be sure to align the way you speak with the result you are hoping to bring about.

Before you even attempt negotiation, it is wise to practice some self-observation and evaluate your motives. Are you asking your partner to change because the issue is really important, or are you just trying to establish control? Be honest with yourself. It may be that all that is necessary in order to restore happiness is for you to let go of the issue. For example, on the occasion when my husband *has* put the dishes in the dishwasher but has not done it the way I think it "should" be done, I have had to stop and ask myself whether it really matters and have had to admit that it does not. It is far more important that I appreciate his efforts than it is to correct him with my perception of the right way of doing things—especially since there isn't really a "right way" and a "wrong way"; there are just "my way" and "his way." A good policy to remember if you're going to give "constructive criticism" is to first ask yourself if it is purposeful to tell the other person. Is it in support of their highest good and that of the relationship? Are you willing to help them through their hurt to a more positive place? These issues are discussed in more detail in Chapter 8, "Managing Emotions and Communicating Clearly."

In your efforts to negotiate, you may encounter challenging situations in which a mediator, such as a counselor or a therapist, would be helpful as a facilitator of communication between you and your partner. Sometimes, the things we want our spouses to address are deeply imbedded behaviors, a lack of consideration or thoughtfulness, or major differences in values that aren't easily changed. There are also things that your partner may not want to change or may not believe he or she can change. At times, the expectation that the other person *needs* to change can hurt their feelings or cause them to get defensive. When we think our concerns will hurt the feelings of someone we love, we often suppress the information, and it comes out in other ways—little barbs, teases, hints, and resentment—that can hurt them even worse. The whole scenario can leave you feeling powerless because, again, you have no control or power over the event or the other person.

Knowing your own values really helps, not only for negotiating with a partner but also in knowing what you are and are not willing to change in yourself at a partner's request. We will look more at values clarification in the next chapter, "The Guideposts."

Love Tip: Relationships require negotiation and compromise; however, the one area that should never be compromised is self-respect.

Resistance

When we opt not to try negotiation or when it doesn't work, a common response is to resist "what is." Resistance takes place when we don't like something and yet choose to stay in the relationship anyway. When we go into resistance, we get locked into control battles in which there are no winners. By "resist," I mean we get upset about the behavior or situation or complain about it; we may even try to deny that it is the way it is. This choice (which we usually don't recognize as a choice because it is generally what we do automatically) often results in nagging, barbed comments, sarcasm, ridicule, putdowns, arguing, and fighting, all of which lead to unhappiness. Some people internalize their resistance to what is by quietly suffering, blaming themselves, believing that they are bad, helpless, or deserving of the poor treatment, or finding subversive ways to fight back.

For them, resistance can lead to lowered self-esteem, depression, apathy, or passive-aggressive behavior rather than overt agression. Some people slip into a quiet resistance that is not obvious until their anger and resentment explode in a way that may seem extreme in the context of the current situation. Their anger may be "slow to boil," but when it does, watch out!

The choice to resist the other person always leads to blocking the flow of love in the relationship. When we begin resisting the other person—withdrawing our affection, making sarcastic comments, casting put-downs—it shows we are hoping that the other person will "get a clue" and change his or her behavior. *Resistance is really an unskilled attempt to negotiate for change.* We think if we drop enough hints or criticisms, the other person will "get it" and behave differently. It very seldom works this way! Usually the person being resisted just gets angry, and then finds ways to get even. Resistance leads to resentment and resentment leads to revenge. Because we focused on changing the other person or the event, we have once again been rendered powerless.

In the example of the dishes, resistance on my part would mean that I refuse to accept the reality that my husband doesn't do dishes by thinking I can change that reality. I would make sarcastic comments, maybe put him down in front of other people, and criticize him at home. The more I resisted, the more angry and resentful I would become and the more angry and resentful he would become. We would be no closer to having the dishes done, and now we would also be angry at each other. The expression of love between us would be damaged—*not because my husband didn't do dishes, but because I choose to respond with resistance.*

Responses to an event that are based in ego always block love. Let me repeat that. *Responses to an event that are based in ego always block love.* Ego by its very nature generates responses that are based in fear, judgment, control—whether covert or overt. Any time we think we are right and the other person is wrong, our ego is intervening. Any time we think we know what is better for the other person, our ego is showing up. Any time we are feeling judged or hurt, it is our ego reacting. To stop reacting from ego, we must learn about other aspects of ourselves that are more powerful, more authentic, and more in alignment with what we are trying to create (loving relationships). The chapters ahead will guide you to discovering or reinforcing these aspects of yourself so that you are better able to create the outcomes and solutions you desire.

♡ *Love Tip:* Take a look at your attitude and ask yourself whether it is contributing to your well-being or detracting from it. Is your attitude building obstacles or clearing them? Then, realize that attitude is a choice.

Acceptance

The third response option—acceptance—doesn't mean that the situation is necessarily your preference, but simply that you accept the fact that it is *what is.* You don't have to like the effects of gravity to accept that gravity *is* a reality. You don't have to like the president to accept that he *is* the president. You don't have to like that your spouse does something, or doesn't do something, to accept that it is so. If instead you were to accept the fact that changing your spouse is not in your realm of power (remember, that's trying to change the event rather than the response), you would be much better off.

Acceptance is easy when the other person is doing things the way you want him or her to or has complied with your negotiation efforts. Acceptance gets harder when you think the other person *could* change what is, or rather that they *should* change and be different.

When the other person is unwilling or unable to change, acceptance requires changing *yourself* instead of changing him or her. After all, it may not really be in the other person's best interest to change because the consequences they are creating may be the exact life lessons they need to encounter in order to grow on their path. Who are we to say what is right for another person? The challenge we must deal with is the impact the other person's behavior has on us. By accepting *what is,* you are free to make a decision about what *you* want to do about it. You may decide to stay in the relationship, continuing to explore ways to make things better and addressing the issues with a solution-focused attitude. In fact, when you move into a state of acceptance, you are better able to see more possible solutions.

> *Love Tip:* When you find yourself in conflict, take a deep breath and let go of your need for control and your need for approval. Take another deep breath and accept what is; let go of resistance. Then, look for solutions outside the influence of your ego. Allow your creativity to solve the problem.

So, back to the dishes. As long as I am resisting the reality that my husband doesn't do dishes, I am still trying to find a way to get him to do them, and this becomes the only solution I can see to my problem. Consequently, I am miserable (and, undoubtedly, so is he). As soon as I accept the fact that he truly doesn't do dishes, my energy shifts into finding another outcome and solution. As soon as I stop energizing my belief that he is wrong, as soon as I disengage from the control battle to get him to change, I start to see other options. For instance, I can just accept that I am the one who does the dishes and that he handles other things I don't like to handle, for example, mowing the lawn, maintaining the car, fixing things around the house. Such a state of affairs has been recognized as "division of labor" throughout the centuries, and it is certainly possible for me to accept it as an alternative. Or I can begin using paper plates. Or I can hire a housekeeper. Or I can delegate dishwashing to the kids (in our case, it would have to be the neighbor's kids). Or we can eat out. Or we can do a combination of these options. The point is that as soon as I stop resisting and accept what is, a bunch of other options emerge that I couldn't see through my resistance.

The reality is that whether I am accepting or resisting, my husband still doesn't do the dishes. The event doesn't change; only my experience of our relationship changes.

> *Love Tip:* Rather than looking outside for the source of your problems, try looking inside yourself for the source of your solutions.

Getting Out

If you want to stay in the relationship, doing so from a place of acceptance of the other person can lead to a healthy and loving solution. However, even if you accept the fact that a certain event took place or that the other person is the way he or she is, you may still find it unacceptable to stay in a relationship with him or her. Your fourth option is to get out.

While it is unlikely that my husband and I would get divorced because he doesn't do dishes, it is certainly possible that we could end up getting divorced over the anger, fighting, and hurt feelings that would erupt if, at the end of each meal, day in and day out, I resisted the fact that he doesn't do dishes.

If you decide that getting out is the response option you are going to choose, it is important to stress that you still need to first accept what is. If you decide to leave your spouse over something you are resisting, your resentment, anger, and hurt will get lodged in your system and you will carry these emotions with you into future relationships. This is because you are still stuck on thinking that the event should change (or that your former spouse should have changed). The outcome will be that you will remain angry and the hurting will continue. You will likely resist anyone who does anything that remotely resembles your spouse's behavior, and the cycle will start all over again with your trying to change the next event (or person). Acceptance will set you free of this relentless sequence.

Don't get me wrong: You don't have to accept the behavior *in your life*, but you do have to accept that this behavior is what is. For instance, if your partner is gambling uncontrollably, you don't have to accept being married to a compulsive gambler as your lot in life, but you do need to accept the reality that your husband or wife is a gambler. When you are not accepting, you are focusing on trying to change the event rather than utilizing the opportunity to figure out what to do about it. The behavior may not be right for you, and you may not *think* it is right for him or her, but you are not responsible for that part; that is the event. As long as you keep focusing on changing the event, you will only create a negative outcome. If you want the outcome to be positive, switch your focus to your response. Believe it or not, when you shift into acceptance, you may even be able to come to peace with your partner's behavior as the perfect stimulus for you to learn something really important about yourself.

 Love Tip: When in doubt, take responsibility.

When I am really taking responsibility for my experience, I can see that I am actually the one who *trained* my husband *not* to do dishes! After all, he did dishes as a bachelor until I moved in, but I had watched my mom do the dishes every day, so whenever he got up to take his dishes to the sink I would say, "It's okay, I'll do them," and let him watch TV instead. *Voilà!* In just a little bit of time *I created* a husband who didn't do dishes!

Partner reads porn

Dear Eve,

I had a boyfriend who loved to read and look at different kinds of porn or erotic magazines. He bought them every month. He also liked to stare at women when we were out together, but he always said he loved me. I told him it hurt me when he acted that way and that I felt I didn't measure up. He told me I should get over it and that it was normal for a man to act that way. I eventually broke up with him.

Why would a man need those magazines and be interested in gawking at other women when he had me?

Aloha,

This is a perfect situation to which to apply the EROS equation: Event + Response = Outcome and Solutions. This formula shows that your power lies not in trying to change the events but rather in changing your responses. Hope-fully, understanding how to apply the equation to this particular situation will help you to create a different result when you encounter it again—which you probably will, because your ex-boyfriend is certainly not alone in his interests and because getting rid of the boyfriend didn't really get rid of the whole problem.

In this case, your boyfriend's interest in looking at erotic magazines and at other women is the event.

What makes you feel like you don't "measure up" isn't his looking at the magazines and the women; it is what you think about yourself on account of his looking at magazines or other women. It is your response, not the event, that makes you feel the way you do.

In my own experience, I have come to the conclusion that the real problem here is a self-esteem issue — not his, but mine; not your boyfriend's, yours. What I mean is that if I felt completely comfortable with my body and my level of fitness, I would not have the same reaction when my partner looked at other women's bodies. I may still dislike it, but the part that flags a self-esteem issue is the feeling that you/I don't "measure up."

Basically, you have four choices about how to handle this situation, few of which involve getting him to stop his behavior.

1. You can negotiate. This means that you can respectfully let him know how you feel and request that he stop. However, it sounds like you tried this and it didn't work. Attempting to get someone else to change his behavior is worth a try, but it seldom works (unless the person wants to change). It is important, however, to notice how you have communicated with him about your feelings and how you have gone about making the request for change. Sometimes people think they have requested change from their partner, but upon further investigation they discover that they have pouted or have gotten depressed, sarcastic, and argumentative while assuming that their partner would automatically know what was wrong and fix it. Seldom does this work; in fact, it actually falls into option two (resisting what is). Make sure you have clearly expressed to your boyfriend that you feel this is a matter of respect and that you do not feel properly valued when he looks at other women, especially while you are with him. You may find that as your level of self-respect increases — and as your words and behavior reflect that sense of self-worth — the respect you receive from others will increase as well.

If the real issue is your self-esteem as it relates to your body image, changing your boyfriend's behavior won't help you; it will only stop reminding you of your discomfort. Rather, you need to work on improving your self-acceptance, a task that may include modifying your diet and exercise habits. Regular exercise and a healthy diet do wonders for self-esteem!

2. You can resist "what is" and stay in the relationship. This choice always blocks love and leads to the destruction of the relationship, as it did yours. The sad thing is that even when the relationship ended, undoubtedly your feelings of inadequacy didn't, unless you made some internal shifts in your self-esteem.

It is said that in India, one of the tests to evaluate whether someone is sane enough to be released from a mental hospital is to turn a water faucet on in a room with a plugged sink. Once the water is running all over the floor, they give a mop to the patient and tell him or her to clean it up. They then watch to see whether the patient just starts cleaning up the water or whether they are sane enough to turn the water off first.

With all due respect, in some ways trying to change your boyfriend's behavior is like trying to clean up the water, when the real source of the problem is how confident and comfortable you are with yourself.

3. You can accept "what is" and stay in the relationship. This choice requires that you change your responses rather than trying to change his behavior. It means accepting the fact that he enjoys looking at pictures of other women and believing that it really isn't about you. It is just something he enjoys.

Imagine that you were looking at a *Playgirl* magazine. My guess is that your appreciation of the men's bodies in the photos would not hurt, in any way, your appreciation of your boyfriend. The same holds true for gorgeous men and women on the big screen. Just because we drool over Johnny Depp or George Clooney doesn't mean we appreciate our sweethearts any less. The same holds true of looking at naked women. As you build your self-esteem and confidence, you won't experience twangs of inadequacy when your partner appreciates someone else's beauty.

Now, this is not to suggest that you accept the unaccept-able. If it absolutely goes against your personal values to have someone in your life who looks at erotic magazines or pornography, or if the real issue is your partner's lack of respect or a lack of trust or a difference in mo-rality, then you can turn to choice number four.

4. You can get out. Sometimes the best thing we can do is to leave a relationship. If you find yourself unable to shift from resisting what is to accepting what is, then by all means get out. But keep in mind that the problem goes with you when your responses are the problem in the first place!

I know it sounds as if I am "blaming" you. I want to as-sure you this isn't a matter of blame; it is a matter of responsibility. It is your responsibility to do something different if what you are currently doing isn't yielding positive results for you. However, had your ex-boyfriend been the one to write to me, I would have put the respon-sibility on him, suggesting that he take a look at his choices to see if there was something he might be able to do to be more respectful of your feelings. I might also have suggested that he take a look at his use of pornogra-phy to see if it was getting in the way of his ability to have an intimate sexual relationship with his real-life partner. One thing guys seldom realize is that the sexier, more beautiful, and more respected they make their partner feel, the more likely she is to enjoy engaging in sexual activities and the less threatened she will feel about other women. Since he didn't write, though, the choice of responses is up to you.

I wish you the best.

With aloha,

Feelings of jealousy and insecurity in our romantic relationships can present a challenge. As you continue reading you will find related is-sues addressed in later chapters. Chapter 4 discusses self-esteem. Chapter 6 addresses the importance of self-observation so that you can become aware of what you are thinking and feeling. Chapter 7 offers some solutions for dealing with jealousy. Chapter 8 discusses uncovering all the emotions that can contribute to anger and hurt. Chapter 10 addresses body image and sexuality.

My Partner, My Teacher

Whenever my husband does something I don't like, once I get conscious about applying the EROS equation (yes, you do have to consciously apply this concept, especially at first), I can often see how he is showing me something that I need to learn or is providing the perfect balance to my personality. I tend to work too much, so when he wants to do something fun instead of work, he is teaching me to lighten up and remember to play. With regard to our different styles of approaching certain tasks, I tend to be the type who wants to simply plant seeds to start a garden, while he is the type who will use a rototiller, make rows, fertilize, and then plant seeds. Although I may initially react by thinking he is taking the fun out of the project, in reality he is showing me the value of doing it properly. Thus, the "fun" comes later, in the results, when we have a successful and satisfying garden. If you choose the response option of accepting what is and looking at everything your partner does as a perfect lesson for you, you may discover that it is no accident you are together. Your differences are likely to be perfectly balanced to make you better teachers for each other.

Perhaps one of you is more responsible than the other—one teaches responsibility, one teaches lightening up. Maybe one of you is more energetic than the other—one teaches getting things done, the other teaches relaxing. One of you is more self-disciplined than the other—one teaches moderation, the other teaches about enjoying life. One of you is stricter than the other—one teaches the importance of responsibility, one teaches compassion. One of you is more emotional than the other—one is teaching to feel, the other to think rationally. If you stop resisting (and judging) the way the other person is and instead accept it, you will start to see the blessing added to your life by the other person's way of being—and vice versa.

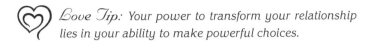 *Love Tip:* Your power to transform your relationship lies in your ability to make powerful choices.

Taking EROS Deeper: When the Event Is Infidelity

Now let's look at the EROS equation applied to a harder situation. A married couple, Dan and Jean, came to see me because she had had an online affair that had turned into a real sexual encounter. They were wondering what to do. After they told me their story we identified the "event" as the affair. They needed to decide how they wanted to respond to that event and thus how to create the outcome of their situation. Their first thought was that maybe they should get divorced. I suggested that they put that option aside for the time being and consider *what they would choose to do if divorce were not an option.* The truth was that they truly loved each other, and although they were upset and hurt, their preference was to be together. They just weren't sure how to do that after such a blow to their marriage.

Jean and Dan considered their response options for a while. Since the event had already taken place, they could not negotiate to change it. Jean had already stopped seeing and communicating with the other man, so that didn't need to be addressed further. Neither Jean nor Dan wanted to live a soap-opera existence, so they chose not to go into a state of resistance to one other. In honesty, they had already done that for weeks prior to coming to see me, and all it did was lead to fighting. They came to me because they wanted to stop the fighting that resulted from resisting. Thus, the only remaining options were either to accept the circumstances and each other and look for solutions within their relationship, or to get out of the marriage.

As I said, their first reaction was to get out, but once I asked what they would do if divorce were not an option, they started exploring other possibilities. They decided that rather than end the relationship, they would both take responsibility for their part in the situation to see if they could figure out what had led to Jean's looking outside of the marriage for companionship. Dan realized that he was taking the relationship for granted and wasn't really engaging in any activities or conversations with Jean. He was spending a lot of time on his computer or watching TV when he wasn't working. Jean acknowledged that she was bored and lonely and that rather than talking to Dan about it, or initiating any personal time with him, she took the easier route of seeking attention from someone who was offering it freely (her online lover) rather than from someone with whom she was going to have to negotiate for attention (Dan).

It is interesting to note that our relationships, and our lives, are a long string of events and responses that lead to new outcomes, which in turn become events to respond to . . . and on and on. In reality, although the affair was the event in this isolated situation, it was also Jean's response to the previous event of Dan's lack of involvement in the relationship. Jean's decision to have an affair was essentially the choice to get out. Now she was trying to figure out a new response that would inspire her to get back in.

Jean acknowledged that she had neglected to hold the marriage as sacred ground, protecting it at all costs. By both taking responsibility for their part in the problem, both felt as though they could choose different behaviors to make their marriage stronger. They came up with a list of things they would actively work on, individually and together. They recommitted to prioritizing the marriage as something they wanted to nourish and grow rather than something they wanted to be lazy about tending while it withered and died.

Love Tip: Catch yourself when you are assigning blame, and ask yourself, *"How can I respond differently to this situation that will create a powerful result?"*

I am not trying to imply that simply moving on is an easy thing to do when something like this happens in a marriage. Rather, I'm saying that if you have a certain goal or outcome that you want to create, how you respond to events will be what determines whether or not you reach your goal. Taking some time to consider your options, rather than merely reacting, will empower you tremendously.

Jean was reacting when she had the affair. Dan and Jean were reacting when they immediately thought about getting divorced. When we look outside of ourselves for the reasons why we feel the way we do or why things happened the way they did, we end up assigning blame. When we blame circumstances outside of ourselves, we give up our power, becoming victims rather than taking responsibility for what we are creating. I'm sure you can see that different responses could have created a very different outcome. Jean could easily have blamed Dan for not paying enough attention to her, and Dan could easily have blamed Jean for being unfaithful. From here the accusations would have flown back and forth, building only more anger. By taking the time to step back and consider other options, Jean and Dan were able to choose responses that were in alignment with the goal of saving their marriage. As a result, they were freed to move forward creatively and constructively. By taking responsibility for our own actions, we are empowered to create many different results. Of course, the maxim "a stitch in time saves nine" applies here. Had one or both of them been trained sooner in taking responsibility for their part in the relationship, they could have avoided the painful situation altogether.

Love Tip: Assumptions and blame are seldom the ingredients to a happy, healthy relationship. Start instead with personal responsibility.

Although I've shared Dan and Jean's story to illustrate the EROS equation and the power of carefully choosing your responses to create the results you desire, let's look a little deeper at infidelity since it is obviously a huge issue when it happens within a marriage. I don't want to oversimplify the matter by implying that you can or should simply accept it and move on. I do mean to suggest, however, that what you choose to do, think, and say will affect the outcome you experience, and how you choose to respond will severely impact how you feel. Therefore, it is important to realize that how you respond is a choice, and that the solution you arrive at will depend upon that choice.

When a partner strays, it not only dishonors the vows of the marriage, it also brings up issues of guilt, embarrassment, betrayal, and trust. It causes issues of self-esteem, self-worth, and self-doubt to flare. It triggers abandonment issues that may loom from childhood. In general, it throws the whole relationship for a loop. Sexually transmitted diseases and pregnancies can impact the stress of the situation. These issues affect both spouses as they examine themselves, each other, and the validity of the marriage. As it did with Dan and Jean, it brings the issue of divorce into the picture where it may not have been before. Infidelity and the challenges that accompany it are usually difficult to recover from.

Although infidelity is seldom a fun thing to go through, most of us realize that it can be handled, renegotiated, resolved, forgiven, and survived. Almost all of us either know someone who has dealt with it, or we have dealt with it ourselves at some point in our lives. We've even watched a president of the United States and a first lady manage infidelity. We've watched plots revolving around extramarital affairs unfold in thousands of movies and television shows and we've read them in novels. Unfaithfulness is now so nonchalantly displayed in the media that it barely shocks us anymore—until it happens in our own marriage. Although no one wants to experience it, most of us are acutely aware of the possibility that we *could,* and, thus, some forethought has likely crossed our minds about how we would handle it. Even if we think we would leave our spouse immediately, we often discover that our love for our partner doesn't go away just because we are disappointed and hurt.

If you want to stay together, the one who strayed is going to have to accept the reality that there are consequences for one's behavior. These consequences may include ongoing suspicion on the part of the other spouse while trust is being re-earned. The consequences may be that no matter how badly the offended partner *wants* to choose healthy responses that lead to positive outcomes, he or she may lack the skills or emotional resources to do so. It is possible—even likely—that there will be an emotional withdrawal while the offended spouse grieves, heals, and readjusts. It is also very possible that the dynamics of the relationship will change after such an event. When one partner has been revolving his or her whole life around a relationship only to discover that the other person has cheated, the healing process may very well bring about a reevaluation of how he or she has been living and prioritizing things. A spouse who once took precedent over all else—including the other person's own happiness—may suddenly find that this is no longer the way things work. In the big picture this is probably a good thing, because making someone else happy at the expense of one's own happiness is generally unhealthy for the individual or for the relationship. But in the short term it may take some getting used to.

It is interesting to note that one is only "cheating" if the partners have an agreement that engaging in physical encounters with others is "against the rules." While certainly for most of us this is the case, many married couples have chosen to take the issue of infidelity out of the picture by agreeing that, under certain circumstances, exploring their sexuality with others is acceptable. For some this means it is okay as long as they know about it; for others it is okay as long as they don't know. For some it is acceptable as long as they are both involved; for others it is acceptable if it happens only occasionally. Although I am not suggesting that you make this kind of agreement in your marriage, the value of looking at alternative arrangements such as these lies in recognizing that they simply provide a different response option to the event of infidelity. These couples have chosen to negotiate, and the solution they came up with works for them.

> **Consider this:** Even people who have the best relationships find other people attractive. Monogamy is not a matter of the absence of opportunity or interest; for both men and women it is a matter of choice about what you want to honor. You can have a relationship that is so fulfilling that you will always make choices to honor it, but you still may face desire, attraction, and interest in other people; thus you need to make the choice to honor monogamy.

Hopefully, if you do encounter infidelity in your marriage—or the temptation for it—or if you already have, rather than reacting from ego, you will utilize the EROS equation and will choose authentic responses in alignment with your true goals and values. There are a lot of different ways to handle the issues that arise. What is critically important is that you and your spouse communicate and agree on what works *for you*.

To choose responses that serve you when dealing with all the issues raised by an event like infidelity, you will need to strengthen and fortify yourself. The information provided in Chapters 4, 5, and 6 will help you do so. Chapter 4 will also take an in-depth look at how ego influences us; this may help you to recognize when an issue really matters (in the big picture) versus when the issue has more to do with a bruised ego. In addition, Chapter 7 will assist you in coping with the changes and the fear evoked by events like extramarital affairs, and Chapter 8 will help you to manage your emotions when someone breaks an integrity agreement with you—or will help you to make amends if you are the one who did the breaking. Chapter 8 also provides guidelines for hearing and receiving your partner's emotions. Chapter 10 provides intellectual foreplay questions for you and your spouse, to help you explore issues of sexuality more deeply. Chapter 12 looks at the bigger picture of making choices that serve your soul and feed your spirituality. Even if leaving your partner is the choice you make, you will still want to find a place of forgiveness and compassion in your heart or you will carry resentment with you throughout your life beyond the marriage. These are the greater life skills that only relationships offer us the opportunity to master.

You are not a victim

Dear Eve,

I'm a man whose finances were ruined by an overspending partner, whom I am now divorcing. Unfortunately this makes it impossible for me to be self-sufficient in my retirement years once they come. How do I best approach this issue with women whom I may wish to date? I seem to get a lot of rejections once my financial situation is understood.

Aloha,

While I empathize with your total frustration over what has happened, I'm a great advocate of taking responsibility rather than assigning blame. The benefit you can gain from this shift in mindset is that by taking responsibility you will be honoring your personal power rather than honoring a sense of being a victim. I encourage you to consider the perspective that your finances were not ruined due to an overspending partner, but rather from your lack of attention to what was happening in your marriage. The payoff of accepting your responsibility for your situation will be that you will see the power you possess to avoid having something similar happen again. You will not need to enter a new relationship with fear and trust issues, because you will see that you are not a victim; you are a responsible, powerful human being.

Most people would like to have a sense of financial security and self-sufficiency in their retirement years. At the same time, there are many single, divorced, and widowed women out there who are financially self-sufficient and who truly and deeply desire a man who cherishes them, loves them, and makes them laugh, one who will care for them in ways beyond finances. Indeed, if you can offer true love, compassion, respect, and kindness, you are a definite catch, whether or not you have money.

I encourage you to move forward to a place of forgiving your previous spouse and a place of taking responsibility for your circumstances. If you do not, you are likely to come across as bitter, angry, and distrusting rather than loving, compassionate, and endearing.

With aloha,

Eve

Thoughts Lead to Feelings

The E + R = O & S equation can be applied to every situation you encounter. You'll know you need to apply it any time you feel "off," like something isn't okay. The reality is that your thoughts create your feelings. Your thoughts are your *response* to an *event*, while your feelings are the *outcome* that results. When you don't like the feelings you are experiencing, begin your search for a *solution* by looking at what you are thinking that may be causing you to feel that way. When you do this, you may find that you are thinking things that you actually don't know to be true or that are simply *not* true, like "He never loved me in the first place." Thoughts like this will undoubtedly make you feel worse. Or you may find that you were thinking negative things about yourself that the other person never said or even thought, for example, "He thinks I am too fat and that is why he did what he did." If you are angry or your feelings are hurt, look to see what response you chose in the form of thoughts that made you feel hurt or angry. I am not suggesting that you suppress your anger; expressing your feelings is an important part of communication. However, when you take responsibility for what you are feeling, the other person is far more likely to be able to hear you, and you are far more powerful and far more able to create a better solution. This requires that you express your feelings from a place of acceptance rather than resistance. (More about sharing the full range of emotions will be discussed in Chapter 8.)

Here is another example that illustrates how thoughts (responses) lead to feelings (outcomes). Uncomfortable feelings are the flag that signal to us that we have a response that is out of line. However, the outcome is often what we become aware of first, *before* we recognize our response to an event.

> **THE EVENT:** I get dressed up for an evening out and my husband doesn't say anything about how I look.
>
> **RESPONSE:** Thinking my husband is judging me, I start judging me— and him.
>
> **OUTCOME:** I start feeling irritable and angry. Note: He hasn't said anything to influence how I feel.

If I am being particularly unconscious and reactionary, I start thinking that my husband is judging me or isn't attracted to me anymore, and then I get mad at him. I may even accuse him of thinking I don't look okay and in order to get even may begin to criticize the way he looks. A chain of bad reactions takes place.

If, instead, when I start feeling bad, I stop and ask myself what thoughts I am thinking that are causing me to feel upset, I would see that I am choosing to think negative things about myself and am assuming that my husband is doing the same. When I become aware of the response that is causing me pain, I can choose a new option. Since I am just making up a story anyway, I can make up a new one in which my husband thinks I am beautiful and just didn't tell me because he assumes that I know how he feels about me. Or I can decide for myself that I look fine and not worry about what my husband may or may not be thinking. Or I can ask him what he thinks and consequently deal with the truth instead of my imagination.

By carefully choosing your responses instead of just reacting to the events around you, you can create solutions that are in alignment with your goals. To help you choose your responses with more consciousness, Chapter 4 will address self-esteem enhancement. Self-esteem obviously affects what you think about yourself, what you think your spouse thinks about you, your ability to love others, and your ability to receive love from others. As you strengthen your self-esteem, you will be better equipped to choose responses to events that are in alignment with the outcomes you desire.

This is nonnegotiable

Dear Eve,

My fiancée and I have been together for about three years. She is a good person and I enjoy her company. My concern is that when she is distracted, she gets forgetful — dangerously so. On four different occasions she has left the stove on in my house. She'll be cooking and then the phone rings and off she goes, forgetting that the stove is on. I have tried just about everything I can think of to make sure it never happens again, but I resent having to watch her or worry about whether she is doing something careless. When I'm home I can monitor the situation, but I travel a lot for my work, and I'm always concerned that something is going to happen while I'm gone. She feels terrible about it and says it won't happen again — and then it does. I just don't know what to do about this; it isn't something I feel can be compromised on. What do you suggest?

Aloha,

You are right. There are some things that can't be compromised, and this is one of them. Another might be the
appropriate care of children or being careful to lock
doors and windows for security. In fact, some of the most
challenging aspects of relationships are those issues that
compromise safety and simply can't be done any other way.

When we encounter things we don't like, we have four
choices: negotiating for change, resisting what is, accepting what is, or getting out.

It sounds like you have tried negotiating by explaining to
her the importance of changing her behavior. The tricky
part is that she agrees with you and knows that she has to
become more conscious — but so far has not done so.

Currently, you are "resisting what is" as an unskilled
means of trying to bring about change. Rather than working, it is destroying the love in your relationship.

Your next option is to accept that the fact this is the
way she is, and that she may be unchangeable. Sometimes
physical deficits due to age, illness, hormonal imbalance,
and other issues come into play, so you may want to have a
doctor check for anything that can be treated. If you
decide to stay in the relationship regardless, you may
have to continue taking responsibility for things where
she falls short. As you accept the situation, other solutions will start to pop into your head. Perhaps you post a
checklist she agrees to go through before she leaves the
kitchen or the house, or you don't allow her to cook at
your house, or she has to call you or someone else before
she leaves home, or you find some sort of timer for the
stove that automatically turns it off. I realize that what
I'm suggesting requires you to get really creative in your
problem solving, but when you accept the reality that this
is the way she is, you will be able to see other solutions. When we resist the things we don't like, we become
blinded to the solutions.

The fourth option you have, if this all proves to be
more than you can handle, is to get out of the relationship. If you decide to stay in, recognize that you
are accepting the consequences (and responsibilities)

of that decision. When it comes to relationships we
need to either love them or leave them. When we realize that hating them (or resisting them) and staying
in the relationship isn't a viable option, other solutions become obvious.

I know you were hoping I would offer a magic way to change
your fiancée, but, unfortunately, sometimes change isn't
possible — whether the other person won't or can't change.
What is always changeable is the way we approach the
problem. If you stay in the relationship, approach the
situation in a manner that enhances the love rather than
destroying it.

With aloha,

CHAPTER 3

The Guideposts

It's pretty hard for the Lord to guide you if you haven't made up your mind which way you want to go.

MADAME C. J. WALKER

In order to align your responses with the outcomes and solutions you want to create, it is important that you determine what you want. Once you've done this, you will need some guideposts to assist you in achieving your goals. This chapter is designed to help you identify your own guideposts, which you can think of as road signs to help keep you on track during your journey. Rather than a set of rules to live by, enforced from the outside or artificially imposed on you by society, you will develop a set of guidelines and a code of ethics based on your own values and beliefs, as well as on your intentions and desires for your marriage.

For some, the first step, identifying what they want, is a challenge. If you have endured years of a difficult marriage, it may be hard to clearly and confidently say, "I want my marriage to work." If you have been closed down emotionally to your partner for a long time, it may be hard to honestly say, "I want to love and be loved unconditionally." When you are facing a partner who is unlikely or unable to change, or when you yourself have resisted changing for so long that the task seems overwhelming, it may be hard to let down your guard enough to even acknowledge what you want. When you know (because you've already been told) that you will have to do some work to bring about your goals, it may be really hard to state with conviction, "I want to love, honor, and cherish, till death do us part."

What Are You Feeding On?

Something else that can make it confusing to determine what you want is the fact that drama, chaos, and disharmony can actually become an addiction. Although you may think you want a peaceful, healthy, loving marriage, you may be addicted to the drama of a chaotic marriage. In much the same way, we often hear people talking about wanting peace, and we as a nation claim we want peace, yet we are so addicted to the drama of war and conflict that we use them as entertainment. I was in line at the market reading the covers of the tabloids and magazines while I waited. I was surprised to see "war words" used as selling points to entice readers: "Regis wins war with Kelly"; "Brad and Jen's battle just beginning." We, as a society, feed on battles. The worse the people's behavior, the more ratings the show gets and the more magazines are sold.

Consider how much of your time and entertainment are dedicated to conflict and chaos. Consider whether you are playing war games on computers and watching soap operas filled with drama. Does your favorite music have lyrics in which one person can't live without the other, or, worse yet, in which one person demeans another? Are your favorite books the ones in which true romance always equals unrequited love? When this level of drama constantly bombards us, it becomes an addiction. We thrive on the agony. The melodrama becomes normal. Then we start creating drama simply because it's familiar, because we need the infusion, the next fix. As you consider these things, also ask yourself at what point your inner world starts to reflect your outer world.

Entertainment and the media feed on misery. Our celebrities, in their *real* lives, are generally not good role models, particularly in the realm of marriage. Consider also the possibility that constantly exposing yourself to these forms of entertainment serves as a type of "education" (albeit not often a good one). When you try to figure out how to handle a situation with your husband, wife, or kids, you may be quick to draw on a dramatic example rather than one that is truly in alignment with what you want to create. What a shock to suddenly hear yourself screaming at your spouse the very words you heard shouted on Jerry Springer's nightly assault on humanity. I'm not suggesting that you stop entertaining yourself in these ways; rather, I'm suggesting that you become aware of how the input affects the output. I'm encouraging you to make the connection so you can consciously choose what you create instead of unconsciously reacting or mimicking. When you begin to develop a strong sense that the "true you" is not the drama and chaos, but rather is the calm, still, peaceful, wise, loving aspect of yourself, then you begin to realize that you can choose drama or choose harmony. The choice is yours. You are not a victim. Even staying in the relationship is your choice.

Hopefully, as you work your way through this book you will be able to clearly define what you want to create with your partner and confidently commit to that goal. Acknowledging that some of you may not be fully committed to your marriage at the moment, I am going to arbitrarily assume that your underlying goals are to love your marriage, your mate, your life, and yourself. Using these as your goals for the time being will help you do the following exercises, which call for you to identify your values, your desires, a clear vision for your marriage, and a code of ethics—all guideposts to assist you along the way. If you find that the goal of loving your marriage is not an authentic goal for you, this, too, is an important revelation to accept and acknowledge.

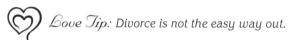 *Love Tip:* Divorce is not the easy way out.

Define Your Values

Before we launch into taking a look at what you want, it will be helpful to identify your values: the qualities and principles you deeply believe in. When you create a vision of what you want, you will find that there are often many ways to get where you want to be, but some of the routes to getting there are not in integrity or in alignment with your value system, and some may be out of your control. For instance, let's say your definition of success is to have a million dollars. To achieve this, some of your options are to earn it through work, earn it through wise investments, inherit it, steal it, or win it. However, if your values are such that you don't believe in stealing, then acquiring the money through robbery won't make you feel successful. It is not in integrity for you. Inheriting or winning the money would be wonderful but may still not make you feel successful if your value system honors hard work more than luck. In any case, while being kind to your relatives or buying a lottery ticket is in your control, winning is not, nor is having a wealthy relative. If your values don't honor gambling, then taking your goal to Vegas won't be in integrity for you either, and, again, winning while you're there is not entirely in your control anyway. This brings you back to earning and investing. If you acquire your goal by being out of integrity, you will find that the goal won't make you happy and you will remain unfulfilled. In order to stay in integrity (and thus happy about your choices), identifying your values, writing them down, and defining what they mean will serve as excellent guideposts to help you make decisions along the way.

In the realm of marriage, knowing your values—and recognizing and honoring your partner's values—is particularly helpful. Prioritizing your values will help you make decisions when work and relationship, or relationship and spirituality, or marriage and children come into conflict.

Following the terrorist attacks of September 11, 2001, *USA Today* published a poll of Americans' values before and after the event.

PRIORITIES PRIOR TO AND AFTER 9/11

Prior to 9/11, Americans rated their values in this order:	After 9/11, Americans rated their values in this order:
1. Career	1. Family
2. Heart	2. Heart
3. Wealth	3. God
4. Health	4. Health
5. Family	5. Country
6. Home	6. Home
7. God	7. Career
8. Country	8. Wealth

Most of us found that day to be a huge wake-up call with regard to what truly mattered. Many questioned their life choices and the way they spent their time. People suddenly recognized that work and wealth were unlikely to be the things that truly mattered most when their lives and lifestyles were threatened. Family, relationships, and spirituality moved to the top of the list. The problem, of course, was sustaining the reprioritized values without having the skills to do so. As time passes, many of us are unconsciously slipping back into our old way of prioritizing things—not necessarily because we want to, but because that is what we know. We know how to do our jobs (because we've been trained). Making our relationships work and our spiritual lives thrive is not as simple (in part because most of us haven't been trained). In light of how important these things are, however, the benefits of doing the work are well worth the effort. Since we haven't been taught, we must make the effort to teach ourselves how to make our deepest relationships work and how to determine our highest priorities.

➤ PAUL AND CINDY, MARRIED TEN YEARS

Paul and I ran a marathon on the day of our wedding. It was such an intense thing to go through, and I remember the great natural high we felt when we finished the race holding hands. We looked at each other and made the commitment that we wanted to have the greatest relationship a husband and wife could possibly have. That is just how Paul and I are. When we decide something is important, we give it 110 percent. We agreed that we would always make our relationship our highest priority. I really believe that is what it takes to make a great marriage.

Making my relationship with Paul the number-one priority in my life makes all my decisions and actions part of a team effort. It actually has gotten easier. Even when Paul is not with me, when I'm faced with some decision, I try to think about how he would respond. Now that we have been married ten years, it's become automatic. We have our own interests and opinions, but we work on things together.

This leads to the most important part of making the marriage the priority: constant communication. It is especially important through tough issues—raising children, for example. We call it the "ultimate team sport." It is a constant challenge but has the hugest rewards.

EXERCISE ∾ *Brainstorm about your list of personal values. Write each one on a Post-it Note so you can easily reorder them. Prioritize the list, identifying the ten most important values. These are your core values, and they will guide you when making decisions. Keep them consciously in mind and aim to live by them. Invite your spouse to identify and prioritize his or her values as well, and share your results with each other.* ∾

If you have been married a long time, it is easy to think you know what your spouse's values are, but I guarantee that if you have never had the discussion you will be surprised. As I said earlier in the book, it is not necessarily important that you and your spouse have the *same* values, but it is important that you have *complementary* values. If one of you has career and wealth at the top of the list and family shortly thereafter, while the other has family at the top of the list and financial security shortly thereafter, this arrangement could be the perfect one for creating both financial security and a nurtured family. However, if one of you prioritizes family first and the other prioritizes family last, you could encounter constant conflicts. If both of you have career and wealth at the top of the list, the emotional health of the family may be jeopardized.

If you and your spouse find that your priorities conflict or don't serve your vision of having a loving marriage and healthy family, then doing this exercise affords a perfect opportunity for you to reprioritize and make decisions together about what you value as a couple. Remember, this doesn't mean that your values have to be exactly the same or in the same order, but they do need to be supportive of your common goals. Knowing, understanding, respecting, and honoring each other's values is more critical than having the same values in the same order.

When doing this exercise with your spouse, try to avoid making it about whose priority system is right or better. This isn't about judging the other person; it is about discovering and understanding him or her. If you know that your partner's career is his or her first priority, then you will not be surprised (and hopefully not angry) when he or she makes decisions based on that priority. If you and your partner agree that your relationship comes at the top of the list or that your spiritual lives are number one, then you will be better equipped to make decisions that support your values—and to let your values guide your decisions. Since the priority of values can change when tragedy strikes or new events (like children or grand-children) come onto the scene, revisit the list from time to time to make sure it still serves you as a useful guidepost.

When I did this exercise the first time (before I was married), I found myself humming a song while I was identifying my values. My initial list included:

1. service to God

2. having an "attitude of gratitude" and expressing my appreciation

3. kindness, compassion, and love

4. honesty, trust, and sincerity

5. health and strength

6. personal and spiritual growth

7. creativity and artistic expression

8. knowledge and intellectual growth

9. beauty, peace, and aesthetics

10. productivity and financial self-sufficiency

Once I finished, I began to wonder what the song was that had been going through my head. As I put words to the tune, I realized that it was the Camp Fire Girl Law. (Camp Fire Girls is a club, similar to Girl Scouts.) The lyrics went like this: "Worship God, seek beauty, give service, and knowledge pursue. Be trustworthy ever in all that you do. Hold fast onto health and your work glorify, and you will be happy in the Law of Camp Fire." As I looked down at my journal, I was amazed to see that virtually every one of the values declared in that little song was on my paper.

EXERCISE ∾ *As you identify your values, consider where you got them. Did your family teach them to you? Did television? Do you really honor them, or have you just unconsciously listed them without commitment? Be sure that the values you list are truly your own and that you are dedicated to living in alignment with them, and then commit yourself to doing so. The results will be enhanced self-esteem and greater clarity, focus, and problem-solving ability.* ∾

To live in alignment with your values, it helps to define what they mean to you. What "service to God" and "appreciation" mean to me may be very different from what they mean to my spouse. Once you are clear about what each value means, then you can actively take steps to live it. For instance, to me, "appreciation" means having a constant attitude of gratitude, remembering in every moment to be thankful for the blessings that surround me—both those that are obvious and those that are harder to recognize. To act in alignment with this value I literally say, "Thank you" out loud when I get a parking space in a crowded lot, when I find something I have lost, when I sit down to a meal, and even when I encounter a challenge or difficulty. I trust that everything is a blessing, and my task is to see it that way.

EXERCISE ∾ *After you have identified your values, define what each one means to you. Then jot down a few different ways that you live in alignment with your values in your daily life, or ways in which you could live in alignment with them. If your spouse is willing to, ask him or her to define his or her values as well.* ∾

Defining your values may be harder than it seems. Putting abstract concepts like "love" into words is not easy, but doing so is important in making sure that you and your spouse are on the same page, using the same language, and getting the definitions out of the same dictionary. Sometimes it is easier to begin by determining what *does not* define a value. For instance, "Love is not possessive. Love is not jealous. Love is not confining or controlling. Love is not limited. Love is not judgmental. Love is not scary. Love is not dramatic. Love is not conditional." Then move on to what *does* define the value: "Love is accepting. Love is appreciating. Love is supportive. Love is compassionate. Love is open and abundant. Love is the core essence of spirit."

It is also helpful to recognize that just because you and your partner have identified the same values or have defined them similarly, it doesn't necessarily mean that you have the same understanding of how a value should be *put into practice*. If you simply state "service" as a priority, one of you may think that means joining the military while the other may think it means going on a mission with your church. In such cases a potential for miscommunication exists. My husband and I both value our spirituality very highly; however, how we *practice* our spiritual lives is different. Recognizing the difference in what "spirituality" means to each of us in terms of behavior, we have chosen to honor and support each other on our individual spiritual paths while simultaneously finding ways to share our spiritual journey.

As you explore what "living in alignment" with each value means to you and to your partner, you both may find that you are not living in alignment with your stated values, which provides an excellent opportunity to make some changes. For instance, if you highly value health, but you smoke, you are out of alignment. If communication and honesty are important to you, but you aren't talking to each other or telling each other the truth about how you feel, you are out of alignment. See if you can agree to support each other in living in alignment with your values.

We'll talk more about living in alignment in the chapters ahead, but for now, knowing what your values are and what they mean to you will help guide you toward deciding what you want—and toward getting it.

♡ *Love Tip:* We have been brainwashed to think that attraction is all about a person's outsides (weight, physical appearance), when in reality what is inside (attitudes, perspectives) is equally important, if not more so. Outer attractiveness serves to reel people in, but inner attractiveness is more likely to build strong, lasting relationships.

What Do You Want?

What do you want from your marriage? Really spend some time thinking about your answers to this question, because to love your marriage you are going to have to *want* to love your marriage. To create harmony, love, and joy with your partner and family, you are going to have to hold this desire as a constant goal and choose all your words, thoughts, and actions in alignment with that goal. To create the outcomes and solutions you desire, you need to know what they are. Use the list of values you have generated to help you to determine what you want.

EXERCISE ⮞ *Make a "Most Wanted" list by answering the question "What do you want?" You are welcome to list anything in the whole world that you want, but be sure to also make the list relevant to what you want in terms of your marriage.*

Some examples:

- *I want my husband and me to be friends, to be on the same team.*

- *I want my wife to love me without criticizing me.*

- *I want to love my marriage.*

- *I want my husband to be more considerate.*

- *I want my wife to be more sexual.*

- *I want my husband to be more romantic.*

- *I want to be more responsive and less reactive.*

- *I want to take a vacation every year alone with my spouse.*

- *I want to stop fighting over money.*

- *I want the kids to grow up to be contributing members of society.*

The list may be very long if you discover that there are a lot of things you want, or it may include only a few things yet still feel complete. ⮞

In terms of the EROS equation, the items on your Most Wanted list are the outcomes and solutions you want to create in your marriage. Therefore, they come at the end of the equation. When something happens (an event) to which you need to respond, hold the vision of what you want as the goal, and use your values as guideposts to help you get there. As you do, it will become clear to you that certain behaviors and responses will lead you away from what you want and others will lead you toward what you want.

Did you know? In a study, 160,000 high-school seniors in the United States were asked, among other questions, "As you look ahead to the future, what's the one thing you want most out of life?" The most frequent answer was "To be loved."

What is tricky is that a lot of things on the Most Wanted list end up being things we want *other* people to do. We want our spouse to…, we want our kids to.… When we put what we want other people to do or not do on our Most Wanted list, we are focusing on the event instead of on our response. We are making their behavior responsible for our happiness. Even trying to get your spouse to read this book or do these exercises with you would fall in the "trying to change the event" category. Remember, when you focus on trying to change the event or the other person, you are rendered powerless. Always turn your focus toward your responses, while clearly keeping your goals in mind.

EXERCISE ∾ *Look at your list of wants. Make the exact same list again, only this time rewrite any wants that depend on other people's behavior, turning them into desires for your own behavior. Rethink them as actions that lie within your realm of responsibility and your circle of influence. This is where your power dwells.*

Some of your wants may turn into two or more statements as you start to realize what you can do to impact the result. For instance, for the first one on the list above—"I want my husband and me to be friends, to be on the same team"—you definitely have a contributing part over your half of the friendship, but you don't have any control over your spouse's part. Change the wording to reflect only the part you are responsible for, the part you have power over. In this case: "I want be to my husband's friend. I am a team player."

Next, take the desires on your list a step further by describing what each one would look like in terms of your thoughts and behavior. What does it mean to be a friend? What does it mean to be considerate? ∾

The above list would be altered to read something like this:

1. I want be to my husband's friend. I am a team player.

   Taking it further: I will listen when my spouse has a problem; I will be supportive without trying to fix it or take it personally. I will set time aside for just being with my spouse; I will make my relationship with him a priority. I will show up on "his side" in his life, rather than as the "opposing team."

2. I want to love my wife without criticizing her. I want to stop reacting to criticism in a negative way.

   Taking it further: I will look for what my wife does well and compliment her. I will stop judging her and putting her down and instead seek to understand her perspective. When she criticizes me, I will not take it personally because I know that is just her style. Instead, I will calmly tell her, "I would appreciate it if you would tell me what you need without criticizing me."

3. I want to love my marriage.

   Taking it further: I will honor my marriage with my time and attention. I will participate in recreational activities with my spouse. I will show my spouse that I love him or her, through both my words and my actions. I will be attentive to my spouse and show up as a life and love *partner,* not as his or her parent, or child, or boss. I will pay attention to and appreciate the ways in which my partner shows his or her love for me—even if they are different or more subtle than I might prefer.

4. I want to notice when my husband is considerate. I want to ask for what I need.

   Taking it further: I will respectfully let my husband know when I am feeling hurt or taken for granted and give him specific examples of what would work better for me. I will assume the best rather than the worst because I know he does appreciate me and that he is just busy. I will watch for the subtle ways in which he expresses consideration and appreciation and acknowledge him when he does so.

5. I want to pay more attention to what makes my wife sexual. I want to turn my wife on physically.

   Taking it further: I will spend more time on foreplay and helping her to be "in the mood." I will touch her throughout the day in nonsexual but loving and tender ways so she will know that my affection is not limited to the bedroom. I will romance her like I did when we were courting, with occasional flowers, cards, unexpected calls, and regular "date nights" so she feels my love. I will make sure that she is satisfied when we have sex, not just that I am.

6. I want to notice the ways in which my husband is romantic. I want to inspire romance in my husband.

   Taking it further: I will make that extra effort to be attractive to my husband. I will be kind and loving with my husband to inspire his appreciation. I will notice and acknowledge and appreciate the ways in which he is romantic and the kind things he does for me. I will do romantic things for my husband, and not expect all the romance to come from him.

7. I want to be more responsive and less reactive.

   Taking it further: When my spouse says or does something that hurts my feelings, I will stop for a moment before responding and choose my words and actions in alignment with the goal of having a loving interaction. I will listen not just with my ears but also with my heart to see what my spouse is really trying to say and do. I will stop focusing on the event, and instead will focus on my response to the event.

8. I want to invite my spouse to take a vacation alone with me every year.

   Taking it further: I will set money aside for a vacation (even if just for one night away). I will let my spouse know that I look forward to spending time alone with him or her. I will initiate making the plans and arrangements for time away together.

9. I want to stop fighting over money. I want to stop worrying about money and start trusting. I want to use my money more wisely.

   Taking it further: I will use our money wisely and discuss expenses with my spouse. I will set up a budget for both of us so that we know what our financial parameters are. I will ask about money issues rather than blaming and accusing.

10. I want to be an encouraging and accepting parent who gives my kids every opportunity to have a great life. I want to trust my kids to make decisions that lead them to exactly what they need to learn.

    Taking it further: I will teach my children how to make decisions and then trust them when they exercise that skill. I will teach my children that every choice has consequences and then let them experience the consequences of their decisions (within limits). I will guide and support them as best I can and let go when need be.

Notice that this exercise alone is powerful in that it shifts the responsibility for what *you* want off of other people (i.e., your spouse, kids, parents, the event) and onto yourself (your response). Any time you expect someone else to alter your experience, you are turning your power over to them. By contrast, any time you take responsibility for your experience, you become powerful for manifesting what you want.

When you are done with this exercise, you may find that you know how to love your marriage already; you just have to *do* it. When an event happens or someone says something to you that causes a reaction, stop. Take a deep breath. Remember the behaviors and desires that you have listed above, and *choose* your next words, thoughts, and actions in alignment with what you are trying to create. Allow these guideposts to steer your decisions.

After you have done all you can possibly do, you may feel that it is time to get out of the relationship. That is one of the options. However, you are encouraged to consider the following question: What would you do if divorce were not an option and living miserably were not either? What would *you* do differently?

Although it may feel as though you are the only one doing the changing here, when you change the way you are showing up in the relationship, the people around you are likely to change in relation to you. For example, if I nag at my husband, he gets defensive and argues back. When I request something respectfully, he is more likely to respond respectfully. How I behave directly impacts how he behaves.

Amazingly enough, this principle also applies to the way we think. People have the ability to feel on a subtle level when they are being judged, even if we haven't told them. If someone across the room is sending you anger and hatred without saying a word, you will likely feel it. When someone is sending you love and appreciation, you can feel that too. So, as you look at your responses, remember that your thoughts impact both you and your spouse, even if they remain unspoken. Sometimes we communicate our disapproval through unconscious communication—sighs, rolling our eyes, a certain look on our face—and the other person can see those signs. The same is true for complaining about your spouse to your friends and family. Part of the addiction to drama is played out in the story you tell about your spouse. If you keep repeating the same complaints long enough, you suddenly find that you are addicted not only to the drama itself but also to the telling of the story *about* your drama. Pay attention to what you are doing, saying, *and* thinking in response to various situations, and allow your guideposts to help you align your thoughts and actions with what you want to create: a loving marriage.

Create Your Vision

Just as you might create a vision statement if you were building a business venture, write a vision statement for your marriage and/or family. Write it in the present tense, as if it were already so. Include your values, what you want, how you feel, and the quality of your marriage. Here you can include your partner's behavior because this is your vision for the big picture, your vision for both of you. This is what you want to manifest. Here is an example:

> Our marriage is joyful, harmonious, and able to endure all challenges placed in its path. When we are upset about something, we talk to each other and work it out. We both see our relationship as our spiritual path and thus prioritize it above all else. We are mutually supportive and know that we are individually only responsible for our own behavior. We trust each other to make wise decisions that protect and nourish our relationship, our family, and our quality of life. We continuously aim to get ego out of the way so that we can love authentically. Our home and our marriage are our sanctuary—the place where we rejuvenate so we can better face the world.

Make sure that what you have written feels good to read and inspires you. Then, if need be, read it daily to keep your focus on what you are creating. If possible, write and read your vision statement with your spouse. Create your vision together. If that is not possible, write and read it yourself. Post it on your refrigerator. Put it in your day planner. Reading it daily will work a bit like saying a prayer. A minute a day spent envisioning the quality of your marriage will by itself impact your marriage, in part because it will impact you. When you set this kind of intention, your mind goes into effort to help you create it.

Code of Ethics

Another necessary set of guideposts to help you manifest a loving marriage is a personal code of ethics. Your code of ethics should be based on your values, which you listed and defined in an earlier exercise. All of us have a code or set of rules we live by. Some rules are looser than others, and some are less conscious than others. To create a code of ethics that will assist you in your marriage, you are going to need to become aware of the rules you currently operate by, whether consciously or unconsciously. Here are some rules that may automatically come to mind: "Honesty is the best policy." "If you can't say something nice, don't say anything at all." "Marriages should be monogamous." "Children are to be seen and not heard." "The man is the head of the household." Keep in mind that although you were exposed to many of these rules as a child, they may not actually be guideposts that you or your spouse *really* believes in.

> ♡ *Love Tip:* People only treat you the way you allow
>   them to treat you. When you know your own value, you
> will change what you allow.

For example, the Golden Rule, which says, "Do unto others as you would have them do unto you," is another common rule that many people automatically think of when asked to list their code of ethics. However, it can be a tricky one to live by because the only way it truly works is if the individual has a strong sense of self-esteem and truly knows his or her worth. If a person feels undeserving of love and therefore is comfortable being treated horribly, he or she might allow others to mistreat him or her. Consequently, treating others poorly in turn may seem acceptable, when obviously it is not. Ultimately, the Golden Rule really should be, "Do unto others as they would have you do unto them." Treat people the way they want to be treated, which is not necessarily the way you want to be treated. A funny example of how this works is that I like back rubs and to be touched firmly, like a massage, whereas my husband likes to be touched more lightly, like a tickle. Consequently, in light of the Golden Rule, he touches me with a feather-light touch and I touch him with firm, massaging strokes—that is, until we remind each other to "do unto us" the kind of treatment we each really like.

....

EXERCISE ⤷ *What rules do you live by? Make a list of every rule you can think of that you may be currently living by, whether* *consciously or unconsciously. If you are doing these exercises with your partner, invite your partner to make his or her own list so you can explore each other's rules.* ༀ

After you have made your list, examine each rule to see if it is really yours or if it was imposed on you by someone else. Then determine whether you are truly committed to abiding by it. You may find that you and your spouse have some rules on your lists that you don't really believe in. Or you may have included some rules that you believe in and your spouse doesn't (or vice versa), a scenario that could impact your marriage. When I asked participants in a relationship workshop what rules they lived by, one man raised his hand and said, "Don't get caught"—much to his wife's dismay. Another woman said she had a rule that every marriage should be allowed one major "mistake," or infidelity, per year. Obviously, if you hold these beliefs as your personal code of ethics and your spouse does not feel the same way, trouble could develop. See which rules you have in common, which rules you or your spouse might like to adopt from the other's list, and which rules the two of you wish to discard because they don't fit your relationship. The point isn't whose code is right and whose is wrong, but rather that you are (individually or together) living by a code that supports your vision of creating a healthy, loving marriage, and that you both agree to the "rules."

EXERCISE ༀ *Now create a new code of ethics that is made up of only the rules you really believe in. It is best if you and your spouse can work together to create a code you are both committed to living by, but if that isn't feasible, create your personal code of ethics that honors your desire for loving your marriage.*

If in the earlier exercise you listed a rule that, upon examination, you find you are not committed to, don't include it in your personal code of ethics. Once you've created your code, an easy way to test it is to ask yourself which of the rules you have broken or think there is a good chance of breaking. If you're not committed to a rule, don't pretend that you will live by it. Instead, only

*add to your code the rules you deeply believe in, or create new
rules that you are willing to abide by.* ∽

Your personal code of ethics may look something like the following (or it may consist of entirely different rules). If you created your code with your partner, each would be written with "we" rather than "I":

- Honesty is to be expressed with purpose and a commitment to the other person's well-being. If I (we) have to say something that may be hurtful, I commit to staying with the other person through his pain and helping him to understand.

- I am here to grow spiritually and am committed to always choosing the highest path that is visible to me. That path is one in which I honor love instead of ego and aim for the highest good of all involved.

- My spouse is on his own spiritual journey, and although his choices aren't always the ones I would make, I trust that he knows what is best for his journey.

- Honoring my marriage vows is important and I'm committed to living by them. I am committed to being faithful and doing everything in my power to make the marriage work and to make it joyful.

- I will treat my spouse as I know she wants to be treated.

- To the best of my ability, I will strive to support my spouse and our marriage and to opt for forgiveness, understanding, and compassion rather than anger, judgment, and blame.

Interestingly, one of *Webster's* definitions of "integrity" is "behavior in accordance with a strict code of values." Hence, when you have defined your values and your personal code of ethics, and when you actively live in alignment with them, you will be living authentically, expressing who you really are in your words, thoughts, and actions. I guarantee that your relationships, which are dependent on your integrity, will be healthier.

Once you have developed your code of ethics, revisit it from time to time, along with your vision statement. This will help you when you face decisions that may conflict with your goal of loving your marriage.

➤ **MARK AND NANCY, MARRIED TEN YEARS**

For Nancy and me, two things are important: (1) expressing appreciation, thanking one another, and feeling gratitude (not criticism) in general; (2) recognizing and bringing up concerns and resentments in a loving way, with a positive intention.

Both require excellent communication and a spirit of loving-kindness.

Love Tip: When it comes to relationships, very few situations are clearly right/wrong or good/bad. When it comes to determining what to do, refer instead to your own internal meters that indicate wise/unwise, healthy/unhealthy, nourishing/toxic.

Rules for Arguing, Disagreeing, and Resolving Issues

In addition to your code of ethics, or perhaps as a section of it, create some guidelines or rules for fair fighting.

If you search on the Internet for "rules for fair fighting" you'll find many websites that offer suggestions. Some of them will make sense to you and will fit your personality, and some of them won't, so pick and choose based on your own and your spouse's personalities. When you approach this topic with your spouse, do so when you are not fighting or in the middle of an argument. Undertaking this project will definitely work better if you develop these guidelines hypothetically rather than in a moment when you need them.

Here are some examples:

1. Save important discussions and disagreements for alcohol- and drug-free moments. It is nearly impossible to have a

conversation of value when one or both partners are under the influence.

2. Keep your voices to a conversation level. Avoid yelling. This can be difficult when you are really upset, but getting louder does not equal being heard.

3. Keep the issue about the present situation. Avoid bringing the past into the argument or mixing issues together (unless they are relevant to the current topic).

4. Clean up small issues before they compound into big ones, but avoid being nitpicky about every little thing.

5. Let go of the ego (i.e., the need to "be right") and focus instead on the goals of resolving the issue and maintaining a loving relationship.

6. Move on quickly. Once something is resolved or has been expressed, let go of it and move on. Don't bring it up again and rehash it unless it hasn't been resolved.

7. Take responsibility for your part of the problem.

8. Keep it a clean argument. No name calling or swearing at the other person.

9. No violence under any circumstances. This means no hitting or hurting each other or yourself, and also no damaging property.

10. Whenever possible, discuss heated issues out of earshot of the children. Although it is important for them to see their parents engaged in healthy problem solving, it is also important to avoid causing them unnecessary worry and fear.

11. Always remember that you love each other, even though you are disagreeing. The goal of "fighting" is to restore harmony, not eliminate it.

Hopefully, you will be able as a couple to establish and agree on rules that work for both of you. Then agree on a way to remind each other of the guidelines in the heat of the moment, if one or the other forgets. Make sure your agreed-upon technique won't compound the problem. For instance, stop participating in the discussion and hold up your hand as a signal that the two of you need to return to the rules. An excellent guide for working through anger appears in Chapter 8, "Managing Emotions and Communicating Clearly."

Even if your partner won't participate in making rules, make your own. This is part of living in alignment with your values and ethics. If only one of you is fighting "fair," it will be better than if neither of you is. In keeping with the EROS equation, it is always a good rule of thumb to see if there is anything *you* can do differently, before asking or expecting *your partner* to do something differently. This is really all about your response to the events, so keep clearly in your mind the outcome and solution you are aiming for, and always start by taking responsibility.

On the television show *I Love Lucy,* Ricky and Lucy were in the middle of a huge fight and were no longer talking to each other. Ricky was complaining to Fred about it when Fred asked, "Ricky, when you and Lucy fight, how long do you usually go without talking to each other?"

Ricky answered, "About three days."

Fred asked, "What happens after three days to resolve it?"

Ricky explained, "I apologize and we make up."

"Well," Fred reasoned, "why don't you just apologize and make up *now* and avoid three days in the doghouse?!"

Love Tip: When you find yourself in a battle in which the only thing at stake is your ego, the best way to get out of the battle is to let the other person win.

➤ CHERYL AND MIKE, MARRIED FIVE YEARS

Mike and I handle our issues by taking "microscopic truth" breaks. We have set up the ground rules so that when we are sharing a microscopic truth, the other person is not to take it personally or to feel in any way that it is his or her problem. I will tell Mike, "I have some microscopic truth to share. When you said (or did) this (whatever it was), what came up for me at that moment was..."—and then I describe what I felt. It is taking the role of the observer—rather than the judge or the victim—to try to see where the emotions were coming from, to analyze why you are feeling a particular emotion as a result of something the other person has done or said. It is making you responsible for your own feelings as opposed to blaming the other person when you are not happy. I believe I am the only person who controls whether I am happy or not. My mate is not given that responsibility. If I don't enjoy something or am not happy, I have to look at it and analyze why I'm feeling that way.

Consequently, we never have angry outbursts or lack of harmony. The biggest challenge to this kind of problem solving is that uncomfortable feelings can come up at inappropriate times. It's really important that you take the time when you are feeling something to stop and breathe into the emotion and examine it and see where it is coming from. Sometimes it is hard for a partner who may feel a bit threatened or too busy to just stop and hold hands and be quiet until the emotional storm has passed. But that is the reason we are in relationship. And when either one of us says, "I have some microscopic truth," it means we have to stop and take a few minutes and work through it.

In the long run, there really is nothing more important, even though supper may be cooking or something else is going on. We care about each other enough to hold a space for each other and to acknowledge that there needs to be a healing at that moment. We care enough to recognize that the healing is the most important thing in our lives right now. Forget the job or the kids or the deadlines. If my mate is emotionally distressed, he is the most important thing in my world.

A Look at the Vows ...
and Renewing Them

The vows you shared when you got married are in essence a code of ethics. They definitely serve as guideposts. If you have them, look at a copy of your marriage vows. Review exactly what you committed to doing and for how long. As you read them, ask yourself how you feel about them. Have you ever really thought about what they mean? Do you still agree to them—*all* of them?

Although there are variations on the theme, here are the traditional wedding vows:

I take you to be my husband (or wife),

to have and to hold from this day forward,

for better, for worse,

for richer, for poorer,

in sickness and in health,

to love and to cherish,

until death do us part.

This is my solemn vow.

A couple of things strike me as I read them. One thing I notice is that they aren't conditional. They don't say, "I love you for richer, for poorer—but not through gambling and bankruptcy. I promise to love you in sickness and in health—but not through a debilitating disability in which I have to be the caretaker. I promise to love you for better or for worse—but not if you cheat on me. I promise to love you until I don't feel like I love you anymore." The idea here is that these vows are not meant to be conditional at all; marriage is a partnership that is designed to help get you through life's challenges, through the "conditions," but that in itself can be one of life's challenges. The other thing I notice is that the quality of the relationship isn't emphasized, only the quantity—the "no matter what" theme. We tend to think of marriage more as a destiny than a process, when in fact we would all do well to continuously aim at evoking the elation in our *relation*ships.

In a moment you are going to be asked to reconsider the vows you took when you got married and to determine, just like you did for your code of ethics, which ones you really believe in and are committed to, taking into consideration the quality you are dedicated to creating in your marriage, not just the quantity of years.

In the wedding ceremonies I perform, I offer an alternative to the traditional vows and a blessing that speaks more to the quality of the marriage:

With this ring, I marry you,

And promise my faithful love.

I have chosen you above all others

For my partner and companion.

I shall love you,

And honor you,

And share with you life's joys

And life's difficulties.

In sorrow, I shall comfort you,

In times of need, I shall be there for you,

In good times, I shall rejoice with you,

From this day forward and forevermore.

May your love grow and bring you peace and joy on life's path. From each other, may you always find communication, compassion, tolerance, understanding, and forgiveness. And to each other, may you always be best friends, companions, lovers, partners, and teachers. May your home always radiate an environment of happiness and unity, and may whoever enters your home be blessed and inspired by the harmony and love that dwell there.

While the vows are "till death do us part" or "forevermore," I've often thought that a "renewal plan," like we get with a driver's license, might make more sense—at least when no children are involved. My husband and I have jokingly pretended that our marriage license required a renewal every five years. On every fifth anniversary we discuss what is working and what is not, what might need improvement, and whether we're both "in" for five more years. "Forever" is a bit daunting, but committing to giving the relationship your all for the next five years is less so. Although for the most part we were joking (because our commitment is "forever"), it is an interesting inquiry and discussion. What I really like about the concept of marriage renewal is that the rule (in our make-believe system) says that getting out (divorce) is only an option in five-year cycles. Consequently, if you were upset with your spouse during any year other than the fifth, tenth, fifteenth, etc., divorce or nonrenewal would not be an option. So, since getting out isn't an option, the couple is "forced" to resolve the issue. When divorce isn't an option and living miserably isn't a preference, one finds that there are a lot of other things one can do instead. This system minimizes the time you waste contemplating getting out, because it simply isn't allowed except during a "renewal year." Generally, by the time you do get to the five-year interval, things are restored and thriving again.

> **Did you know?** *The Case For Marriage*, by Linda Waite and Maggie Gallagher, reports that in a study of more than 550 adults from a national database, 64 percent of those who said they were unhappy but stayed together anyway reported that they were happy five years later, while 50 percent of those who divorced or separated were still unhappy five years later. Here is the good news: Unhappiness doesn't have to be a permanent condition!

....

EXERCISE ∾ *While the marriage renewal plan is obviously not a reality in today's society, consider how you could put the concept to use in your marriage anyhow. What if you were to pretend during the years that weren't up for renewal that your only option was to really practice the EROS equation and take responsibility for what you were creating with your spouse? What if every five years—or every three years, or every anniversary— you took a serious look at your marriage and at what you both wanted to change, and then renewed your commitment accordingly? What if you, individually, evaluated your responses, and rather than renewing your marriage you renewed your commitment to aligning your words, thoughts, and actions with your vision?* ∾

....

One couple opted not to get married in the traditional sense but still wanted a legally binding agreement that outlined exactly what they were entering into by choosing to live together. They put a lot of thought into what they both wanted, what they were willing to commit to, and what they expected of each other in terms of time, space, and financial obligations. They visited a lawyer and drew up a very official agreement, which they both signed. It included articles such as "Recitals of Intention," "Relationships with Others" (in which they agreed to maintain sexual fidelity), "Care and Use of the Living Space," "Property, Debts, Living Expenses," "Evaluation of the Partnership," "Decision Making," and "Termination." Ironically, they put more thought into what their partnership meant than most couples who say "I do."

One very important clause was the "Evaluation of the Partnership." It reads:

> Pat and Wally recognize the importance of change in their relationship and intend that this agreement shall be a living document. They agree to engage in periodic evaluation of the partnership (at least twice a year). They agree that either party can initiate a review of any article of the agreement at any time to reflect changes in the partnership. The parties agree to honor such requests for review with negotiations and discussions at a mutually convenient time. The parties agree that in the case of unresolved conflicts between them over any provisions of the agreement, they will seek mediation, professional or otherwise, with a third party.

By mutual consent the agreement could be terminated and the relationship ended with thirty-days notice. This thoughtful agreement has carried Pat and Wally through thirty-five years of partnership—so far!

Think outside of tradition

Dear Eve,

I've been with the man in my life for twenty-five years, nineteen of those married (we lived together for six years before that). We've had a wonderful life, but now we each want something different. For most of the last twenty-five years we've lived in the country, where we overlook the coastline of Maui. I love it here. Now my husband wants to move to another part of the island, where there is no ocean view and it is very hot, windy, dirty, and loud. This has caused an upheaval in our lives, and the worst in each other is coming out. We do love each other, but I'm

not sure we like each other. I think we should probably
have a period of separation, but we have talked about
divorce. We don't have children and we both have good
jobs. This is a horrible time in my life. Any advice you
could give would be greatly appreciated.

Aloha,

Whenever I hear married couples talk about divorce, unless
the situation is totally abusive or unsafe I encourage
them to consider what they would do if divorce were not an
option. Ultimately, you would have to make a conscious
choice either to continue living miserably or to do something different within the marriage. My guess is if you
had to stay married, you would seek ways of making the relationship work. Sometimes just knowing that getting out
is an option is what keeps us from seeing other solutions.

My immediate reaction to your situation — and this may not
be practical — is for you to stay where you are and for him
to get a place where he wants to live. Rather than viewing
it as an official separation, maybe you could think of it
as an opportunity to totally revitalize your relationship.
You stay married and committed, but live in separate homes
within visiting distance. You could date, meet for dinner,
and sometimes stay at each other's houses. You may find
that not having to be together allows you to remember what
you most love and enjoy about each other. You may find
that you are more attracted to each other when you aren't
together every night. You may also find that being apart
is totally unacceptable, in which case you then figure out
how to compromise and improve the relationship. You have
to also know that this may be the first step out the door
of the marriage, so you really need to consider whether
you want to open that door. It certainly would be a step
to take before divorce, as it may be just what you need to
find your way back together again.

If you split up simply because you don't want to work on
things or get the necessary assistance, unfortunately, you
will likely find yourself in another relationship with
similar issues that need to be resolved. Relationships are
the ultimate spiritual-growth experience. The point is
that we learn from each other, learn from the relationship, and gain wisdom in the process. We get to "practice"

finding ways to return to love, to transcend our egos, to
love unconditionally, to serve, to grow, to learn, to let
go. What a practice ground marriage is! The important
thing here is to find ways to bring out the best in yourself — and in each other.

With aloha,

Eve

When author and speaker Maryanne Comaroto and her partner,
David, were courting, they contemplated the concept of "prenuptial
agreements." They decided that rather than creating a contract of
withholding, or "what you won't get from me," they would agree to
be "enriched no matter what" from the experience of being in a relationship together. They created and signed a "Consciousness Contract" that acknowledged their intention of staying conscious and
aligned with the goal of love and harmony.

➤ MARYANNE AND DAVID'S CONSCIOUSNESS CONTRACT

It is my purpose in this life to serve and to continue to grow. I offer
you this consciousness contract as a gift, given out of love and fierce
compassion.

This work is not about me, it is about *we,* and I promise to continue to
seek the truth in my heart, body, mind, and spirit.

I promise to stay committed to my path of consciousness and agree
to do all that is in my power to stay awake so that I may better do
God's will.

I promise to be true to myself and to be true to all that I teach and
share with you.

I will do my very best to refrain from judgment.

I agree to clean up any situation where I may have caused harm.

I agree to stay even when I want to run, and to stay open even when
I want to shut down to protect myself, knowing that in my vulnerabil-
ity I will eventually find true strength. I agree not to always have to be
right and not to always have to know everything.

I will allow myself to stand alongside you and be fully human with all my flaws and ugliness, as well as all my beauty and radiance, so that I may fully share this journey with you.

I agree to be your mirror as you are my own.

I agree to let myself fall off my path without ridicule or judgment.

I agree to let you fall off your path with the same grace and dignity and invite you back to the celebration of your life as seamlessly as possible.

I agree to remind you, as you remind me, that in every moment there is an opportunity to reunite with God and to stay awake in consciousness.

I agree to aspire to a life filled with gratitude, abundance for all, and peace on earth. I pray that we all find that peace in ourselves so that we practice goodwill toward each other.

I agree to laugh at myself regularly, and to laugh aloud as often as I can.

I ask that you hold me in my highest light, wishing only that I become the best version of what God would have me be as a whole, loving human being; I will do the same for you.

I ask that you honor my sacred boundaries of time and space with courtesy and care, as I honor yours.

I ask that you be responsible in your communication and also that you own that your experience and your reality stem directly from inside of you.

I ask that you communicate your feelings and thoughts with care, from the heart and with the sole intention of creating love and peace.

I ask that we agree to self-inquiry first, seeking answers to all of our issues within ourselves.

I ask that we agree to engage in responsible and respectful communication, refraining from harsh judgment, remembering the precious words "There but for the grace of God go I."

It is my mission to help end human suffering and to do all that is in my power to help as many people on the planet as I can.

It is our vision to transform the culture that shapes young people.

May God bless you always and keep you safe from harm.

EXERCISE `∾ *If you were to write your own marriage vows now, knowing what you know that you didn't know when you got married, what would your renewal vows say? What are you willing to commit to? How would you create a conscious relationship? If your partner agrees, consciously create personalized vows that you both are willing to commit to together and that incorporate your values, your vision, and your code of ethics.* ∾

The next few chapters will guide you through a process that will help you apply the EROS equation in your marriage every day, using your guideposts to help you. Let's first turn our attention to understanding the role of self-esteem in your relationship, and the impact of your relationship on your self-esteem.

If, so far, you have been reading without taking the time to actually write down your responses to the exercises, I invite you to stop here, go get some paper and a pen—and perhaps your spouse—and do the work! Self-discovery is a great adventure, and the benefits— love, peace of mind, wisdom, strength, and the chance at a loving marriage—are well worth the time and effort.

CHAPTER 4

understanding the
Role of self-esteem

If we do not love ourselves, how can we love others?

THE DALAI LAMA

To explain what happens to love between two people, we need to begin by understanding what happens to self-love, or self-esteem. Since you are the primary ingredient—and the common denominator—in all of your relationships, you will see the definite correlation between the strength of your self-esteem and the health of your relationships. Understanding the dynamics of self-esteem, what happens to it as we grow up, and how to put it back on the right path will not only help you feel better about yourself, which will certainly contribute to your relationships, but will also assist you in enhancing the self-esteem of the people you love the most: your family, spouse, and children.

Some Misconceptions

First, let's clear up some serious misconceptions our society has about self-esteem.

- We have mistakenly thought that ego or conceit is the same thing as self-esteem. It is not. Self-esteem is based on our inherent worth and strength as human beings, that is, on our soul essence. Ego is based on our minds—what we think—

95

not on who we are at our core. In relationships, ego pushes people away, while self-esteem attracts them.

- By the nature of our common language on the subject, we have created the misunderstanding that self-esteem is "high" or "low." Self-esteem is referred to here as "high" or "low" simply for convenience, but we don't really have high or low levels of self-esteem. By its nature, our soul essence has an abundance of self-esteem. We have either easy access or blocked access to that self-esteem. The same is true for love. Love doesn't go away; it just gets blocked.

- We have mistakenly thought that once we achieve easy access to our self-esteem, it is ours for good. In actuality, self-esteem, much like physical fitness, has to be continuously and consciously maintained. The good news is that once healthy self-esteem has been achieved, the "lows" don't go as deep, and a pathway out of the depths has already been forged so you don't stay down as long. Relationships also require this ongoing maintenance.

- We have mistakenly thought that self-esteem is "global." That is, we think that if someone has self-esteem, they have it across the board in all areas of life. In reality, someone can feel good about his performance at work and terrible about his relationships at home. Someone can have high self-esteem with regard to her productivity or creativity and low self-esteem around her body image.

- We have greatly underestimated the impact of self-esteem on our relationships by mistakenly thinking that the health of our self-esteem only impacts how we feel about *ourselves*. In actuality, our self-esteem also impacts our ability to feel loved by others, to feel worthy of the love of others, and to share our love with others. If we do not love ourselves, we cannot fully believe that others love us. If we do not feel worthy of love, we will sabotage our relationships to prove that we were right about our lack of worthiness. If we do not feel love within us, we are unable to share our love with others. If we cannot love ourselves unconditionally, forgive ourselves for our mistakes, and experience joy and happiness on a daily basis, we cannot love others unconditionally, forgive them when necessary, or share our joy and happiness with them.

Love Tip: Remember that we are custodians of each other's self-esteem and each other's heart. We must be cognizant of the words we use, while still honoring the truth and our personal boundaries.

Who You Really Are

Consider the positive qualities of small children before they have been "contaminated" by the world around them. They are inherently playful, funny, creative, honest, imaginative, curious, wonder-filled, loving, joyful, and enthusiastic. They are adventurous risk-takers. They are authentic and in the moment with their emotions; they laugh when they are happy, cry when they are sad, and forget about whatever upset them as soon as it is fixed or something new happens. They are natural learners, wanting to know what everything is called and how things work. They are creative and imaginative, able to build a magnificent fort out of a few blankets and chairs. Children are able to take compliments simply because they know their own worth and are confident that the compliments are true. Small children get along with others regardless of race, religion, gender, or handicap because they haven't yet learned to judge. Small children are forgiving because living in the present moment doesn't allow them to hold a grudge. Children are closely aligned with their esteemed self because they haven't yet had life experiences that have separated their egos from their spirits. Small children know their divine essence. All they do is an authentic expression of who they are. When you consider the qualities of someone with high self-esteem, they are very similar: confident, risk-taking, adventurous, authentic, eager to learn, happy, loving, lovable. . . .

Keep in mind that this is true not only about the children *outside* of you but also about the child *inside* of you. You were like this as a child, too! These childlike qualities are an expression of your soul; they represent who you really are. The good news is that these qualities never go away; they just get covered up. Our access to them gets blocked. With a little concerted effort, we can regain access to all these childlike, esteemed qualities.

> *Love Tip:* It is interesting to note that the qualities of high self-esteem and the qualities of ego often look the same—assertive, passionate, confident, carefree—but they feel very different! Behavior based in true self-esteem is never done with an intention to hurt others. Self-esteem attracts others; ego repels them. Pay attention to how you feel when you are with another person, and you will be able to tell if one or both of you are coming from ego or self-esteem.

Who You Think You Are

As we grow up, important people in our lives—parents, relatives, siblings, friends, teachers—through both their words and their actions give us negative input that impacts our self-esteem. They say things to us that don't feel good: "You're stupid." "You're ugly." "What is that C doing on your report card? You will never amount to anything." Sometimes the messages weren't so blatant but rather came through loud and clear when a parent couldn't make time for us, or we were picked last for the baseball team, or someone gave us a dirty look, or a teacher rolled her eyes when we answered a question, or a close friend whispered and pointed behind our back. Regardless of whether the other person was really upset with us, we would take in these experiences as information about who we were and what we were worth. From there, we began to form beliefs that defined us.

For instance, when I was young I was not very athletic and was always chosen last for sports teams. Whenever I was up to bat or kick, the other team would chant the familiar "Easy out, easy out." Since my name was Evey, it quickly became "Evey out, Evey out," and I would promptly strike out. Over the years I developed a belief that I was not good at athletics, and I began to hate physical education classes, particularly if they involved a team sport. When I got into high school and could choose my P.E. classes, I chose activities that didn't put me at risk for public ridicule and, preferably, which I could do by myself or with only one other person, like archery, dancing, or Frisbee. The messages I was sent caused me to take on a belief that I, in turn, used to limit my life experiences and my relationships. While it was true that I wasn't good at athletics, what wasn't true was that I couldn't *become* good at athletics with proper training, practice, improved coordination, and physical growth. However, I let the belief that I wasn't good stop me from becoming good. Effectively, I blocked my self-esteem in the area of athletics by blocking my natural ability to learn, play, and take risks.

When I got older I moved to Hawaii and wanted to participate in competition outrigger canoe paddling, even though it was a team sport. I gave it a shot and much to my surprise discovered that I had a natural ability to paddle. I began training extensively as part of a team that was going to compete in the forty-mile Molokai to Oahu race. Just days before the big race, my back went out and I was unable to compete. I am absolutely convinced that my underlying belief that I would let my team down or that I was not athletic was physically manifested in my back problems. Ironically, I let my team down regardless of my performance. My underlying beliefs that I was not a team player, that I couldn't do it, and that I was incapable impacted my relationship with others.

We have all adopted limiting beliefs about different parts of ourselves. Something undoubtedly happened along the way to communicate to you that you were not good at something, and you bought into it, turned it into a belief, and began acting out your life in alignment with it. It wasn't a belief that served you, and yet perhaps you still live your life in accordance with it. At what age did you take on the belief that you couldn't sing or speak in public or that you were not good at art, or math, or reading, or spelling? Maybe these beliefs were based on the truth about your skills and abilities at age eight, ten, or twelve. What *wasn't* true was that this belief defined who you were, what you were capable of becoming, or what you were capable of overcoming by learning new skills.

Consider how this shows up in your life. Did you ever take on the belief that you didn't deserve love? Or that you couldn't make or manage money? How about the belief that you can't make someone else happy in a relationship or that relationships don't last or that you can't be faithful? How about the belief that to really open your heart and show up 100 percent in a relationship makes you too vulnerable and is dangerous? Or that if you told the whole truth about yourself no one would want to be with you? How about

Did you know? Two out of three Americans suffer from low self-esteem.

the belief that you are nobody without your partner and you could not possibly live if he or she were to leave you? Maybe yours is the belief that if you allow yourself to fully love someone else, you will lose control; therefore you remain reserved (otherwise known as "emotionally unavailable"). These are simply beliefs—who you *think* you are—that are only true as long as you believe them, and they only stay alive as long as you feed them with the fuel of your energy.

As we take life experiences and begin turning them into limiting beliefs, we mistakenly begin to believe that who we are is someone limited, fearful, undeserving, reserved, incapable, dependent, jealous, possessive, and weak, instead of who we really are: someone powerful, abundant, capable, friendly, energetic, creative, imaginative, expressive, authentic, and loving.

Now, consider which you would rather be.

Then, consider which you would rather be in a relationship with!

Love Tip: Feeling confident and beautiful is an inside job, not an outside one. Confidence is a very attractive feature, so start noticing all you have to offer.

Who You Want Everyone Else to Think You Are

Remember, who we *really* are is being covered up and smothered by who we have come to *think* we are, based on our limiting beliefs. Since it is so painful to believe all these negative and limiting statements about ourselves and to allow others to see these things in us, we develop defense mechanisms to try to keep more pain out. So we put on a façade to keep others from hurting us further or to keep them from seeing (what we think is) the truth about us (that we are limited and weak). We may begin judging others in an effort to relieve the pain by trying to prove that we are better than everyone else or by acting as if this were true. We may show up as really angry or distant, unconsciously figuring that if we are angry enough or aloof enough, people will not get close enough to hurt us. In order to hide our negative beliefs about ourselves, we may try to impress other people by dressing a certain way, driving fancy cars, buying expensive things, or trying to be perfect. We may flaunt our sexuality or become promiscuous, unconsciously thinking the kind of attention we receive can make us feel better about ourselves. We may try to avoid being hurt by not trying new things, thus avoiding the potential failure that would add to our negative beliefs. We may smile even when we don't feel happy or friendly because we figure if we just keep on smiling, other people will think we are okay. We may crack jokes ad nauseam in an effort to keep people laughing so that they will like us. We may take drugs or abuse other substances in an effort both to numb our pain and to divert others' attention toward our addictions and away from our painful beliefs. We unconsciously think that if we throw them off track, they won't notice how bad we feel about ourselves. We may even work out excessively or develop eating disorders in an effort to cover up what we believe to be true (that we are not okay the way we are).

Our unconscious efforts to protect ourselves cause us to become more and more inauthentic until we feel totally disconnected from other people and, worse yet, disconnected from ourselves. If we no longer know who we really are, it is impossible to believe that the people we are in relationships with know us. Worse yet, it is impossible to truly believe, to truly receive, their love because we don't feel worthy.

If one or more of the above statements describes you, it's important to remember the following:

Even though we no longer know who we really are,
our essence is still there. It has simply gotten blocked.

Keep in mind that there is nothing wrong with being funny, or doing your best, or being sexual, or working out, or having nice things—when they are an authentic expression of who you really are or when they are a celebration of your joy. The problem enters when you believe this is who you *have to be* to keep others from hurting you or to make them like you. It requires a huge amount of effort to put on this show, as opposed to the effortless task of just relaxing into your true nature, your true self-expression.

Let me give you a graphic analogy. Imagine that "who you really are" is a glass full of sparkling, clear, pure, bubbly water—refreshing and delightful. Then, your life experiences and the people around you begin pouring dirty, grimy motor oil into your glass. Since oil floats on water, a mucky layer of oil forms on top of your beautiful, pure effervescence. Now when you look at yourself you see the oily muck instead of the clear, refreshing water, and you begin to believe that this mucky layer is who you are. Who you really are is still there, but your access to it is blocked.

Then, because you don't like the way this oily muck looks or feels, you begin sprinkling glitter on top. You want other people to see the glitter instead of the muck because, hopefully, they won't hurt you more by pointing out the muck. The pure, bubbly water is covered up by the oil, which is covered up by the glitter. Who you really are (your soul essence) is covered up by who you think you are (your mucky thoughts and thought-generated feelings), which is covered up by who you want everyone else to think you are (the façade you present to the world for self-protection).

The irony here is that we think our glittery ego layer will protect us or make people like us more, and maybe even make us like ourselves more. So we all go around bumping into each other, glitter to glitter or muck to muck (that is, ego to ego). And while the glittery ego layer may sometimes protect us from feeling more pain, it also "protects" us from feeling more love. Our inauthentic connections with others leave us feeling isolated and lonely. In actuality, ego, in both its damaged, mucky form and its bandaged, glittery form, is what blocks our access to self-esteem—to heart, to truth, to connection, to intimacy, to love—every time.

So, as you can see, there is a huge difference between ego and self-esteem. Self-esteem is expressed when you know your own true essence and live in alignment with it. Ego is what blocks your ability to do so.

The secret to turning all of this around will be explained in detail in Chapter 6, but for now keep in mind that it is simply a process of growing who you really are and simultaneously letting go of who you really aren't. Taking the water, oil, and glitter analogy further, if you were to pour more pure, bubbling water into the glass, the levels would rise, causing the glitter and oil to spill over the edge. The good news is that for many of our self-esteem issues, when we simply start paying attention to who we really are and growing that aspect of ourselves by acknowledging our positive, authentic qualities, our negative beliefs and defense mechanisms start to fall away. The bad news is that sometimes it is a painful process. In an effort to grow our goodness we may identify our good qualities, citing, "I am a good friend, trustworthy spouse, and honest person." Then we may hear a small inner voice say, "Oh yeah, if you are such a good friend, how about the time you...." Or, "If you are so honest, what about when...."

> **Did you know?** Enthusiasm comes from the Greek root *en theos,* meaning "in God."

As the negative and limiting beliefs rise to the surface, they often make themselves known—and felt. Instead of simply caving in and thinking, "You are right, who am I fooling? I am a worthless person," do a process of self-inquiry to determine if the "voice of doubt" is true, and if so use it as feedback for developing a strategy for improvement. If it is inaccurate or is old news—if it is not a current description of you—let it go. As you continue to grow who you really are and let go of who you really aren't, you will soon discover that the oil and glitter barely leave a trace and all you are left with is your pure, authentic, joyful, enthusiastic self.

An exercise for working through this process is provided in the upcoming section in this chapter on creating empowering beliefs. Guidelines for how to take a deeper look at your "self-talk"—the things you tell yourself—are found in Chapter 6.

My self-esteem, my child's self-esteem

Dear Eve,

I had really low self-esteem as a teenager, and I still
have a lot of self-doubt. I now have a two-year-old daughter, and I really don't want her to suffer the same thing.
What can I do to ensure that she grows up with a healthy
self-image?

Aloha,

I admire your ability to recognize that this concern needs
to be addressed now, while your daughter is still young.
It can, of course, be addressed at any time, but creating
healthy self-esteem is easier as prevention than cure.
The older a person gets, the more they become responsible
for changing their own self-esteem and the less you can do
for them.

Young children (before they've been "contaminated" by
negativity) have a natural state of self-esteem. Our job
as parents (and teachers, friends, family, and community)
is to help maintain this esteemed state. Our job as individuals is to regain access to it in ourselves. It never
really goes away; it just gets covered up.

The challenge is that when our own self-esteem is low, it
is difficult to enhance self-esteem in others because
children learn from what we do; they learn by example. The
best possible thing you can do for your daughter is to
actively work on raising your own self-esteem and treating
yourself with respect. The other thing you can do is to
become very aware of the words you use and the messages
you give your daughter throughout the day, making sure you
use language and the power of your words in a healthy,
esteeming way.

There was a study done many years ago in Iowa in which
two-year-olds were followed around for a day. The researchers counted the number of positive and negative
comments made to the children. The results revealed that
the average two-year-old received 432 negative or controlling statements a day and only 32 positives. That is a

ratio of 13.5 to 1. Although everyone knows that two-year-olds need constant monitoring, to create a child with a healthy self-image the ratio of positive comments should be two to three times that of the negative and controlling statements. This is known as the "sandwich theory": sandwiching your corrective words between encouraging comments.

Raising your own self-esteem begins in exactly the same way: becoming acutely aware of your self-talk and replacing or balancing the negative and critical comments you give yourself with positive, encouraging statements.

Consider this: If you said to your friends the things you say to yourself, would you still have any friends?

We tend to be incredibly hard on ourselves. Many of us emotionally "beat ourselves up" with constant negative self-talk, which results in low self-esteem, fear, unhealthy relationships, self-sabotage, and depression. We each must take responsibility for turning that process around.

First, begin to "self-observe" so that you become aware of what you are doing, saying, and thinking. Next, start to make new choices about what you do, say, and think so that your actions, words, and thoughts are in alignment with your goal of creating healthy self-esteem. Although there are many ways to raise self-esteem, these two simple tasks are a huge step in the right direction.

Remember, regaining access to your self-esteem (or any personal growth) isn't achieved instantaneously. To even attempt that would be overwhelming. All change takes place one moment at a time. And that means every moment is an opportunity to start fresh!

With aloha,

Eve

Love Tip: When you change the way you think about yourself, you disarm the power others have to make you feel bad.

The Impact of Self-Esteem
on Relationships

A marriage has the potential to be a mutually supportive classroom, playground, and safe sanctuary. Marriages provide the perfect arena for us to learn, love, laugh, and serve. They are the ultimate place for us to share ourselves authentically, transcend our egos (the mucky, glittery obstacle to love), practice our relationship skills, and gain new ones. In fact, relationships are often the *only* arena in which we are truly able to grow and improve. It is only in relationships that we get feedback about how we show up, how we communicate, how we treat others, how our mood or energy affects our behavior, and how we solve problems. Our intimate relationship shows us how our ego tries to make us right—instead of happily married. The ego often forgets the goal of having a healthy relationship.

Because most of us have approached our relationships (and our lives) from ego instead of spirit, we have "mucked up" our marriages. Our egos bring out our possessive, judgmental, controlling, and needy tendencies, generating pain, a loss of freedom, and a lack of authenticness. Because this is so painful—and completely out of alignment with who we really are—we sprinkle more "glitter" on top, trying to portray to the world (and perhaps to our spouse and children) a happy marriage when inside we desperately wish for something, or someone, else. Sometimes the ego manifests as anger, sometimes as apathy, sometimes as addiction. . . .

When there is a difference (a gap) between who you really are at your core (your soul) and how you are showing up (your ego), your self-esteem suffers—and so do your relationships. It's as though your self-esteem and the health of your relationships fall into that gap.

- If you value honesty but regularly tell lies, there is a gap. (which causes blocked self-esteem and unhealthy relationships).

- If you value being kind to others and you act kindly, there is no gap. (and thus you have healthy self-esteem and healthy relationships).

- If you value monogamy but cheat on your spouse, there is a gap (and thus low self-esteem and damaged relationships).

- If you value taking responsibility for your actions and you admit your mistakes and learn from them, there is no gap (and you enjoy high self-esteem and repairable relationships).

- If you value communication but don't listen to others or express your feelings, there is a gap (which blocks your self-esteem and isolates you in your relationships).

- If you value being a good friend and you show up for your friends in thoughtful, consistent, and fair ways, there is no gap (and thus high self-esteem and strong relationships).

- If you value being fit but you know you could improve your diet and exercise habits, there is a gap (and thus a bad feeling about yourself that impacts your relationships).

When access to our esteemed, authentic self is blocked, our relationships suffer. When we think we don't deserve love, we sabotage our relationships to prove ourselves right. As author and speaker Byron Katie points out, "Our mind's job is to validate what it thinks." If we think we are unworthy of love, we may do or say things that push the other person away so we can prove ourselves right. If we think we are incapable of having a healthy relationship, we unconsciously create unhealthy situations to validate our perceptions. When we think we are unattractive, we don't trust that others could be attracted to us. Although our relationships definitely have an impact on our self-esteem (if we allow them to), our self-esteem can make or break a relationship (whether we mean for it to or not).

The good news is that the blockages to our self-esteem can be removed. But here is the deal: No one can really damage your self-esteem without your consent. You had to take on the beliefs as your very own; otherwise, they wouldn't have impacted you in a negative way. Your father could have said you would never amount to anything; if you believed it, your self-esteem was blocked. If you didn't believe it, you may have actually been inspired to prove him wrong by achieving all of your dreams and being the best you could be. It isn't what your father said that impacted you; it is how you responded to it. By the same token, no one can fix your self-esteem for you; you have to do the work. Your mother can say wonderful things about you ad nauseam, but if you don't believe her it won't change the way you feel about yourself. Your spouse can tell you and show you daily that he or she loves you, but if you believe you're unworthy of that love you won't be able to feel it.

Love Tip: When a relationship challenges your core values, you should challenge the relationship. When the relationship challenges you, rise to the challenge.

Creating Empowering Beliefs

We often think that just because we believe something, it is the truth, which is not always the case. As you know, the majority of people prior to 1492 believed that the earth was flat. That belief turned out to be wrong. Many, many of our beliefs—about everything from science to society—have been proven wrong over time with the addition of new information and new tools. Many of the beliefs we as individuals have held about ourselves and about our lives have also been proven wrong—or will be over the course of our lives. Therefore, the concept that "belief equals truth" is disputable.

The problem is that few of us are trained to question our beliefs, and unchallenged false beliefs have the power to alter our decisions and to limit what we can accomplish. When we use limiting beliefs as guideposts for our decision making (instead of the powerful guideposts we developed in the last chapter), they impact every aspect of our well-being, including our relationships. If we think something is dangerous, impossible, or too hard, we may not venture to do it. Can you imagine how many people didn't try sailing around the world based on the belief that they would fall off when they reached the edge? Can you imagine how many marriages have ended in divorce because of the belief that nothing could be done to make the marriage work?

It is interesting to note that the *Encarta World Dictionary* lists the following definitions of "belief": "1. Acceptance by the mind that something is true or real, often underpinned by an emotional or spiritual sense of certainty; 2. confidence that somebody or something is good or will be effective; 3. a statement, principle, or doctrine that a person or group accepts as true; 4. an opinion, especially a firm and considered one; and 5. religious faith." Nowhere does the dictionary imply that a belief is actually a fact, and yet most of us treat our beliefs as if they were the absolute truth, often without testing them. This is where self-examination and inquiry come in.

It is time to examine your beliefs about yourself and your relationships, challenge them, and determine whether they are serving you. If your beliefs make you feel good and serve your goal of having healthy self-esteem and a loving marriage, great. If not, it is time to develop a new mindset—one that emphasizes your personal power for creating and maintaining love in your life and in your marriage. The good news is that beliefs are something we *choose*. When your current choices aren't serving you, you can make new ones.

The following is a list of common beliefs that don't serve relationships well. As you read them, notice whether any of them are beliefs that *you* hold, consciously or unconsciously. Notice also how you *feel* as you read them.

False beliefs to challenge:

- Once I've fallen out of love with someone, that is that; I can't get it back.

- What I have experienced in the past is likely what I will experience in the future.

- My spouse has to do something different in order for our marriage to work.

- I can't improve the relationship by myself; it takes two.

- I need different conditions to make my marriage work (if only I had a job/we didn't have kids/we had kids/we had more money/I weighed less/I were more trusting/he hadn't cheated/she liked sex more . . .).

- I am powerless to change my life.

- Love relationships don't require work. They should be purely magical. (Or, conversely, relationships always require constant hard work.)

- If this relationship doesn't work, I will never have love again.

- I've never been in a relationship that lasted; this one probably won't either.

- Men (or women) aren't trustworthy.

If you hold any of these beliefs to be true, I encourage you to try on some new ones—at least while you are reading this book. Holding on to beliefs that limit your ability to create what you want will not serve you.

 Love Tip: It is never too late to make a new decision and adopt a new, more empowering belief.

As you read through the following list of empowering beliefs, notice the difference in the way you feel as you read them. Notice if an old belief or way of doing things is being challenged and, just for the sake of the exercise, try on some new beliefs to see if they serve you better. (You can always have the old ones back, in the unlikely event that you ever want to feel that way again.)

Empowering beliefs to try on:

- I can fall in love again. In fact, love has never left me; it has just gotten blocked. I can clear the obstacles between love and me—and between me and my partner.

- With new skills and tools, I can create new experiences.

- It is *my response* to circumstances—not the circumstances themselves—that dictate the quality of my relationships.

- I take full responsibility for the quality of my marriage.

- I can improve my experience of this relationship with or without my spouse's involvement.

- I am powerful and able to change—or simply enjoy— my life.

- Love is unlimited. As long as I am loving, I will never be without love.

- No relationship lasts until one does! This one can be the one.

- I trust myself to be able to handle any situation I encounter. I trust God to provide me with experiences that will help me grow wiser, stronger, and more compassionate.

This set of empowering beliefs speaks of possibility, while the set of false beliefs speaks of impossibility. If you want your marriage to work, if you want to reignite or maintain the love there, it is much easier to do so when you are open to the possibility that it *can* work and that *you* hold the power to transform it. Here's how: Simply become aware of when you are "feeding" a belief that limits possibility, and consciously switch to a belief that serves you—and your marriage—better. Your willingness to challenge old beliefs will make a huge difference in your ability to transform the way you approach your marriage.

....

EXERCISE ∾

1. Make a list of your limiting beliefs about yourself and about marriage and relationships. Write them down so you can examine them.

It may be easier to identify your limiting beliefs by working backwards. That is, start by looking at decisions you have made, and then identify the beliefs that led to those decisions. For instance, did you stop yourself from participating in sports because you didn't believe you could compete? Did you avoid trying out for choir because you didn't think you could sing? Did you stop yourself from having kids because someone told you that you were just like your mother or father—or because you didn't be-lieve you would be a good parent? Did you stop yourself from applying for the job you really wanted because you didn't think they would accept you? Did you take a job you didn't want be-cause you believed that no one else would hire you? Did you stay in a relationship you should have left because you thought you would never find someone else? Did you avoid writing the book you've always wanted to write because twenty years ago a teacher told you that you couldn't write—and you believed him or her? Do you stop yourself from sharing your ideas and dreams with others because you believe they will think you are stupid or a "dreamer"? Have you avoided trying to make your marriage work because you believed there was nothing you could do? Do you avoid telling the truth to your spouse about how you feel be-cause you believe he or she doesn't feel the same way, or won't care? The idea here is to simply become aware of the limiting be-liefs you have allowed to affect you—and which still may be im-pacting your choices and your happiness.

2. Look at each belief and ask yourself, "Is this really true?" Is it true that you cannot sing, or spell, or compete in sports? Often you will find that the belief is absolutely not true. Sometimes you will find that you don't really know if it is true because you have no concrete evidence. Other times you will find that even if it is true now or was true when you adopted it, the reality may be changeable. Ask yourself: "Can this reality be changed with les-sons and practice? Can it be changed by simply choosing a new belief?" What would your life be like if you simply stopped be-lieving that you were depressed, or lazy, or untalented...?

If you know the belief is true with no hope for change, then you need to practice self-acceptance by changing the way you talk to yourself about that issue. This will be discussed further in Chapter 6.

3. For each of the limiting beliefs you wrote down in step one, write an alternative, empowering belief that you could replace it with, as was done above in the lists of relationship beliefs. Re-

*member, your beliefs and thoughts are simply the responses you
choose to certain events in your life. Remember also that it is
possible in every moment to make new choices. m*

Ultimately, one of our main tasks as human beings is to align our
outer self with our inner self, to clear the blockages between the two.
Otherwise, we engage with others gap to gap instead of aligning heart
to heart. Meeting another person gap to gap forms a hole that the relationship can fall through.

In the next chapter you will find a "Self-Esteem Self-Assessment"
and a "Marriage Assessment." These tools will help you identify the
gaps in your self-esteem and in your relationship, and the information they yield will assist you in bridging the gaps step-by-step.

Love Tip: As you discover what is wonderful about
yourself, what you have to offer, and why someone
would want to be in a relationship with you, you will find that
others suddenly discover all of those things about you, too!

CHAPTER 5

Assessing the Gaps

Love is the great miracle cure. Loving ourselves
works miracles in our lives.

LOUISE HAY

The word "esteem" comes from the root word "estimate." Consequently, self-esteem is a self-estimation or self-assessment. Most people define self-esteem as simply how you feel about yourself, or your self-confidence, but the concept goes much deeper than that. The California Legislature's Task Force to Promote Self-Esteem and Personal and Social Responsibility was made up of national self-esteem experts who together defined self-esteem as follows: "Appreciating my own worth and importance and having the character to be accountable for myself and to act responsibly toward others." This definition is important because it broadens the meaning of self-esteem to include its effect on others, which is directly based on a person's actions and words. My personal definition of self-esteem is "Knowing your own divine essence and behaving in alignment with that essense." Having "high" self-esteem is really of little consequence if it doesn't manifest in your behavior. Interestingly, sometimes the only way to measure your self-esteem is to look at your actions and see if they are in alignment with your beliefs and values. If not, simply changing the action can impact your self-esteem.

A Self-Esteem Self-Assessment Tool

The following exercise offers you a tool for assessing your self-esteem. Completing the exercise will reveal to you any gaps between your perception of yourself as you are now and your vision of the way you

114

would like to be. Your self-esteem will be indicated by the width of the gaps *and* by how you feel about the gaps. As we discussed in Chapter 4, these gaps are the obstacles that block our self-love, and blocked self-love interferes with our ability to give love to and receive it from others.

You will find a list of paired words (generally extreme opposites) with numbers from 1 to 10 between the members of each pair. You will be asked to determine where on the continuum you think you are now, and where you think you *should* be. In some cases a gap between the two will be revealed; in other cases, there will be no gap. No gap means that where you are and where you want to be are the same; they are in alignment.

Here are examples of a few of the paired words so that you can have an understanding of how the assessment works as you read through the instructions:

EXAMPLES OF SELF-ASSESSMENT CONTINUUMS

	1	2	3	4	5	6	7	8	9	10	
Unattractive											Beautiful/handsome
Out of shape											Fit
Frigid/no libido											Sexy/sexual
Ignorant											Educated
Shy											Outgoing

It may at first appear that there is a "positive" end to the continuum and a "negative" end. While for several of the paired words, it is true that there is a societal bias toward one or the other, in some cases it would be preferable *not* to be at either extreme; instead, you may prefer to be right in the middle. It is important for you to recognize that this assessment is not about society's evaluation of you, or about what is right or wrong. The importance of this tool isn't at which end of the spectrum you place yourself for any individual item; its value lies entirely in helping you to see where there is a gap between *how you see yourself* and *how you want to see yourself*. In general, the wider the gap between the two, the lower or more blocked your self-esteem is around that particular issue. The narrower the gap, the higher or more accessible your self-esteem is.

If you find that the chosen words for opposite pairs get in your way of doing the exercise or even enjoying the assessment, *change the words!* Don't let the tool get in the way of your self-discovery. This is your tool, and if the words cause you stress or discomfort, it is easily remedied. Simply take responsibility for wording the pairs more appropriately, as you see fit. If there are other areas you want to look at that are not already listed (e.g., violent/peaceful, depressed/happy, etc.), you are welcome to put additional paired words on a separate sheet of paper.

As I explained in Chapter 4, self-esteem is not "global," meaning you may feel great about yourself in one area and terrible in another. This tool will help you figure out which areas need your attention. We are primarily looking for both narrow gaps, to flag areas of "high," or easily accessed, self-esteem, and wider gaps, to flag areas of "low," or blocked, self-esteem. In addition, this tool can guide you through the process of bridging the gaps, which we'll talk more about later.

How to Do the Exercise

After you have read these instructions, for each pair of extremes you will be invited to place an *O* in the box beneath the number that you believe currently describes where you are. For instance, on the scale between "unattractive" and "beautiful/handsome," determine how you honestly feel about the way you look, and place an *O* in the proper place. If you generally like the way you look but don't think you are beautiful, perhaps you would rate yourself an 8. If you don't like the way you look, perhaps you would rate yourself a 2 or 3. For example:

EXAMPLE OF A SELF-ASSESSMENT WITH AN *O* MARKING WHERE YOU ARE NOW

	1	2	3	4	5	6	7	8	9	10	
Unattractive			*O*								Beautiful/handsome

As you assess yourself with each pair of words, remember that you are rating *how you feel,* not necessarily *what is really true.* After you have placed your *O* in the box for all the paired words, you'll be asked to go back and place an *X* on the continuum where you feel you should be or would like to be. For instance, on the failure/successful continuum, I feel I am about a 7, so I would place an *O* in the box under the number 7. I would place an *X* under the number 9 because that is where I would like to be. My self-assessment would look like this:

EXAMPLE OF A SELF-ASSESSMENT WITH *O* REPRESENTING WHERE YOU ARE AND *X* MARKING WHERE YOU WOULD LIKE TO BE

	1	2	3	4	5	6	7	8	9	10	
Failure							*O*	*X*			Successful

Notice that the meaning attrributed to each pair of words and to each number on the continuum is entirely up to the person doing the assessment. For one person, being "successful" means becoming a millionaire; for another, it means being on *Oprah;* for another, it means overcoming an illness; for another, it means raising healthy, happy children; for another, it means having a happy marriage. What these values mean is entirely up to you.

As I already mentioned, although these paired words are extreme opposites, one extreme or the other may not be better or more appropriate. That is, being a 10 isn't necessarily preferred. In some cases, a 7 or 8 may be a more appropriate placement. For instance, "workaholic" isn't generally a "good" thing; it is just the opposite of "lazy." It may be ideal for you to be a 5 on this continuum. Someone who is a 10 in fitness may be a body builder, which requires way more time and commitment than most of us have and is not necessarily desirable. Being a 10 on the "outgoing" continuum may mean that you dominate all conversations and overpower your relationships; thus you may prefer a placement around 7. Being a 10 on the sexual continuum may mean you are promiscuous or so sexual that you can't get anything else done. In the atheist/religious continuum, you may feel you are very spiritual but just not religious, and in fact "religious" may not appeal to you at all. Again, a 10 isn't necessarily the goal; it is just the other extreme in the pair. The goal is not any particular location on the continuum between the two extremes; the goal is to assess the width of the gap between where you see yourself now and where you want to be. The point is not someone else's assessment of you; it is your assessment of yourself. If you are "out of shape," but contentedly so, then rejoice! If you are atheist and quite comfortable as such, again, celebrate, and place both your *O* and *X* in the first box. The problem enters when you perceive yourself a certain way *and wish you didn't*. That is when an alignment of the gap becomes necessary.

Although we could assess ourselves using an extensive list of paired characteristics, the words in this inventory were chosen to give you a sampling of your self-assessment in the realms of body, mind, spirit, career, and relationships.

Assess Yourself

There are six steps for utilizing the assessment; here are the first two. After you complete them, you will receive further instructions. (Note: A second assessment tool for your partner to use is provided at the end of the six steps.)

STEP ONE: For each pair of words, be honest with yourself and put an *O* where you feel you are now.

STEP TWO: Place an *X* where you think you should be.

SELF-ESTEEM SELF-ASSESSMENT

	1	2	3	4	5	6	7	8	9	10	
Unattractive											Beautiful/handsome
Out of shape											Fit
Frigid/no libido											Sexy/sexual
Ignorant											Educated
Shy											Outgoing

SELF-ESTEEM SELF-ASSESSMENT (CONT'D.)

	1	2	3	4	5	6	7	8	9	10	
Unattractive											Beautiful/handsome
Unreliable											Responsible
Incompetent											Capable
Reserved/private											Communicative
Failure											Successful
Poor											Rich
Hateful											Loving
Stagnant											Creative
Atheist											Religious/spiritual
Fraudulent											Trustworthy
Paranoid											Trusting
Lethargic											Energetic
Ill											Healthy
Judgmental											Compassionate
Lonely											Have companionship
Hate job/career											Love job/career
Lazy											Workaholic
Selfish											Generous
Mean											Kind

Be Self-Observant

Once you have assessed both where you are now (with an *O*) and where you would like to be (with an *X*) for each pair, consider that what you have just assessed is *who you think you are* (the "oil") and *how you want the world to see you* (the "glitter"), which we spoke about in Chapter 4. Take a look at the graph. Are your *X*'s and *O*'s close together or far apart? How do you feel about the placements, the gaps, and the alignments?

Notice if your X's are all really high numbers. This can be an indicator of unrealistic expectations or expectations adopted in childhood in an effort to cover low self-esteem. The logic here is "I have to be perfect to be okay." Ask yourself if your expectations are really your own or whether you have taken them on as beliefs that now limit your joy. Did a parent make you feel that you had to be a 10 on the religious scale? Did society make you feel that you needed to be a 10 on the rich scale? Are these expectations true for *you?*

If all your X's are very low numbers, pay attention to that as well. True self-esteem never revels in hurting others. If you have narrow gaps between your O's and your X's but they are all at the lower end, this is known as a "false self-esteem" and is generally an indicator of a defense mechanism. The logic is, "I'm no good and I don't care; it is just fine with me." That kind of apathy is not to be confused with self-esteem, even though the gap is narrow. When you find yourself consistently placing your X's near the bottom of the scale, where you and other people may be harmed by your behavior, it is a definite red flag signaling that who you really are is deeply blocked. You may need counseling to realign your goals with those that will serve you and others instead of hurting yourself and others. Love cannot easily flow through blockages such as these. In order to love yourself, your mate, and your marriage, you will need to attend to this inner state of affairs.

Notice also if all or most of your O's are at the lower end. This could be flagging that you are too hard on yourself and too judgmental, an obvious indicator of the need to work on improving your self-image. If this is true for you, it is a great discovery! Awareness is critical in order to turn your self-esteem around. I guarantee, if your self-esteem is low, your marriage is suffering from it.

What Is Authentic for You?

Now we are going to assess your *authentic* placement on the continuum—the one that aligns with who you really are (the bubbly, pure water discussed in Chapter 4)—versus your ego's judgment or expectations. If you think that your expectations (your X's) are unrealistic, this is your opportunity to choose new, more realistic expectations. If you feel you were just being apathetic or defensive and thus placed an *X* lower than you believe is truly an authentic placement for you, this is your opportunity to set your sights higher.

The quick test for the proper, authentic placement is to assess your joy by imagining what your behavior would be like if you actually were where you think you should be. Aligning with your ego won't make you happy; aligning with your true self will. For instance, if I currently rated myself at 5 on the shy/outgoing continuum and rated where I thought I "should" be at 9, for this step I would imagine what I think it means to be a 9 and see if it makes me happy to imagine being that way. To me, being a 9 means going out of my way to talk to strangers and being social at every opportunity, but when I visualize those things I realize I value my privacy and my time alone. It doesn't make me happy to imagine being a 9. Therefore, I will put a star or asterisk (*) in the number 7 column, as that feels more truthfully aligned with who I am. It feels authentic to me.

STEP THREE: Go back through the paired words, and place an asterisk (*) beneath the number that feels most joyful and authentic for you to target as your goal.

In some cases, the asterisk will align with where you want to be; sometimes it will align with where you already are. In other cases, it will be somewhere in between. In the cases where your *O* and your *X* already align, pay attention to how you feel about that alignment. If it feels just right, that is also where your asterisk will go.

Are there any categories where you think you are overachieving and you need to go down a notch or two in order to be authentic or joyful? One woman placed her *X* under the number 10 on the judgmental/compassionate continuum, but when assessing what was truly authentic for her, she felt a 10 belonged to someone like Mother Theresa and realized she wasn't comfortable with that extreme. She felt "at home" with an 8, so that is where her asterisk went. A man became aware that his high level of energy allowed him no time for rest or relaxation and that he was pushing his partner away (and possibly damaging his health) by never simply relaxing. He rated himself a 10 on the lethargic/energetic scale for both the *O* and the *X*, but when considering what really felt authentic, he determined a more healthy alignment for him would be an 8. That is where he placed his asterisk.

EXAMPLE OF SELF-ASSESSMENT WITH AN ASTERISK MARKING YOUR AUTHENTIC PLACEMENT

	1	2	3	4	5	6	7	8	9	10	
Lethargic								*	*X*		Energetic
									O		

Color the Gap

STEP FOUR: Now, color in the space between the *O* (your assessment of where you are now) and the star or asterisk (where your authentic placement is).

This will become a "bar graph" of your self-esteem that will lead you more easily toward achieving self-improvement. When you are done, you'll have a graph of the "gaps" that looks something like this:

EXAMPLE OF SELF-ASSESSMENT SHOWING GAPS IN SELF-ESTEEM

	1	2	3	4	5	6	7	8	9	10	
Poor					*O*		*	*X*			Rich
Ill							*O*	*X**			Healthy
Judgmental		*O*					*	*X*			Compassionate
Fraudulent								*OX**			Trustworthy

Depicting your self-esteem on a graph is powerful because it puts it out in front of you where you can really look at it, study it, and make decisions about it. This self-assessment tool makes improving your self-esteem manageable and tangible instead of ethereal and illusive. It also makes the measure of your self-esteem specific to individual issues, which is an accurate reflection of how self-esteem really works. Now let's take a look at what to do with this information.

Love Tip: The first step to change is always self-awareness, which comes about through self-observation. When we become aware of what we are doing (or not doing) and saying (or not saying), then we can consider other options. When we are able to see our choices, we have the power to change.

Determining What to Change

STEP FIVE: Evaluate the results through self-inquiry, and set appropriate goals.

Here are some self-inquiry questions to use in determining what to change:

- How big is the gap?

- How do I feel about the gap?

- Can this issue be changed?

- Is it true that it needs to be changed?

- Is my self-perception accurate, or am I being unfairly harsh with myself? A good test of this is: Do my self-perceptions match the feedback I receive from others?

Now you will be guided in evaluating your graph. Ultimately we are aiming toward determining which gaps need bridging and which don't, and how to go about making the necessary changes. Before we begin looking at the action steps necessary to bridge the gaps, we are going to look at some considerations that will help you determine what kinds of changes to make.

The size of the gap and the importance of the issue will make a difference as to whether anything needs to be done about it. As you look at your graph, consider whether the *size* of any of the gaps takes you by surprise. Are some smaller than you would have guessed while others loom much larger? How do you feel about these gaps? For some of them, the gap may be so small that it isn't really a big issue for you, and consequently you may only need to make a tiny adjustment in your behavior to bridge the gap. Or perhaps you aren't motivated to make a change at all because the gap doesn't make you feel bad. Generally, the bigger the gap the more uncomfortable you are and the more motivated you will be to make the necessary changes to improve your self-esteem.

When a gap looms too large, there is often a temptation to give up, as if it were hopeless. If you have this feeling, simply aim to narrow the gap by one step on the continuum rather than by the whole distance. Once that step is successfully mastered, you can narrow the gap by one more step at a time.

Also, ask yourself if this particular issue really matters to you. The more an issue matters, the more it affects your self-esteem, particularly if the gap is large. Refer to the list of values you wrote in Chapter 3. The items that are a high priority on that list are the ones that matter to you the most and that have the greatest ability to affect your self-esteem. For instance, you may like the idea of having more money but are comfortable with the amount you have right now. Thus, the gap is more a matter of preference than importance. Consequently, your self-esteem is not blocked by this gap because it does not matter that much. However, if you were unable to pay the bills, feed yourself, or provide shelter, low self-esteem would undoubtedly result from the gap. As you determine where to start making changes, start with the issues that matter the most to you—the ones that will make you feel better when you change them.

Generally, to achieve alignment, we take steps to move the O closer to the asterisk or to the X by determining what we would need to change, or do differently, so that *how we are* more closely aligns with *how we want to be.* The other way to move the O closer to your goal is to reassess the truth of your self-perceptions and adjust your expectations and self-image accordingly. Sometimes reality doesn't need changing; rather, our perception of ourselves needs a heavier dose of reality. For instance, one woman I worked with perceived herself to be overweight when in fact she was very thin, almost dangerously so. In this case, getting thinner in order to bridge the gap wasn't appropriate. Rather, working on changing her self-perception (moving the *O* closer to the *X* or asterisk) was more appropriate. If you are assessing yourself as lower than you deserve, your *O* may be a long way from your *X* simply because you need to be trained to see yourself in a more positive light. Sometimes, with issues like this, it is helpful to share your graph with someone you trust who can help you to see where your self-perception is off base. In addition, practicing the steps for turning it all around that are outlined in Chapter 6 can help you shift your self-perception.

In determining what to change, you also need to consider whether or not the issue is something that *can* be changed. Sometimes we are unhappy about things that can't be changed, are not easily changed, or should not be changed. For instance, you may think you'd be more attractive if you were just three inches taller, but, so far, changing one's height is not an option. Or you may be lethargic due to an illness that you are fighting. When you find that a gap results from something you cannot change, recognize that *the gap exists because you are choosing to resist what is.* This is what is causing you pain. Instead, if you practice acceptance of what is, you will be able to bridge the gap by moving the expectation of where you feel you should be closer to where you currently are—that is, moving the *X* or the asterisk closer to the *O.* This is a great time to practice the Serenity Prayer: "Grant me the serenity to accept the things I cannot change, the courage to change the things I can, and the wisdom to know the difference."

Love Tip: When seeking that which makes you happy, turn your attention to what is permanent. Test it: Is this true? Is this real? Is this lasting? You will discover that the only thing that meets these criteria is your spiritual life—not things, people, or money.

Achieving Alignment

STEP SIX: Take action to bring about change. Make sure the action you take is aligned with the guideposts you developed in Chapter 3.

Once you have determined which issues you want to work on
and which issues really merit change, for each of the paired words explore these questions:

- What steps would it take in terms of your behavior to bridge
  the gap? In other words, what would you need to do to close
  or narrow the gap?

- What would you need to do to close the gap by one step on
  the continuum? Two? Remember, this is your behavior you
  are changing in order to raise your self-esteem—not anyone
  else's behavior.

To make this exercise the most powerful it can be, take time to
write down your answers to the questions regarding degree and type
of change for each area of change. For example, "In order to move
from an 8 to a 10 on the health continuum, I would need to participate in an exercise regimen every day for a minimum of half an hour.
I would also need to eat more protein." (Then get specific as to what
"more protein" means to you so you will know when you have accomplished this particular action step.) If the gap looms too large to
manage a complete bridge, just list what it would take to move one
step closer to your goal. For instance, "In order to move from a 2 to a
3 on the compassion continuum, I would simply become aware of
when I am being judgmental so that it is no longer unconscious behavior." Then, when you're ready, tackle moving to a 4: "In order to
move to a 4 on the compassion continuum, when I am aware that I
am judging someone, I'm going to stop and look at the situation
through their eyes."

By making a list of what you can do to close the gap, you will begin setting goals and feeling empowered to bring about change one
step a time. This will help you to actively and consciously make the
effort to close the gaps and improve your self-esteem.

Love Tip: Any investment you make in improving
your self-esteem will bear returns throughout all areas
of your life in your abilities to love, make wise decisions, and experience happiness and joy.

An Ounce of Self-Esteem

EXERCISE ∾ *Take a moment to make a list of what you would do or how your life would be affected if you had just a tiny bit more self-esteem. Be sure to also include on the list anything you would stop doing if you had a little more self-esteem. We're not talking about a lot, just an ounce more self-esteem. What would you do differently? Would you learn to play an instument? Join a choir? Start taking better care of your body? Be kinder to your spouse? Would you try harder to make your marriage work? Would you stop smoking? Would you stop judging others? Would you stop putting yourself down? With just an ounce more self-esteem, what would you do?*

Then make a list of what you would need to do to get an ounce more self-esteem. What would that require? ∾

The irony here is that you will find that the things you would do if you had more self-esteem are often the exact same things you need to do to *get* more self-esteem. If we had more self-esteem, we'd stop smoking, start working out, be less critical of our family members, be more loving toward ourselves, take more risks, speak in public, sing in front of people, take art lessons.... And to raise our self-esteem, these are the very same things we need to do.

So, which comes first: the self-esteem or the action? The easiest way is to take the action first. Every risk you survive enhances your self-esteem and leads to the ability to take a new risk. It is a domino effect in your favor! Every time you transcend your ego and behave in alignment with who you really are, you strengthen and grow who you really are. Of course, the good news is that you do have more self-esteem than you are currently accessing; it is just blocked. So pick one thing from the list of things you would do to narrow the gap between you and loving yourself more, reach deep within to access the strength that is already there, and go for it! Once you survive that step, pick another.

Remember, change only happens in a moment. When we first set out to make changes, we often expect the entire task to be handled once and for all on our first try, usually an unrealistic hope. Change is a process, not an event. Generally, the process of change works like this: First, you set your intention to begin a new behavior. Then, as you move through your day, right after you do something in the old way you become aware that you meant to do things differently. Awareness comes too late to make the change. You then reset your intention, and set out once again. This time you might become aware in the middle of doing things the old way. Again, awareness comes too late, but not as late as last time. So you set your intention again (that is, if you haven't already given up; it is important not to give up when aiming to make changes). This time awareness comes just before you begin to do things the old way, so you self-adjust, aligning your behavior with your goals. Next time, you set out with your new intentions, and you don't even try to do things the old way; awareness of the new way has become part of your being. When you forget and slip back into the old way, simply reset your intentions once again.

A Self-Esteem Self-Assessment for Your Spouse

STEP ONE: For each pair of words, be honest with yourself and put an *O* where you feel you are now.

STEP TWO: Place an *X* where you think you should be.

STEP THREE: Go back through the paired words and place an asterisk (*) beneath the number that feels most joyful and authentic for you to target as your goal.

STEP FOUR: Color in the space between the *O* (your assessment of where you are now) and the star or asterisk (your authentic target).

STEP FIVE: Evaluate the results through self-inquiry, and set appropriate goals for bridging the gap.

STEP SIX: Take action to bring about the desired change. Make sure the action you take is in alignment with the guideposts you developed in Chapter 3.

SELF-ESTEEM SELF-ASSESSMENT TABLE FOR YOUR SPOUSE

	1	2	3	4	5	6	7	8	9	10	
Unattractive											Beautiful/handsome
Out of shape											Fit
Frigid/no libido											Sexy/sexual
Ignorant											Educated
Shy											Outgoing
Unreliable											Responsible
Incompetent											Capable
Reserved/private											Communicative
Failure											Successful
Poor											Rich
Hateful											Loving
Stagnant											Creative
Atheist											Religious
Fraudulent											Trustworthy
Paranoid											Trusting
Lethargic											Energetic
Ill											Healthy
Judgmental											Compassionate
Lonely											Have companionship
Hate job/career											Love job/career
Lazy											Workaholic
Selfish											Generous
Mean											Kind

A Marriage Assessment

In addition to applying these concepts to your self-esteem, you can apply them to your marriage. The wider the gap between how you want your relationship to be and how you perceive it to actually be, the worse you feel about your partner and your marriage. If you want to love your marriage, it is very helpful to take a look at where the gaps are and what it would take to close them.

To do this, you need to explore the following:

- How do you want your marriage to be?

- What do you perceive to be the current state of your marriage?

- How big is the gap between the two?

Below you will find another chart of paired words. This time, though, you are assessing your marriage rather than yourself. Place an *O* where you perceive the marriage to be now. Then place an *X* where you think it should be. Next, go back and place an asterisk where you feel the truth of the marriage could be. The hard part here is to remember that you aren't rating your *partner;* you are rating *your experience* of the marriage. The marriage is made up of both of your behaviors, not just your spouse's. So, as you fill out the chart, assess the marriage as a whole, not your partner. If you are parents, also include your sense of the marriage as a parenting partnership. (If you are not, skip the parenting-related continuums.)

Every time you place an assessment on a continuum, ask yourself, "Is this really true?" Give yourself permission to have an emotional, reactionary assessment. If need be, mark it with a checkmark (?), and then ask yourself if your assessment is really true. If you think it isn't, place your *O* more accurately. For instance, as an emotional reaction you might place a checkmark under 3 on the hate my marriage/love my marriage continuum. In that moment, you may really hate being married. But, once you've marked it, you can take a deep breath and ask yourself if, overall, this is really true. You may then decide to move your answer (your *O*) to a 6. Then, mark with an *X* where you want your marriage to be. Again, ask yourself if this rings true or whether it is an unrealistic expectation. Finally, place the asterisk under the number you feel would be an accurate, authentic target to aim for.

**EXAMPLE OF HOW TO MARK THE CONTINUUM TO SHOW AN
IMMEDIATE REACTION VERSUS AN ACCURATE ASSESSMENT**

	1 2 3 4 5 6 7 8 9 10	
Hate my marriage	? *O* *X**	Love my marriage

Remember that these are paired extremes. Again, a 10 may not be the goal; your goal may fall right in the middle or somewhere else on the continuum. For instance, you may not feel it is important to parent with strict or loose discipline but rather that discipline should fall somewhere in between the two extremes.

To assess your marriage (see the chart on page 132), use the same steps you followed to assess your self-esteem. Notice that the first pair of words has to do with how you feel about your marriage, while the others assess the quality of your marriage.

STEP ONE: For each pair of words, place an *O* where you feel your marriage is now.

STEP TWO: Place an *X* where you feel it should be.

STEP THREE: Place an asterisk (*) where you believe an authentic target for your marriage would be, one that you are willing to strive for and realistically feel you can reach.

STEP FOUR: For each pair of words, color in the gap between where you perceive your marriage to be right now (your *O*) and where you feel it authentically could be (your asterisk).

STEP FIVE: Evaluate the results through self-inquiry, and set appropriate goals for bridging the gap.

How do you feel about the gaps? Are some bigger than you would have thought? Are some narrower? Can they be changed? Does the "reality" need to be changed or does your perception/acceptance of reality need to be changed?

Ask yourself, "What would I need to do in terms of changing my behavior to narrow the gap?" What would I need to do to move one step closer? Two? Take the time to write down the behaviors you could change that would close the gap.

MARRIAGE ASSESSMENT

	1	2	3	4	5	6	7	8	9	10	
Hate my marriage											Love my marriage
Indifferent											Loving
Sexually unsatisfying											Sexually satisfying
Lonely											Companionship
No communication											Good communication
Judgmental											Supportive
Conflict-filled											Peaceful
Jealous											Trusting
Stagnant											Growing
Argumentative											Solution-focused
Dysfunctional											Functional
Conflicting goals											Common goals
Financially unstable											Financially stable
Abusive											Respectful
Dependent											Independent
(We are) bad parents											(We are) good parents
Loose discipline											Strict discipline

Remember, all goals for change need to be focused on your actions, that is, on your responses to your spouse or to the events that happen. You cannot make changes for someone else, but you can make changes in your own behavior. For example, you could write, "To move from a 6 to a 9 on the 'love my marriage' continuum, I would need to be more sexual with my husband. I would need to stop reacting harshly to him. I would need to start talking to him more honestly about how I feel about things. I would need to stop blaming him and instead take responsibility for my own happiness." Then, to break it down into smaller steps, imagine what it would take to move just one step closer. Perhaps you could write, "To start, I can move from a 6 to 7 on the continuum by setting aside an evening just for us twice per month. I will either fix his favorite dinner or we can go out to a restaurant. I will initiate some sensual cuddling. On those date nights, I won't default to turning on the TV in the bedroom." Then, imagine what it would take to move from a 7 to an 8.

> *Love Tip:* The distance between "what is" and "what should be" can create an unmanageable rift. In relationships, sometimes one is living in the past while the other is living in the future. If instead both were to bring their attention to the present moment, they may be surprised to find perfection in this halfway point.

STEP SIX: Take action to bring about change. Again, make sure the action you take is in alignment with the guideposts you developed in Chapter 3.

Satis*faction* requires action. Set your intention and begin taking the necessary steps to bridge the gaps. You may find, ironically, that the very things you want more of are the things you need *to be* more of. When I want my husband to love me more, I find I need to be more loving. When I want my husband to stop judging me, I find *I* need to stop judging me—and him. Remember, this is all about you. Right now we are simply looking at what *you* can do differently to change your experience of your marriage. *What three things could you do immediately to open your heart to more love?*

Ideally, it would be wonderful if your spouse took this assessment

> **Did you know?** Married people are twice as likely as those who are single for whatever reason to say they are "very happy." Some 40 percent of married couples say they are very happy, compared to 15 percent of those who are separated and 18 percent of those who are divorced. What's surprising is that only 22 percent of the never-married and of cohabitants are very happy, the same as widows.

also and you could compare your results. Thus, an assessment tool has been provided below for him or her. However, if you are doing it alone, you will still find that *your experience* of your marriage lies in your hands. If your partner is willing to work through the process with you, it will help you discover things that each of you can do to improve the marriage and develop a plan together on how to bridge the gaps. When comparing your individual assessments of the marriage, you will discover whether there are mutual areas of discontent or enjoyment. Do your very best not to take your spouse's assessment personally, but rather see it as an education. The only way we can fix things is if we become aware that they are broken or damaged in the first place. Take a deep breath, transcend your ego, align your energy with who you really are—and with your goals—and choose your thoughts, words, and actions carefully, in support of bridging the gaps and creating a loving marriage.

A Marriage Assessment for Your Spouse

STEP ONE: For each pair of words, place an *O* where you feel your marriage is now.

STEP TWO: Place an *X* where you feel it should be.

STEP THREE: Place an asterisk (*) where you believe an authentic target for your marriage would be, one that you are willing to strive for and realistically feel you can reach.

STEP FOUR: For each pair of words, color in the gap between where you perceive your marriage to be right now (your *O*) and where you feel it authentically could be (your asterisk).

STEP FIVE: Evaluate the results through self-inquiry, and set appropriate goals for bridging the gap.

STEP SIX: Take action to bring about change.

> *Love Tip:* Allow the world to be your mirror, reflecting back to you what you need to see in yourself. Then, instead of blaming the world or trying to fix "it," determine what you can adjust within yourself that will transform your perceptions and experiences.

MARRIAGE ASSESSMENT FOR YOUR SPOUSE

	1	2	3	4	5	6	7	8	9	10	
Hate my marriage											Love my marriage
Indifferent											Loving
Sexually unsatisfying											Sexually satisfying
Lonely											Companionship
No communication											Good communication
Judgmental											Supportive
Conflict-filled											Peaceful
Jealous											Trusting
Stagnant											Growing
Argumentative											Solution-focused
Dysfunctional											Functional
Conflicting goals											Common goals
Financially unstable											Financially stable
Abusive											Respectful
Dependent											Independent
(We are) bad parents											(We are) good parents
Loose discipline											Strict discipline

steps for turning
it all around

*The Constitution only gives people the right
to pursue happiness.
You have to catch it yourself.*

BEN FRANKLIN

Every new relationship—or new situation within an existing relationship—provides us with a new mirror in which we get to see ourselves. It is only through this reflection that we *can* see ourselves. Just as we cannot view our physical being unless we have a mirror, we cannot truly see our personality and interpersonal skills except through the mirror of our relationships. The quality of our relationships is the indicator of how we are doing; it is the "report card" for our interpersonal skills.

Thus, it is only through relationships that we are able to achieve self-mastery—and it is through self-mastery that we are able to love our relationships. Sounds like the chicken and the egg, doesn't it? Which came first? Relationships. Then came trial and error and lots of mistakes, which created the drive for self-mastery and the desire for loving relationships. Hopefully this is where you stand right now, because you will need this drive for what comes next.

Until now you've been gaining an understanding of what happens to block self-esteem and self-love and, consequently, what blocks the love in our relationships. Now comes the work to break down the walls, clean up the muck, transcend the ego, and restore a free flow of self-esteem, love, and joy in your life. Now comes the work to restore your marriage by restoring yourself. Remember, right now it is still all about you.

Here are the steps for turning it all around:

1. Wake up and become conscious of who you really are.

2. Pay attention, self-observe.

3. Let go of ego and reconnect with your authentic self.

4. Take action that is in alignment with your authentic self and with your goals.

These steps are also essential life skills for self-mastery.

Step One: Wake Up and Become Conscious of Who You Really Are

The first step to accessing your esteemed self is to *remember* who you really are: a playful, expressive, honest, imaginative, creative, funny, joyful, talented, curious, capable, and loving person. Now, some of you might immediately think, "How can I *remember* if I *never knew* in the first place? In fact, how can I remember if it isn't true?!" If this is the case for you, you are invited to simply consider the *possibility* that this is who you really are and to allow each day to be an adventure in which you look for, listen for, and discover the evidence that this is true. These actions will grow who you really are.

What do you have to lose? All of your negative, limiting beliefs!

Although this step is the first, it must be done simultaneously with all the other steps, and it must be done consciously and consistently. When we forget who we really are, we resort to behaving as who we *think* we are: weak, possessive, incapable, undeserving, judgmental, superior, inferior, and/or needy. Remember, these traits of the ego block love. When we know ourselves to be strong, powerful, capable, and loving, we show up in relationships that way.

To "remember," you are going to have to take a deep look at yourself. Look for the pure, bubbly essence of your childlike self.

Although I realize it is a vague question, you will find that you can go deep with the answers. When people answer this question they often start with life roles like, "I'm a teacher," "I'm a wife," "I'm an athlete." Most of us can easily identify these aspects of ourselves. But as you continue to answer the question, you will begin to look at who you really *are*, regardless of what you *do*. If you no longer had these particular life roles, who would you be? As you look more deeply at yourself, your answers may include other qualities, such as: "I am creative," "I am a joyful person," "I am a spiritual being"—whatever is true for you.

EXERCISE ∾

Who are you, really?

Take some time to really ponder, and answer, this question—re-peatedly. If you are reading this book with your spouse, take turns asking each other this question over and over and over again, and just allow the first answers to flow out. Don't judge your or your spouse's answers or agree or disagree; just listen. If you are reading this book alone, you are invited to write your answers to this simple, yet often challenging, question in a jour-nal. ∾

If you find that the answers you are getting aren't positive, notice! Maybe your answers are more like these: "I'm a frustrated, discontent person." "I am a victim." These answers can be very revealing of areas in which you are not living in alignment with your most authentic self. They can show you some of the limiting or disempowering be-liefs that come from your "oil" and "glitter" layers that we talked about in Chapter 4. If you find that all you have to say about yourself is negative, you will want to seriously work on your self-esteem and self-concept. Go back to Chapter 4 and do the exercise on creating empowering beliefs. Now, see if you can look deeper to your authen-tic, positive qualities—the ones you were born with and that may simply be lying dormant, just waiting for you to look deeply enough to find them.

EXERCISE ∿

- *Who are you, really, really?*

- *Look deeper.*

- *Who are you, really, really, really?*

- *What are your positive qualities?*

- *What is the good news about you?*

- *What is lovable about you?*

- *What do you like, love, admire, and appreciate about your self?*

I was once on a talk show in which we explored the impact of self-esteem on relationships. The topic was "Would you date you?" When you know why someone should date you, or marry you, or enjoy being married to you, it is more likely that they will know why as well.

EXERCISE ∿

- *Would you marry you?*

- *Why?* ∿

Because we have all spent so much time, maybe our whole lives, with our limiting beliefs and with our egos seemingly running the show (and our relationships), it may take some time and work for you to peel away the layers to reveal who you really are. Harder yet is to bring this aspect of yourself to the surface when interacting with your mate—someone whom you have probably responded to in a set pattern for potentially many, many years. Now you are being called upon to show up in a different way.

Your job is to set your intention on "meeting" your true self and on bringing that aspect of yourself out to play on a regular basis. You are working up to bringing that aspect of yourself forward all the time. The more familiar you get with this part of yourself—the strong, joyful, honest, clear, conscious, wise part of yourself—the more easily accessible it will become. It is a matter of paying attention and growing who you really are. You will know if you are "asleep," or not living in alignment with this aspect of yourself, if you find that you feel unhappy more often than happy, complain more often than resolve issues, resist what is rather than accepting what is, or feel like a victim. Who you really are is powerful and therefore never feels like a victim. Rather, your essence understands that it is always being blessed, even when dealing with the hardest things life throws at you.

> *Love Tip:* Pretend that your inner self is just like the guy in the cell-phone ads who says, "Can you hear me now? Can you hear me now?" Begin to pay attention to what you are thinking and the feelings that result. If you don't like the feelings, change the thoughts and actions that caused them! Turn up your reception and pay attention to your Self!

Our true selves are calling to us in little ways all the time. Remember, this is our esteemed self, the pure, effervescent aspect of ourselves from which little bubbles break through to the surface to get our attention—a divine indigestion of sorts. These are reminder moments that occur so we don't actually forget that our true self exists. Watch for them. Watch for the moments when you suddenly feel a connection to something greater than your normal feelings. Notice when you feel good—and when you don't. Notice when you feel strong, even if it is only for a fleeting moment. Notice when you rise above your ego and soothe your relationships. The more you pay attention, the more you will notice when you are operating from who you *really* are instead of from who you think you *should* be, or who you want the world to think you are. Every time you simply notice when you are being authentic and when you are not, you are a step closer to clearing the blocks to your self-esteem.

All you are doing in this first, wake-up step is remembering that underneath the glitter and the oil, underneath the drama and the pain, underneath the hurt and the frustration, underneath it all is your joyful, spiritual, happy, capable, strong, wise, loving self. You are remembering who you really are or are looking for evidence of it. Then you want to extend this remembering into the definition you hold of yourself. That way, whenever you are *not* feeling strong, wise, capable, and loving, you will simply know that you are not in alignment with your esteemed, authentic self. You are hitting a blockage. Once you are adept at recognizing when you have clear access and when you don't, you will be able to follow the next steps, as though you were on a pathway through the obstacles that exist between your ego and true self-esteem.

Remember, this is also true for your partner. He or she is also a powerful, strong, wise, spiritual, and capable being underneath his or her ego. Underneath the negative beliefs he or she was subjected to and bought into while growing up, underneath the act of trying to be a certain way in the world, underneath the need for approval and the need for control is love. As you recognize this essence in yourself, you will begin to also recognize it in your partner as it bubbles up in little ways every day. Simply looking for, paying attention to, and noticing this essence in yourself and your partner on a daily basis can do wonders for improving your relationship. It is this that reminds you that you are not your ego and that your partner is not his or her ego either. You are both much deeper, wider, and more wonderful. The more attention you pay to these aspects of both of you, the more they will grow and the more accessible they will become.

When I was going through a particularly stressful time in my marriage, I would lie in bed at night and mentally talk "soul to soul" with my husband, totally unbeknownst to him. I would silently tell him (souls can hear without words) that I was calling out to his soul, looking past his ego and persona (and my own), and inviting his soul to come forth and play with mine. I apologized for forgetting who I really was and forgetting who he really was and asked for us both to show up more deeply and intimately. Whether it made a difference in his behavior or not was really irrelevant (because that would have been focusing on changing the event); what it did do is remind me to evoke who I really am and to remember who he really is when interacting with him (which changed my responses). If nothing else, it made me feel better (which was a new outcome and solution!).

EXERCISE ∾ *Answer the following questions about your spouse. Depending on your situation it may be too soon for you to answer authentically, so don't be afraid to come back to these questions again and again, taking the answers deeper each time:*

- *Who is your partner, really?*

- *Who is your partner, really, really, really?*

- *Looking past the "oil" and the "glitter," what are his or her positive qualities?*

- *What do you like, love, admire, and appreciate about your partner?*

- *Why did you marry him or her? Be specific. "I loved him/her" isn't enough. What did you love about your partner? What do you still love?* ∾

I am sure that some of you doubt whether there is a "true self" underneath it all. Understandably, some life situations have made it hard to imagine or recognize that this could be so. This is all the more reason to start looking for that aspect of yourself now! I first learned about self-esteem at a workshop led by Jack Canfield that I attended to learn how to raise the self-esteem of the students in my classroom. I had no idea that I needed help myself. Jack led us through an exercise in which we closed our eyes and imagined that we were looking at a mirror image of ourselves, into our own eyes. I did as directed and closed my eyes, picturing myself in a mirror. No biggie. Then he said, "Now, looking into your eyes, tell yourself, 'I love you and accept you just the way you are,' and watch in the mirror for your reaction." Again, I did as I was guided to do, but this time it was much harder. It wasn't hard for me to say, "I love you and accept you just the way you are," but it was hard for me to *believe* it. I watched sadly as my mirrored image rolled her eyes and responded sarcastically, "Yeah, sure you do."

It wasn't until that moment that I even knew my access to my self-esteem was blocked. Feeling that pain and discomfort was one of the greatest gifts I have ever received in my life. The pain resulting from the exercise was like a spotlight that lit up the obstacles to my self-esteem, to joy, to happiness, to success. If you don't know that the hurdles are there, you are certainly not going to be able to navigate around them. I had a choice right then whether to decide that the inner work was too painful, that my self-esteem was low and that was that, or to utilize this information as the inspiration to do something about it. Thankfully, I chose the latter. I began reading books, taking workshops, and, most importantly, looking for evidence daily that there was more to me than my wounded, sarcastic self that felt unlovable. You have the same choice.

If you are doubtful that there is a healthy, happy, strong, capable essence inside of you, I invite you to prove yourself wrong! The first step is to simply hold the possibility that there really is a "true self" and to recognize that your doubt is just one of the obstacles. Embrace your doubt as a gift; without it, you would be unaware of the blocks between you and your esteemed self and, thus, unable to overcome them. Don't try to make yourself believe something you don't; simply hold the intention of watching for the evidence that it is true. Ask your mind to be on the lookout for evidence of your greatness, for evidence of your childlike qualities, for evidence of your esteemed self, for evidence that who you really are is far more vast and deep than meets the eye. Watch also for those magical moments when you feel deeply peaceful or in which some amazing coincidence happens—a serendipity that appears divinely choreographed. Ask your mind to listen for compliments and appreciation from your spouse that until now you may have failed to hear.

While you are at it, also request that your mind watch for the evidence of your spouse's greatness. Notice when he or she does something kind, honest, generous, or loving. Notice when he or she takes a risk to tell the truth or does something particularly well or is silent when nothing needs to be said. The "evidence" doesn't have to be monumental; it can be subtle—a moment when you catch each other's eyes and see past the superficial into the soul, for just a second. Simply watch. When we give our minds a job such as this, it responds in a full effort to find the information we are seeking.

Unfortunately, the task most of us have unconsciously given our minds is to find evidence that we are not good enough (or, conversely, that we are superior to all others), that we are failures, that our marriage is faltering, that our spouse is a jerk.... When you hold those beliefs and reinforce them constantly, your mind works hard to prove you right. When, instead, you hold the image that you are a good person—loving and deserving of love—and that your spouse is too, your mind will seek evidence to prove you right. Ask your mind to seek that which serves you and empowers you and your relationship, not that which deflates you and adds to the obstacles between you and love. Ask your mind to see what you saw in each other in the beginning. It is still there; it just may be blocked.

I know some readers are thinking that what I'm suggesting is equivalent to being a Pollyanna or burying your head in the sand. In actuality, what I'm suggesting is an effort to regain some balance in your perspective. We become so skewed toward looking at what is wrong, at what we don't like in ourselves or another person, and at what makes us unhappy that we completely stop seeing the love, joy, goodness, and kindness that continue to exist—and persist. Rather than *seeking* love, connection, kindness, and intimacy, start *seeing* the ways in which it already exists. Then you can build from there.

When it comes to seeing your spouse differently, it is a bit like looking at one of those 3-D posters that were really popular a few years ago. When you looked at them automatically, all you saw were colorful lines and dots. However, if you softened your eyes or crossed your eyes, an entire image or scene would emerge that was previously invisible. Nothing in the actual poster changed; only the way you looked at it changed. When you look at your spouse "automatically," you may find that you see his or her negative qualities, the things that drive you nuts. However, if you shift your vision, soften your gaze, and look from your heart, you will see an entirely different person emerge—the one you love. The same is also true when you look at yourself.

To start balancing your perspective, begin to constantly remember who you really are—or hold the possibility of discovering who you really are and watch constantly for the evidence. As you do, you will begin to grow your authentic self so that rather than being a small spark deep within, it will transform into an immediately accessible well of wisdom, strength, and love that you can draw from any time you wish.

 Love Tip: Stop **seeking** love and start **seeing** it instead. Evidence of love is all around us, all the time.

Growing Who You Really Are

In order to experience something different, you are going to have to *do* something different. In order to do something different, you are going to need to begin feeding your authentic self so that it grows—and therefore will be easier to remember and to access. The good news is that this process is fun. Several activities to help you are listed below. Creating the time to do them may be challenging, especially when you have work and kids to contend with, but there are ways to make time for being alone and for being alone with your spouse. Some of these self-strengthening activities can be done with your family to strengthen and restore each of you. Make self-strengthening a priority. It will serve all your other efforts toward loving your marriage and your life.

EXERCISE ∿ *Do what you love.* *To begin growing who you really are, make a list of everything you love. Everything. Sunsets, kittens, good wine, jazz, swimming, reading, sleeping, shopping, time alone, golfing, working out, writing, drawing, singing ... everything! Also list those things that make you feel stronger or more peaceful. Consider including activities that you especially love to do with your spouse or family. List the places that make you feel "at home"—safe, protected, and nurtured (this may not be your actual home, but under a big tree in the yard, or at the beach, or riding a bike, etc.). Then notice how much time you spend enjoying these things, people, and places, and what qualities they bring out in you. Make a point of doing one or several of the things on your list every day, and pay attention to enjoying* *them. Even if you can only spend five minutes a day consciously doing what you love—or noticing that you love what you are doing—it will begin to feed the part of you that you wish to grow.*

Whenever you do what you love, pay attention to how you feel. Notice that you feel stronger and rejuvenated. What you will undoubtedly discover is that doing what you love, noticing what you love, and enjoying what you love all make you feel more loved and loving. Since love is what your true self is made of, every moment dedicated to love will make you stronger. ∾

Make lists of things you want. *This includes things you want to learn, places you want to go, and people you want to meet. Get creative. Avoid boredom—it kills your sense of self. Whenever you feel lethargic or stuck, you just need to make one reasonable step to begin the unsticking process! Pick one activity on your list, and take active steps toward doing it.* ∾

Express yourself! *Write, dance, draw, play music, sing, cook— do whatever allows you to be creative. Our ultimate nature is creativity, and we are most aligned with our authentic self when expressing ourselves in a creative manner. Experience your uniqueness through expression! Create! Imagine! Play!* ∾

Look for your goodness. *Make a list of all your good qualities, strengths, successes, and talents. Add to it daily. Aim to identify fifty positive qualities about yourself. Once you've reached that, aim for a hundred. If you look, you will find them! Take your time.* ∾

Look for what you love in your spouse. *Make a list of all the things you love and appreciate about your spouse and love doing with your spouse. See if you can list fifty things, large and small, and add to the list every time you think of something new. If your spouse is participating, invite him or her to make a list about you. Turn it into a habit to mention to each other every day the positive qualities or actions you notice, then add them to the list. Continue to grow the list. (If you have children, do the same for them.)* ∾

Receive compliments. *Allow yourself to accept valid compliments rather than simply dismissing them. To be able do this you must first be able to compliment yourself! We tend to block incoming compliments, appreciation, and acknowledgements, especially when our self-esteem is blocked. When we refuse to accept a compliment, we don't allow the other person to experience the full joy of giving the compliment and having it be received.* ❧

Give, serve. *A wonderful aspect of our true nature is the joy that we derive from helping others and being of service. Practice conscious acts of kindness. Surprise people unexpectedly. Look for things that you can do to be kind. Do things that will allow you to see the other's response, and then do things that no one will ever know you did. The reward for anonymous acts of kindness is simply internal. Mix them up! Have fun plotting to do the world good! Be the answer to someone's prayer!* ❧

Do the mirror exercise. *Look into your eyes in a mirror and simply "be with yourself" for several minutes. Then, when you are ready, begin telling yourself, either silently or out loud, what you appreciate about yourself. Maintain eye contact. Remember to breathe! End with, "I love you and accept you just the way you are." Breathe; hold the look. Do this every morning as a pep talk for what you will accomplish that day. Do it every night and go over all the successes you had during the day. Do it every day for sixty days minimum. The eyes are the windows to the soul. Look deeply, and see if you can find your authentic self. You may have to look past the glitter and oil, the superficiality, the defense mechanisms—past ego. This only takes thirty seconds, so overcome your excuses not to do it.* ❧

Be a mirror to your spouse, and vice versa. *If your spouse is willing, look into his or her eyes, silently, for several minutes. Then, when you feel moved to do so, tell him or her, "I love you and accept you just the way you are." Only say it if you mean it. Notice how you feel when you say these words of unconditional love and acceptance. Take turns; see what it feels like to receive this kind of support. If your partner is not a willing participant, say the words silently, speaking only to his or her soul, regardless of whether you are looking into his or her eyes.* ❧

❤️ *Love Tip:* The question is not "Is the glass half empty or half full?" The question is "Do you know how to fill your glass back up?"

Step Two: Pay Attention; Be Self-Observant

Hopefully, somewhere in the back of your mind you are beginning to realize that drama and chaos are not your true birthright, but rather that you are here to learn and to love, and that these goals can be accomplished joyfully, healthfully, and wisely. Feelings such as anger, hatred, frustration, jealousy, and hurt are here to teach you, not to grab hold of you and make camp. They attract your notice by waving red flags over areas that need your attention. To heed their lessons, you must become adept at noticing, through self-observation, how you are feeling and what you are doing in any given moment.

Self-observation leads to awareness, which leads to choice, and choice gives you power. If you don't take the time to notice what you are experiencing, you will continue to feel like a victim of your feelings rather than recognizing that you have created them. Becoming self-observant is what will let you know when you are aligned and when you aren't. When you find you are "off center," you can self-correct. If you don't know, or if you forget, that your responses (rather than events) cause you to feel the way you do, you'll get stuck.

Begin paying attention to yourself occasionally throughout the day with the goal of becoming self-observant and self-aware all the time. Right now, as you're reading, stop for a moment to pay attention to what you are feeling. You may notice that you feel great or even excited about what you are learning. Or you may notice that your tooth hurts, or that your leg is in an uncomfortable position, or that your brow is furrowed in doubt, or that you are breathing shallowly, or that you feel like crying—or all of the above. If you never stop to notice what you are feeling, both in your body and in your emotions, you keep operating on autopilot and consequently continue to ignore your warning signs of discomfort. When you become aware of them, you are able to determine what you want to do about them, that is, how you want to respond. Do you need to shift your position? Do you need to focus on different thoughts?

Sometimes you don't have to consciously do anything differently at all; your body will automatically self-correct when the awareness is revealed. When I notice I am breathing shallowly, my auto-response is to take a deep breath. With thoughts, often when we just acknowledge what we are feeling—fear, judgment, criticized, jealous, possessive—the awareness triggers a recognition that our ego is reacting, not our true self. This simple awareness can cause a shift to a more conscious choice of thoughts, one that reflects our naturally healthy level of self-esteem.

Self-observation is a very powerful tool in relationships because it leads you to become aware of what you are thinking or doing (your response) that is causing you pain (your outcome). From there, you have an opportunity to make a new choice to think, say, or do something that is in alignment with what you want to create (the solution). At the same time, self-observation can make you aware of whether the way you are treating your spouse and family is in alignment with who you really are, or whether you are responding from ego—being cruel, judgmental, or too sensitive. Again, a heightened awareness of how you are treating others offers you the opportunity to make a new, more powerful choice.

EXERCISE ∾ *Self-observe. Ask yourself some important questions. Every time you think of it, ask yourself, "How am I feeling now? What am I thinking now? What am I aware of now?" Then, simply notice how you are feeling and what you are doing, saying, and thinking that is causing you to feel the way you do. You can strengthen your practice of this skill by setting an alarm on your cell phone or wristwatch to go off several times a day for a couple of weeks. When the alarm goes off, wherever you are,* simply stop, take a deep breath, and self-observe. Notice what is going on with you in that moment. Over time, extend this practice so that you become continuously self-observant.

With practice, you will begin to have a deeper sense that "you" are not really what you are observing; the "real you" is the one doing the observing. This process will cause you to begin to see that you are not the drama going on around you. You are not the emotions you feel. This is a powerful shift from ego (what you observe) to your true essence (the observer). ∽

Self-inquire. You can take this observation even deeper to empower your relationships through additional self-inquiry. Explore the following questions; write your answers in a journal so you can really examine them: "What is it like to live with me? What is it like to be in a relationship with me? What is it like to confide in me, to talk to me? What is it like to wake up with me? What is it like to take me out to dinner? What is it like to parent with me? What is it like to explore problems and solutions with me? What is it like to make love with me—or to want to make love with me?" Simply become aware of how you show up or when you don't engage with your partner. Every now and then throughout the day, take a "snapshot" of yourself and how you are being in that moment. Inquire also if what you are thinking in that moment is really true. Make a conscious choice from this place of observation to adjust any words, thoughts, feelings, behaviors, or beliefs that are not accurate, authentic, or based in love. ∽

Make a physical assessment. Consider all the senses as you evaluate yourself. How do you put yourself together from a visual perspective? Are your fingernails clean? Are your clothes clean? How do you smell? What is your breath like? How do you sound—what words do you use and what tone of voice? If you can't see yourself clearly, ask friends, your spouse, or professionals for help. If you don't like what you observe, use this awareness to "clean it up." ∽

Train Your Brain to
Start with Heart

Now that you have observed yourself, the challenge is to accept where you are with love rather than resistance. It is very difficult to change "what is" when you are resisting the *existence* of "what is." To be more accepting of yourself, you need to become aware of what you are saying to yourself—your self-talk—and then choose empowering words. Remember, this part of the work is "all about you," but learning to love, appreciate, and respect yourself is critical education for loving, appreciating, and respecting your partner and your marriage.

Self-talk is the relatively unconscious banter that bombards us throughout the day. When we are not paying attention to what our self-talk is saying, it runs amuck and gains full control of our feelings. It makes a commentary on virtually everything, and for most of us it is usually a negative commentary. Our self-talk is more like self-critique. It is also quite often critical of others; it notices whatever is wrong with everyone and everything. Unless we train the brain to start with heart, the brain seems to start with pain. It is like a fault-finding computer system, and unless we retrain it, it just keeps running its critical commentary. When we consciously start observing our self-talk and begin to recognize that as the observer we have some power to choose what we want to focus on, we are able to separate ourselves from this commentary. Thus, we begin to gain control over the way it makes us feel.

For a long time I thought the goal was to figure out how to silence this voice of self-doubt or how to make the self-talk stop. Now I don't think it is so important (or even possible) to stop it. What's important is to know that you totally have a choice about whether or not you honor the voice of doubt by allowing it to affect you. You can choose to ignore it, and you can retrain it so that it is more useful and less frequently negative. One woman shared that she finds it extremely helpful to send love to the inner critic when she becomes aware that it is blasting her or others with judgment. She says, "I realize that my negative self-talk is just coming from a part of myself that is unevolved and unskilled at appropriate dialogue, so it needs my love. It's like loving a small child who simply doesn't know better." Our negative self-talk really is generated from an aspect of ourselves that means well and actually thinks it is helping us with its feedback, but its lack of skill makes it, for the most part, unhelpful.

Before I knew about observing my self-talk, it was always negative and made me feel bad. It would say things like, "That was dumb," or, "You don't know what you are doing." I would simply believe it and feel accordingly. Now, knowing how to self-observe, when I hear critical self-talk I have the ability to decide whether or not to listen to it. I have the ability to believe it or not. I have the ability to let it affect me or not. For instance, if my self-talk says, "You don't know what you are doing," I can consider this message and evaluate if it is true. If it is true, I can use the information to self-adjust (ask for help, read directions, reevaluate). If it is not true, I can simply ignore it. Before I knew how to self-observe this banter, I didn't have this choice.

Love Tip: A great saint once said, "If someone speaks ill of you, first see if he is right. If he is right, try to correct yourself. If it is unjust, then forget." The same holds true of self-criticism. Whenever you find yourself feeling hopeless, stop and examine the thoughts that led to the feeling, and, when appropriate, change your self-talk! As a result, your feelings will also change.

Retraining the self-talk requires consciously thinking new thoughts. For instance, if I am unconscious and I look in the mirror, my automatic self-talk begins to see every flaw, every dimple of cellulite, every scar, every pimple, and every ounce of fat. And it points these things out to me. If I am conscious, when I look in the mirror and the criticism begins, I refocus my attention on what I like about the way I look or on how I appreciate the way my body serves me, above and beyond the way it looks. My unconscious, negative commentary can't run when I am consciously running a positive one. I can override my negative self-talk with positive self-talk—or, at minimum, I can balance it out.

EXERCISE ∾ *Notice your self-talk. What is your self-talk telling you? Are those thoughts true? How do they make you feel? Train your brain to start with heart by focusing on what you are doing right instead of what you are doing wrong and by noticing what is good about you. If your self-talk is speaking the truth about something you need to attend to, choose to take action.* ∾

Although self-talk is generally silent and internal, you will find that paying attention to and retraining *all* of your verbal communication is also valuable. Unless we consciously choose how we communicate, both with ourselves and with others, we are subject to the brain's infliction of pain. I have a friend who recounts her days based solely upon all the bad things that happened. If she goes to a party, she reports on all the negative things about everyone there, what went wrong, what could have been better, bad outfits. . . . When she talks about herself, it is always negative and belittling. When she talks about other people, she is quick to find their faults. Sound familiar? Know anyone like that? Are you someone like that? Being in a relationship with someone who is constantly negative is exhausting. Being someone who is constantly negative is also exhausting. To train the brain to start with heart, we must consciously choose to recount the day looking at the good that happened, and we must help those around us do the same. Consciously set your intention, and eventually your self-talk (and verbal talk) will start to shift—and your experience of your life will start to shift, too.

EXERCISE ∾ *Pay attention to the thoughts you have about your marriage and your spouse, and pay attention to how you speak to your friends about your marriage and your spouse. Shift your attention to what you love about your spouse, what he or she does well, and what you appreciate about him or her. Practice describing yourself with what is good about you. Notice what you and your spouse do right. Make this a conscious shift every time you observe yourself running a judgmental banter tape in your head (or from your mouth).* ∾

Thinking negatively about everything is just a habit. With a little consciousness and attention, the habit can be broken. Your job is to think like a miner. When a miner goes into a gold mine, he has to remove tons and tons of dirt and rock to find a single nugget of gold, but a miner never goes into the mine looking for the *dirt*. You can look for the dirt or you can look for the gold in yourself and your partner. It all depends on which you want to find. It is your choice.

This doesn't mean you have to ignore or overlook the issues that bother you. By all means, notice them, address them, discuss them; just don't make them your constant focus. Balance your attention so that not every word that comes out of your mouth is negative and every thought pummeling you isn't thrashing you—or your partner—emotionally. Train your brain to start with heart. The other stuff undoubtedly will begin to come naturally.

➤ HERCHEL AND LONNIE, MARRIED THIRTY-FIVE YEARS

When Lonnie and I married we agreed about our Christian beliefs and dedication, so our marriage was considered holy matrimony. We took the vows not just as a promise *before* God but as a covenant *with* God and each other. We made ourselves students of love. True love transcends obstacles. We agreed on our purpose in marriage and consolidated our hopes, dreams, and goals. As a result we pull together and push together.

Observation taught us that we would not always be the same in body or mindset or even spirit. We did know, however, that if our foundation was sure and if the life principles we put in place were kept as pillars, then we could manage. We put together a mission statement.

Love gives room to grow. We haven't let personal changes be divisive. Patience has allowed us each to grow and become. This has been a benefit for both of us. The more we are individually, the more we are together. That is what you call synergy!

"Fellowship" is the word I choose to describe our intimacy of heart and mind. In fellowship we discover things about each other. We're still discovering things. Some of those discoveries we make about ourselves, individually. Because of the intimacy of fellowship we are able to fall in love over and over again.

The energy we put into our marriage is not self-serving, though it does serve self. I don't work to find happiness in being married to sweet Lonnie. My labor of love is to see how much happiness I can bring to her. She has adopted the same heartset. As a result, giving facilitates receiving. My life (joy) is in her. Her security (peace of mind) is in me. Our source (faith) is in the Lord.

I'm her biggest fan and she is mine. We encourage each other on an ongoing basis. When we are apart we realize we represent each other and have agreed to bring no shame to our name. When we are out together we attempt to be good ambassadors for our marriage and our love. We guard our affections and live proactively. We don't allow negativity to grow or anything from outside to wage sustained war or win a battle against our marriage. Early on I said our marriage was a covenant with God. We view each other as a gift from God. We treat each other as though we are saying to Him, "Thank You!"

I didn't say there aren't challenges. Of course there are setbacks and losses, but our victories come because we stay in the fight. We fight for what is ours because we feel we're worth it. We feel our lives have destiny attached to them. These are just some of the choices we've made. Lonnie pointed out that we make these decisions every day. She also says that in the reality of everyday living, it's best to choose your fights wisely. Sometimes a win is a loss. Fight for what will be a win for both parties!

Step Three: Let Go of Ego and Reconnect with Your Authentic Self

Let's take a deeper look at who we really are and at how ego gets in our way, blocking the love in our relationships. "Who we really are" at the soul level is love. We are here to love and to be loved; we get married to share that love. Our egos misconstrue that concept by thinking that we *need* to love and be loved, rather than that we *are* loving and loved. The problem isn't in the love; it is in the perception of need. When we perceive that we need something, we go into effort to create it (rather than just being it or enjoying it); we start seeking it instead of *seeing* it. The problem is that the ego is the one seeking, and the ego always blocks love. So not only does it fail at its attempts to seek love, but also it impedes our progress toward loving authentically.

When our ego believes it *needs to love* someone, it thinks, "Well, if they just called me more often or cleaned up their room or sent me flowers or lost weight, then I'd be able to fulfill my need to love them." Thus, the need to love becomes a need to control, and the ego's need to control always blocks love. The one controlling is always seeking to fix or change things to get his or her needs met, and the other person feels inadequate and constantly judged rather than loved.

When the ego thinks it needs *to be loved,* it starts altering its behavior to try to get approval. To gain the other person's approval we may change the way we dress, the way we behave, the things we say, or even the way we think. The problem is that we can't possibly always meet the expectations of everyone else, and the more we try the less authentic we become. The less authentic we are, the harder it is for anyone to love us because they don't really know us; they only know the false representation we have shown them. Worse yet, the less authentic we are, the harder it is for us to love ourselves because we don't really know ourselves. To top it all off, when someone does make the attempt to love us, we don't *believe* they really do because we know we haven't shown them who we really are.

Is this starting to sound familiar? It should, because virtually every relationship is subject to this challenge. These needs—to love and to be loved—are like opposite sides of the same ego-coin. Everybody flips back and forth between the need for approval and the need for control, but most of us have a strong tendency toward one or the other of these ego-needs as our consistent way of showing up. You've heard that "opposites attract." In this case, it is "those with opposite needs attract." Those of us who need control seek out and are attracted to those who need approval (because they are easier to control). Those who need approval seek out those who need control (because they are ready to put their stamp of approval on those who comply with their wishes). If you think about your friendships and your previous intimate relationships, you will probably be able to see that if you are the one seeking approval, you are typically drawn to people with a need for control, and if you are the one seeking control, you typically attract people with a need for approval. In a weird sort of way, we thus form a perfect match, although not generally a very satisfying one, because neither person ever truly feels love when his or her ego needs flare up.

EXERCISE ∽ *Which one are you?* *Consider your current relationship and ask yourself which one you typically are: the one needing control (judging and trying to change the other) or the one needing approval (trying to get the other's approval, attention, and love). Keep in mind that we all have the ability to do both in different situations, but for the most part we tend to consistently respond to events out of one need or the other.* ∽

To turn this love-blocking dynamic around, you are going to need to draw on all that you have already learned so far in this book. First, whenever you are unhappy, uncomfortable, or feeling weak, confused, or irritable, rather than blaming the other person or the event, look at your response. Keep in mind that this "small self" is not who you really are. Become self-observant and ask yourself, "Is this discomfort about my need for control or my need for approval?" This self-observation and inquiry may lead you to the awareness, "Oh, this is about my need for control," which will lead to the recognition, "My need for control is really about my desire to love." At which point, you can transcend your ego, letting go of the need for control and realigning with who you really are. Or, your awareness may be, "Oh, this is about my need for approval. That is really about my desire to be loved. If I let go of my neediness and just show up authentically, I will be able to feel loved." Then take a deep breath and release your need for approval.

When you recognize your need for control or your need for approval at work, take a deep breath and let it go, shifting your energy from ego to heart, from reaction to response, from blame to responsibility. As you become aware of your ego at play, you can shift your energy, aligning with who you really are instead of who you really aren't. This will take practice and it may take several breaths, but the more you practice, the easier it will become. Sometimes you will have to *consciously* choose a new response, new behaviors, and new thoughts based on the discovery that you are being inauthentic; other times the shift will happen automatically just because you became self-aware. For me, "letting go" or "transcending the ego" or "shifting the energy" has been managed through taking and releasing deep breaths while consciously remembering who I really am and actively choosing to be that. It is almost as tangible as letting go of one rung on a ladder and grabbing another instead, or moving your awareness from your head to your heart.

When you are first learning these steps they may seem daunting or laborious, even unrealistic. However, the more you practice them, you will discover that the whole process can happen in a split second. In fact, the goal is to have the whole process happen in *every* second. Every time an event takes place, automatically remember who you are and what you want to create. Become self-observant to see if your thoughts, words, and actions are in alignment with the outcome you desire. If you feel inauthentic, notice whether you are operating from a need for approval or control, then take a deep breath, transcend that ego energy, and realign your intention with your goal and your heart before choosing your next action. This practice transforms *you,* and as it does you will realize your power for transforming your relationship.

If at first you don't succeed...

Dear Eve,

I am about to return to a relationship with a man I am married to but have lived away from for the last five years. I am going to try again, but I need some new communication skills. Please help.

Aloha,

This relationship must have some really wonderful compo-
nents if it has endured living apart for five years and
holds enough promise for you to uproot your current life
and move back into it. I am excited for you and the possibilities your decision holds.

Learning to transcend our egos is critical in creating
healthy relationships. Ego is that part of us that judges,
criticizes, blames, and argues — and it flares up regularly for most of us. Not only does ego block love, but
these ego-elements can interfere with effective communication. The best way to transcend the ego is to become
self-observant all the time. Simply notice what is going
on with you, especially when you are being triggered by
someone else.

When being self-observant, sometimes you will notice that
you are feeling judged by the other person and that is
triggering your defenses and your ego's need for approval.
Sometimes you will notice that you are the one judging,
which is about your ego's need for control. In that
moment, rather than letting ego dictate your behavior,
take a deep breath, and choose words and actions in alignment with your goal of making the relationship work —
joyfully and healthfully.

Ironically, we often declare that we want love, but then
our words and actions are unconsciously generated by ego/
head instead of by soul/heart. In other words, our stated
destination is love and joy, but our steps lead elsewhere.

We need to be honest in our communication, but honest with
purpose. By this I mean we need to pass what we are going
to tell someone through the "test" of asking ourselves,
"Is this purposeful or helpful to the other person? Is it
something they can do anything about? Is there a way to
say it that is not hurtful? Is what I have to say truly a
statement about them, or does it really reveal something
about my need for approval or control? Am I saying this
from heart or from ego?"

I've found that I can be "brutally honest" with people and
tell them exactly what I see going on with them when I say
it 100 percent from a place of wanting the best for them.

If any of my own ego (judgment) comes into play in how I answer or give feedback, they resist and aren't able to receive my words. Thus, their ability to hear what I say is entirely dependent on the energy with which I say it.

With aloha,

Eve

Love Tip: Sometimes the "safety ring" you are holding onto until you have a stable footing elsewhere is actually the very thing that is keeping you out of balance. As you let go of the past with faith and trust, you may find wings unfurling that you never even knew you had!

Step Four: Take Action That Is in Alignment with Your Authentic Self and Your Goals

Once you have let go of ego and reconnected with your authentic self, the next step is to take action that is in alignment with who you really are and what you really want. Doing so will serve your effort to become more authentic by clearing away blockages and revealing your self-esteem. Just as one cannot be lazy in love and expect it to thrive, one cannot be lazy about loving oneself and expect to enjoy life. If you want satis*faction*, you're going to need to take *action*. However, the action must be grounded in your values and aligned with what you want to create. Be sure to refer back to your guideposts from Chapter 3 and allow them to steer you.

Here's how to do this step: Clearly keeping your goals in mind—the goals of accessing your self-esteem and creating a healthy, loving marriage—choose all your words and actions in alignment with those goals. It's that simple—and that rigorous.

EXERCISE ✎ *Give your actions and words the "purpose test." Ask yourself if what you are saying and doing are leading you* *closer to your goals or farther away from them. Consciously choose words and behaviors that move you toward your goals. Aim to have your words and actions based in love. Try to say and do things that make you, and those around you, feel more loving.* ∿

....

Love Tip: You are 100-percent responsible for the quality of your life—and your relationships. Take steps to align yourself with your Self, your true nature, your strong, capable, powerful self, and you will create a strong, healthy, and powerful life.

Putting It All Together

Applying the four steps for turning it all around works beautifully in combination with applying the EROS equation and the guideposts you identified earlier. Here's an example:

EVENT: I walk into my freshly cleaned house and find that my husband has left his things lying around and has made a mess in the kitchen.

RESPONSE: I start to get angry; I feel taken for granted and judgmental. My initial reaction is to vent at my husband and let him know how angry I am that the kitchen is a mess.

STEP ONE: In that moment, I stop and remember who I really am—wise, creative, and powerful (rather than reactive and a victim).

STEP TWO: I become self-observant and notice, first, how I am feeling and, second, what I am thinking that is causing me to feel that way. I realize that I am thinking that my husband doesn't respect me and my efforts. I am thinking that he is taking me for granted. *Notice that neither of these thoughts has anything to do with my house being clean.* The real issue I am dealing with isn't a dirty kitchen; it is a perception of my value to my husband, a very different issue.

STEP THREE: I ask myself whether my upset has to do with my need for approval or my need for control. I clearly see that my emotions are triggered by my need for approval. I want my husband to respect me and be thoughtful of me. I take a deep breath (or several of them), let go of my need for approval, and realign with who I really am. This process of self-inquiry reveals that the quality of my interaction with my husband is more important to me than the cleanliness of my house. I also consider whether my beliefs about my husband's taking me for granted are really true, and I realize that his leaving the kitchen a mess actually doesn't have anything to do with how he feels about me.

STEP FOUR: I choose my words and actions in alignment with both my authentic self and the outcome I am trying to create (a loving, communicative marriage). If need be, I consult with my list of guideposts from Chapter 3 to help remind me of what is really important to me and how to proceed. Instead of blowing up at my husband, I ask him if he can help me clean up the kitchen, or I let him know that I need reassurance of my importance to him and ask him for a hug. Instead of involving my husband in the solution at all, I may consider all the ways that he shows me he loves me and all the things he does for me, and simply let go of the issue—and clean the kitchen myself. There are several options for what I can do or say, and several that I clearly should *not* do or say if I want to maintain the harmony in my marriage.

> **OUTCOME AND SOLUTION:** The harmony is maintained in my marriage (and, hopefully, the order in the kitchen is restored). Even more important, my emotions and attitude are realigned with who I really am and what I really care about. My personal sense of well-being is strong, as is my sense of being valued by my husband.

> *Love Tip:* Set and reset your intention. If your goal is to create a loving, lasting, supportive, thriving relationship in every given moment, you will need to repeatedly reset your intention and realign your words, thoughts, and actions.

She does it this way; I do it that way

Dear Eve,

My wife and I get along well, but we just can't seem to
agree on one particular issue. I'm the kind of guy who
sets the alarm to go off when I have to get up, and when
it goes off I get up right away. My wife sets the alarm
half an hour earlier than she needs to get up and sleeps
through the beeping for half an hour, until I, who can't
sleep through beeps, finally get her out of bed. It makes
me mad that I have missed out on half an hour of sleep
while she sleeps right through the alarm. We just can't
seem to agree on who is right. Can you help?

Aloha,

Your situation is a lot more common than you might imagine. The key is in recognizing that there isn't a "right"
or "wrong" way of doing this; rather, there are two people
involved who are impacted by the choice. As long as you
are both resisting the way the other does it, options are
not obvious to you. As soon as you accept the fact that
she needs a little lead time to wake up, and she accepts
the reality that you'd prefer not to lose half an hour's
sleep or to be harassed by a lengthy beep, possible solutions will become available. This may be one of those
situations where compromise comes into play.

It sounds to me like she has a hard time waking up and is
concerned that she will miss her wake-up time if she does
not have the lead. You, however, wake up immediately to
the alarm. Therefore, if you work together, you could get
a little extra sleep and she could have an extra "alarm
clock." For instance, try setting the alarm to go off with
music rather than the beep fifteen minutes prior to when
your wife has to get up. Then ten minutes or five minutes
before she has to get up, kindly rub her back or gently
remind her that she has to get up in ten minutes. She gets
the extra assurance that you will help make sure she wakes
up, while you get an extra fifteen minutes of sleep and
music to listen to instead of the beep. Knowing that you
will help her wake up should help her be willing to let go

of the other fifteen minutes. Another option is to start
waking her up right when the alarm goes off and put the
time to good use — snuggling and enjoying each other's
company before you go separate ways.

Often in relationships the things we think are the problems seem like "little things" unworthy of fighting over —
wake-up times, toilet seat up or down, toothpaste cap on
or off. It is important to recognize that it isn't really
the issue you are fighting over that creates the problem.
Rather, it is your resistance to the other person's way —
and theirs to yours — that is the problem. What happens is
you launch into a massive control/approval battle where
you both want to control the way the other person does
it and want for him/her to honor the way you do it. If
instead you stop the ego battle long enough to recognize
that there isn't a "right way" or a "wrong way," and to
accept the way your partner prefers it done, many other
solutions will appear that will satisfy you both. Practice acceptance of "what is," and see what presents itself
to you.

With aloha,

Eve

PART II

WORKING AS TWO

A good relationship has a pattern like a dance and is built on some of the same rules. The partners do not need to hold on tightly, because they move confidently in the same pattern, intricate but gay and swift and free, like a country dance of Mozart's. To touch heavily would be to arrest the pattern and freeze the movement, to check the endlessly changing beauty of its unfolding. There is no place here for the possessive clutch, the clinging arm, the heavy hand; only the barest touch in passing. Now arm in arm, now face to face, now back to back—it does not matter which. Because they know they are partners moving to the same rhythm, creating a pattern together, and being invisibly nourished by it.

ANNE MORROW LINDBERGH

embracing change

*The most powerful agent of growth and
transformation is something much more basic
than any technique: a change of heart.*

JOHN WELWOOD

C hange is a double-edged sword in relationships; we crave change and we fear it at the same time. People often come to me complaining about their partner or their marriage. They say, "I've grown and changed and he has remained stagnant; we're growing apart," or, "She isn't the same person I married," or, "Ten years into the marriage I guess I just have to accept that this is it; the marriage isn't changing."

The purpose of life is specifically to grow, gain wisdom, and change as we learn from experiences. Ideally, we never stop learning, whether we learn computer skills, new languages, musical instruments, art, gardening techniques, communication and relationship skills, spiritual studies, or learn about our partners or ourselves. It doesn't matter what the topic is; new input creates new output. Hopefully, reading this book will cause you to change. Oddly, we expect growth and change in children, both physically and developmentally, but we somehow (falsely) think the process stops once we are adults.

Change Happens

Ironically, while we can't go into a relationship expecting to change the other person, we should go into a relationship expecting that he or she will change. The difference is the emphasis on who is implementing the change. We cannot make our partner change, but the forces of nature, as well as their own impetus, will cause them to change. Their bodies will change. Their hormones will change. Their libido will change. Their weight and health may change. Their physical appearance may change. Their friendships may change. Their careers may change. Their hobbies may change. Their athletic activities may change. Their alcohol consumption may change. Their levels of confidence and self-esteem may change. Their minds may even change. So what is it exactly that we expect to stay the same?

Then there is the marriage itself, which will change as a separate entity from either partner. Frequency of "date nights" may change. Level of financial comfort may change. Houses and communities may change. Time available for recreation may change. Family support may change. Number of family members will change. Children (who are always changing) will change the marriage. More children will change it more. Children growing up and moving out of the home will change the marriage again. The loss of family members will change the dynamics. Sexual frequency and ability may change. Skills for problem solving and communication may change. The way you spend your time together—and *how much* time you spend together—may change. Retirement will change the marriage again. So what is it exactly that we expect to stay the same?

The love is probably what we want to have stay the same, but even the expression and experience of love changes. While the core essence of true love is unchanging, as it filters through our egos it appears to change over time. As I've said already, love doesn't go away, but it does get blocked with ego; our experience of it ebbs and flows. Love can deepen over time, moving from infatuation and becoming more secure. Love can be more passionate or less passionate. Love can be conditional or unconditional. Love can be expressed or withheld. Love can be given and not received. The intensity of the love in marriage can wax and wane, as can the level of intimacy. If we want to be successful in our relationships (and in our lives), we have to become comfortable with change—both managing it when it happens and creating it when it is needed.

After about eleven years of being married, living in the same home, and keeping the same schedule, I remember having the passing thought, "So this is it; this is life." I wasn't making a judgment of good or bad, just an observation that things had been on a pretty even keel for a while and appeared to be staying true to course. Then, over the next several months, almost everything changed: My mom got sick and I relocated three thousand miles away to care for her while commuting home to see my husband. Three of my sources of income underwent major changes while I cared for my mom. Then she died, and grief impacted my emotions. When I returned to Maui my husband and I bought a new house, moved into an entirely different community, and embarked on a wholly different lifestyle—complete with new pets. After a few months in our new situation, my husband made a comment like, "So this is it. . . ." I had to kind of laugh at both us for thinking that anything ever stays the same. Change is inevitable. In fact, it is one of life's only guarantees. We will hit those 180-degree turns many times throughout our lives. Learning to manage and even embrace change, and the emotions that come with it, is critical to our well-being. Equally critical is appreciating the way things are, because "what is" can very quickly become "what was."

What is particularly hard on a relationship is when one of the spouse's core values change. For instance, if your spouse is religious when you get married and then decides that he or she doesn't believe in or honor God anymore, or if your spouse is not particularly spiritual when you marry and then becomes intensely religious along the way, havoc can happen—unless you both accept each other's personal path and trust that what is right for you may not be right for your partner, and vice versa. Another difficult change would be a shift in one partner's desire to have children (or not to have them) after having agreed one way or the other when going into the marriage. One couple was in their mid-forties and had been married for several years when the wife, who had initially agreed not to have children, suddenly changed her mind. Since menopause was looming around the corner, having kids suddenly became very important to her. The husband had children from a previous marriage and was definite about not wanting more. They went on to have the child (whom both parents loved) and ultimately got a divorce.

It is also challenging when situations change that cause a reprioritization of values. When my husband and I got married, I had a lot more leisure time. I had a normal job in which my weekends were free so I participated with him in outdoor activities like scuba diving. When I left my job to become an author, consultant, and speaker, I became a lot more regimented in how I spent my time. As they say, an entrepreneur is someone who will work eighty hours a week for herself to avoid working forty hours a week for someone else! This was not a change in values, as I still love scuba diving, but it was a change in how I prioritized my values and made use of my time. It has been a challenge for us, and I have to consciously remember to make time for activities we enjoy doing together. Couples need to be careful that how they prioritize their values doesn't change in such a way as to cause a gradual deterioration of the marriage without their having put any conscious thought into it.

Although "unconscious" change can happen over time, conscious change comes after a deliberate decision and usually requires effort. One of the things I hear a lot when talking to one or the other member of a couple is, "This is just the way I am; it is the way I always have been, and I can't change." The truth isn't that they *can't* change; it is that they *won't* change. This is a very important distinction. You *can* change *if you want to* change. Of course, if you like the way you are and you like the results you've been getting, then there is no need to do anything different. But if you want different results, you are going to have to do something different. How we show up is not set in stone. "I've always been this way,"

> **Did you know?** Dr. John Gottman of the Gottman Institute reports that the average couple waits six years before seeking help for marital problems and that half of the marriages that end do so in the first seven years. This means the average couple lives with unhappiness for far too long and waits until it is on the verge of being too late.

or, "This is just the way it is" are merely excuses for not doing the work. Our relationships *can* change *if we want them to change*. What you can't do is change the other person. They, too, will only change *if they want to change*.

The Moment of Change

When we work to bring about a change—whether it is something we want to start doing (dieting, exercising, being more conscious about the way we speak to ourselves or our partners) or stop doing (being judgmental, smoking, eating unhealthy foods, swearing)—it is usually daunting to think about changing the behavior for the rest of time. Doing so seems too monumental and unmanageable. Our minds start thinking that changing forever is unrealistic, so why bother?

I used to think that when I started a diet, if I screwed up at breakfast the whole day was lost. So I would eat whatever I wanted and restart the diet the next day. This kind of thinking doesn't work very well. When instead I recognized that if I screwed up at breakfast, there was still hope for lunch and dinner, I was much more successful. Even better, if I screwed up with one bite, I could still save the diet with the rest of the meal. We only have to manage one bite at a time, literally. In fact, the reality is that when you are tackling change, all you need to tackle—in fact, all you *can* tackle—is changing the moment. Every moment in which you master change is a victory that leads you to the next moment. The same would hold true if your goal were to become a millionaire. If you held the expectation that you would become a millionaire all at once, for all time, it would be a daunting task and an unlikely phenomenon. If, instead, you started by earning your first dollar, then another, then a hundred dollars, then a thousand dollars, the goal would become attainable, although you'd still have the task of maintaining and growing your acquired fortune.

> *Love Tip:* Imagine for a moment that the goal of a relationship isn't "happily ever after," but rather is "happily right now in the moment."

When you are trying to change your marriage, the notion of changing the whole thing for all time can certainly be hard to face. Instead, just aim to make one moment—one thought, one word, one action—aligned with love instead of ego, then one more moment, and then another. A loving marriage is a new choice in every moment. You can't change your marriage forever and you can't change yourself forever; you can only change the way you show up in any given moment. Mastery of the moment becomes mastery of the marriage, of life, and of your experience.

EXERCISE ∾ *Take a moment to look at your marriage. Evaluate what is working and what isn't, what has changed (both consciously and unconsciously), and what needs changing. Using all that you have learned so far, discuss these questions with your partner. Most importantly, take responsibility for your part in the EROS equation, communicate from your heart rather than your ego, and always keep your goal in mind. To borrow a phrase, "Ask not what your marriage (or partner) can do for you; ask what you can do for your marriage."* ∾

So much to change, so little time

Dear Eve,

With the new year here, there are so many things I want to change about myself that I get overwhelmed and bogged down — and don't end up changing anything. This year I want to lose weight, I want to learn to play an instrument, I want to stop judging others, I want to be more successful, I want a loving relationship...the list goes on and on. How do I move from feeling overwhelmed to actually making changes?

Aloha,

Whenever we look at a total change, we are easily overwhelmed — especially when the change is something that requires time. If we focus on changing our behavior in any given moment, it is much easier to manage and accomplish the changes we desire. Ultimately, all of us have the ability to change what we are doing moment by moment, but few of us experience ease trying to change everything at

once. For instance, take losing weight. Depending on how
much weight you want to lose, it isn't likely going to
happen in a week or even a month. It takes time to healthfully remove excess weight. The key is not to focus on the
twenty, thirty, or forty pounds you want to lose, but
rather to take it one pound at a time. It is far less
overwhelming to plan to lose a pound, and often far more
successful. Success at losing one pound will inspire you
to have success at losing the next pound. It is also
important to give yourself credit for those baby steps.
One pound may not seem like much until you realize that
one little notch on your scale is equivalent to four
sticks of butter!

The same holds true for the other items on your list.
Instead of focusing on bringing more love into your life,
see if you can bring more love into any — and every —
moment. Instead of learning to play an instrument, learn
to play one note or one song. When you have mastered that
one, add another. Even letting go of feeling overwhelmed
is a moment-by-moment task.

As for judging others, it is nearly impossible to simply
"stop judging others" all at once, but it is very possible
to become aware of when you are judging others — and to
stop just for that moment. The key to change is to be
self-observant. When you self-observe, you become aware.
When you are aware of what you are doing, saying, or
thinking, you have the opportunity to make a new choice —
and to do, say, or think something different. This ability
to choose is what makes you powerful. When we use that
power to transform a single moment, and then start string-
ing those changed moments together, we bring about overall
change without the stress and sense of being overwhelmed
that accompany trying to change everything at once.

When your goal is "to be more successful," it is very
important that you take some time to define what success
is to you. For some of us success is related to wealth.
For others success is defined by our happiness, our love
lives, and our health. For still others it is measured by
how well we manage huge amounts of responsibility. If you
don't know how you define success, you surely won't know
(or acknowledge) when you get there! Often when we sit
down to really define what success means to us, we dis-

cover that it wouldn't take much to move into the "more successful" category.

Last but not least, take note of which of your goals are "process goals" and which are "product goals." Process goals are not achieved by a deadline, but rather are ongoing. Exercise is a process goal, because you can't "just do it" and then be done with it. Fitness requires continued maintenance. Cleaning your house is a process goal because it must be done continually. Bringing more love into your life is a process goal. By contrast, finishing a certain project is a product goal — you have completed a task by a certain date. A lot of us have ongoing process goals and never feel successful because we haven't yet "gotten it" that the goal isn't something we'll ever reach; rather, it is something we continuously do. In these cases, we need to redefine success to include the process, not just the product.

With aloha,

Eve

> ♡ *Love Tip:* Success is achieved moment by moment; the time to start is right now, now, now, now, and again now. Look back on what you have accomplished and realize that "now" spelled backwards is "won"!

Turns on the Path

I am a labyrinth facilitator. That means I guide people on walks through labyrinths as a path of self-discovery. The process is a metaphor for taking a pilgrimage, but rather than journeying outward, the exploration is internal. The labyrinth I use is a replica of the inlaid stone labyrinth set into the floor of the Chartres Cathedral, in France (see the illustration on the next page). A labyrinth is not a maze, but rather consists of a single path that leads to the center—the sacred destination. The same path leads you back out.

One of the ways that the labyrinth works for self-discovery is through metaphor. Whatever one experiences while walking the labyrinth is what, metaphorically, one needs to look at in his or her life. For instance, if you find yourself judging others as they walk, judgment is likely blocking your experience of joy in life. Judgment usually reveals a need for control, which, once released, will move you back to center, to heart, from where you can make new choices. Or if you find yourself bored or impatient as you walk, boredom and impatience are issues you need to look at in your life. The labyrinth walk is a journey toward your heart, toward authenticity. The labyrinth is the perfect experiential tool for practicing and mastering the essential life skills presented in Chapter 6 as steps for turning it all around. (To learn more about the labyrinth, read my book *Way of the Winding Path: A Map for the Labyrinth of Life.*)

Chartres Cathedral Labyrinth

If you ever have the opportunity to participate in a labyrinth walk, before you enter, remember who you really are. As you walk, become self-observant and let go of your ego needs for approval and control as they emerge. Realign with your soul and with your heart as you reach the sacred center of the labyrinth. And, on the walk back out from the center of the labyrinth, choose your next actions in alignment with your most authentic self.

When walking the labyrinth you encounter twenty-eight 180-degree turns, both going in and coming out. Paying special attention to how you feel as you encounter the turns can reveal a lot to you about how you deal with change. Often people share that they didn't like the turns, that the turns emerged just as they were getting their rhythm. Or they share that the turns made them feel "off balance." Metaphorically, this is usually true-to-life in terms of what they are going through outside of the labyrinth. I have found that by the time most people get through twenty or thirty turns, they begin to "make friends" with the turns. They start spinning and dancing on the turns and noticing who they come face-to-face with; in other words, they start finding creative ways of managing the turns as they begin to recognize that the turns (which represent changes) are inevitable and that the only way past them is through them. Often they even start looking forward to them. For some, the turns become the "fun part," breaking up the monotony of walking in a single direction.

There is something to be learned from this process as it relates to our relationships and our lives. Since we know that we will inevitably encounter turns and changes in our marriage, in our spouses, and in ourselves, achieving a sense of acceptance, rather than resistance, about these changes will serve us greatly. And although we can aim to minimize some changes—by staying fit, eating healthfully, communicating honestly and regularly, and staying physically intimate—many changes are not within our control. Remember the EROS equation; this is where our ability to respond comes in.

Change affects both the good times and the difficult; thus, it is especially important to remember to consciously appreciate when things are going well and to trust that difficulties won't remain difficult forever.

Love Tip: The root word of "emergency" is "emergence." Trust that every tragedy or difficult time is just the transition to something new and improved. Look for what is emerging, and trust the process.

One of the things I observed as I took my husband on his first labyrinth walk was that although we entered the labyrinth fairly close together, within minutes we were walking on opposite sides of the circle, seemingly going in opposite directions. Then the labyrinth brought us together again; we were suddenly walking side by side and going the same way. Again the labyrinth took us apart, and again it brought us back together. As I observed this cycle throughout our walk, I began to view it as a metaphor for our marriage. I could see how our relationship has been like that. There are times when it seems we are close together and going in the same direction, and there are periods of more distance. Understanding this cycle, I have begun to recognize that when the periods of distance begin, there are things I can do to bring us back together. In my marriage, I've found that the ebbs and flows are directly linked to two things: loving communication and physical touch. Whenever we feel distant and disconnected, in the ebb, we need to talk (either more, more honestly, or more lovingly) and/or touch, or both. (They call it "making love" for a reason!)

 Love Tip: When you want your spouse to be more loving, be more loving toward your spouse.

Attachment to What Was Equals Resistance to What Is

What usually causes us the most pain when we come to 180-degree turns in relationships are (1) attachment to expectations or dreams of what we wanted, and (2) fear of the unknown and made-up stories about what is yet to come.

When a relationship changes and we are attached to the image of what we were hoping the relationship would become (or remain), we feel pain. When I was in my twenties I had a relationship for four years with a man who I imagined would love me, cherish me, marry me, and father our children. He was kind and generous but aloof with his emotions. He lied to me and cheated on me repeatedly. He remained withdrawn rather than engaging in our relationship. One day I was complaining to a male friend about the relationship when he gently pointed out that I had been complaining about the exact same things for a year or more. He asked me what kind of support I needed in order to do something different. As sweet as this offer was, he had held up a mirror for me that I didn't like looking in. I realized that he was absolutely right—I had been resisting "what is" and staying in the relationship, complaining but doing nothing about it. Realizing that the relationship was not what I wanted, I broke up with my boyfriend. Shortly thereafter, while I was sad and crying over the loss, a professor pointed out that I was mourning the loss of what I wanted the relationship to become (an illusion), not the loss of the relationship itself (reality). As I thought about what he said, I could see that it was true. When I focused upon what I'd *actually* "lost" rather than what I *felt* like I had lost, the pain dissipated significantly. Recognizing that I'd never actually *had* the relationship whose loss I was mourning made all the difference in my ability to let go and move on.

Love Tip: There is a fine line between dreams and illusions. Be careful to hold on to your dreams, while being aware of your illusions. In any relationship it is helpful to take a reality check from time to time to acknowledge what you really love about the other person rather than loving what you wish were true. Watch for the truth.

When we got married, most of us held a vision of what we wanted the relationship to be. Perhaps our image was that the relationship would eternally stay as loving and passionate as it was when we were married, or that love, trust, and communication would grow stronger over time. Perhaps the attachment was to a stereotype that didn't play out in reality (she should be subservient, he should be the breadwinner) or to the idea of monogamy, which later was violated. Perhaps the attachment was to the idea that marriage meant you would no longer have to seek sex or to the belief that you would no longer have to endure being pressured for sex. Perhaps the attachment was to the image of physical bodies that stayed young and fit, rather than having to deal with aging or illness. Perhaps the attachment was to the idea that you and your spouse would participate in all the same activities and escort each other to social events. Undoubtedly you had an ideal image of what you thought marriage would be—and maybe it even was, for a time. The point is that we get attached to certain images that are based on expectations, and when they are tested or revealed as false or when they change, we mourn the loss of the image. In many cases the only thing we're losing is some illusion we held.

Attachment to "what was" (or to what we hoped for) equals resistance to "what is," which as we've discussed results in pain and blocks the experience of love in a relationship. As an analogy, let's say someone refills your empty coffee cup. You're expecting a nice, hot cup of freshly brewed coffee. You take a sip, full of your expectations, and discover a cup of chamomile tea. Even though the tea is delicious, your expectations are not fulfilled and you are disappointed. If you'd had no expectations or were flexible about embracing what is, you could have been delighted with the tea.

If you want to turn this dynamic around in your relationship, it is important to become aware of when your attachment to your expectations is interfering with embracing the relationship as is. Then, refocus on what is good about the relationship and what is good about your partner. Make it your automatic response to acknowledge and appreciate, rather than to judge and criticize. Look for what is and celebrate it, rather than looking at what is not and mourning it.

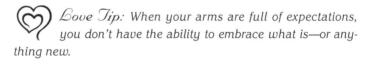 *Love Tip:* When your arms are full of expectations, you don't have the ability to embrace what is—or anything new.

Stories, Stories Everywhere but Not a Drop of Truth

One of the most empowering things you can do when changes begin to happen and emotions begin to rise is to stay in the present moment. This has been said so many times by so many people in the "self-help" industry over the last few years that it sounds cliché, but it is a really important skill to master, especially in relationships.

What does it really mean to remain present? When you begin to feel upset or agitated by an impending change or situation, take a look at yourself—self-observe—and notice what you are thinking. Notice if you are thinking about the past or the future, and then consciously pay attention to what is happening at that exact moment. As you know, the past has already happened and you can't change it; you can only respond to it, honor it, appreciate it, or be glad it is over, but wishing to relive it is not a viable option. Simply pay attention to when you are doing this, and refocus your thinking. If there is something you wish you had done differently, pay attention and make a conscious note of what you learned from the experience, and then bring your attention back to what is happening now, where you can apply that knowledge. Pay attention to what needs attending to now, what you are feeling, thinking, saying, and doing now. This requires practice. I'm sure as you begin to be aware of the time zone in which most of your thoughts take place, you'll be shocked to find that 90 percent (if not more) of your thoughts are about either the past or the future.

Love Tip: Love is purely in the moment. When you are worrying about the past or thinking about the future, you are not in love. Instead you are in ego. Ego worries about "mine," "forever," "jealousy," "more." When you find yourself falling into ego, return to the present moment where love lives, thrives, and is shared.

Future thinking is where fear of the unknown sneaks up on us. Since the unknown is so uncomfortable, we make up stories to fill in the blanks. These stories *could* be true, but they *may not* be true. We don't know whether they are, but we start believing that our theories are true and even make decisions based on these made-up stories. I was working with a woman recently who was planning to move to another state with her spouse. Although they still hadn't decided for sure to move, she started feeling the anxiety of going through the move. She worried about whether her husband would be okay with relocating, whether they would get jobs, whether they would like the house, and whether their relationship would be able to handle all the stress. Although considering possible "worst-case scenarios" can help you plan and strategize to avoid potential problems, the anxiety she was generating from worrying about the future was causing a meltdown and rendering her unable to handle anything.

Interestingly, fear is the *anticipation* of pain, the imagination of pain. The anticipation of suffering is often worse than the suffering itself (and it lasts longer!). We compound our problems tenfold when we make up stories about the pain we *think* we are going to feel. When we expect and worry about the *possibility* of pain, we experience the pain as if the situation were already happening, so we end up prolonging the agony or putting ourselves through the same emotions as if the actual event were occurring—when it may not ever happen. Fear seldom happens in real time, because when a situation really *is* happening, fear gets replaced with other emotions: anger, hurt, or jealousy, for instance. (We'll talk more about those emotions in the next chapter.) Fear exists, for the most part, totally in our heads, and the *anticipation* that something will happen can be debilitating if we allow it to be.

When you start getting panicky about what *might* happen and begin making up stories with worst-case scenarios, practice what you have learned so far in order to manage your emotions:

1. Notice how you are feeling.

2. Inquire about what you are thinking that is causing you to feel the way you do.

3. Determine whether or not your thoughts are accurate.

4. If they are not, let them go and choose new thoughts, thus creating new feelings.

5. If you are not sure, talk to your spouse or a trusted friend and see if he or she can help you get a reality check on what is actually a valid concern and what is not.

When you are inquiring, of yourself or others, about the truth of your fears, if you find that they are valid—that is, you find that the things you fear *are* happening or are very likely to happen—use the information to help you strategize a solution or a means of minimiz-

ing the impact. Again, the beauty of fear is that hiding just underneath it is something you cherish and want to protect. Use your fear
to flag what matters to you, and then create a plan for protecting and
nurturing it. The more work you have done in developing your self-
esteem, identifying your strengths and values (see Chapters 3 and 4),
and learning to trust your intuition, the easier it will be for you to
manage difficulties as they arise.

> ♡ *Love Tip:* Whenever you hear yourself saying things
> like "I know he thinks I'm unattractive," or "I know she
> doesn't trust me," or "I am sure the relationship is over," ask
> yourself how you know. What is your evidence? Do you truly
> know, or are you assuming? Aim to base your decisions and
> communication on truth.

In essence, fear is a form of visualization. A lot of research has
gone into the power of visualization. It is the experience of many
people that visualization is very powerful and is the first step toward
manifestation. Consequently, when you don't know the truth, if you
are going to make up stories and visualize your future, you may as
well make up stories that serve you, empower you, and make you feel
like the world (and your spouse) are out to do you good instead of
stories that make you think the world is out to get you. Visualize a different path altogether, one in which the pain you fear is not inflicted,
or visualize yourself handling your fears competently if they should
materialize. Allow your visualization to be practice for managing and
handling any problems that may arise. Visualize your spouse as behaving in alignment with his or her authentic self—honest, trustworthy, and communicative. Visualize yourself as powerful, capable,
faithful, loving, and authentic. Visualize your marriage as strong, enduring, and thriving.

Years ago, I bought a convertible that had an alarm system. I continuously worried about (and thus visualized) people messing with
my car, so I carefully made sure I set the alarm every time I left my
car. Even so, people repeatedly vandalized my car. At some point, I realized that through my fear-based visualization I was energizing the

expectation that people would harm my car and I decided to stop worrying, stop turning on the alarm, and stop being a magnet for that kind of behavior. Lo and behold, no one messed with my car again. Now that may have been coincidental, but the reason I share this is because changing the way I visualized other people didn't change *them* (directly); it changed *me*. As my energy shifted, my experiences shifted as well.

As we have already established, you can't change your spouse, but you *can* give him or her the *room* to change. When you always expect him or her to behave the same old way, or when because of your fears you always visualize your spouse at his or her worst, energetically you are holding your spouse in a "box" with little room to manuever or show up differently. When, through self-observation, you realize that you are doing this, consciously visualize your spouse's goodness instead. This is not a matter of visualizing your spouse (or your child) as *better than* he or she really is; it is a matter of visualizing your spouse *authentically* as he or she *really* is. This concept is discussed more in Chapter 11 as it relates to helping children change their behavior.

Recently I was writing in my journal to explore some fear I was feeling in my community. I realized that "unreasonable people" caused me fear. People who are racist are unreasonable. People who are mentally unstable are often unreasonable. People on drugs or alcohol are unreasonable. My fear was based upon thinking that I wouldn't be able to protect myself or others in the presence of someone whom I could not reason with. As I inquired whether my thinking was true, I realized I had encountered many situations in which I'd had to deal with "unreasonable" people who were coping with serious mental challenges, the influence of drugs, hatred, or health impairments, and I had always risen to the challenge. As I reviewed past incidents, I recalled that I had broken up a potential fight in a bar, stopped a woman who was having a psychotic episode from harming herself or others in a hotel, counseled suicidal teenagers, and reasoned with people under the influence of drugs and alcohol (or safely removed myself from their presence). As I looked at the "truth" of my fears, I realized that a very strong and capable part of myself has always emerged in the midst of emergencies and I did not need to be afraid. Simply facing my fear and asking myself if it was indeed true helped me to let it go. I don't know if I released the fear or if it released me, but looking it in the eye definitely shifted it from fear of the unknown to fear of the known, and suddenly it no longer had me by the gut. I began to hold the vision of myself as strong and capable instead of in danger.

> **EXERCISE** ❧ *When emotions rise, put your thoughts on paper. Writing about your emotions puts them in front of you, where they are often more manageable than when they are stuck inside of you, invisible but felt. Try pretending you are a relationship advisor; write yourself a question and then answer it. Since most of us are better at helping other people with their problems than we think we are at dealing with our own, if you write your problems in question form and then answer them from the viewpoint of wise outsider, you may discover that you have the answer after all. This process provides a totally different perspective.* ❧

What Are You Afraid Of?

One woman shared her experience of going through a divorce after twenty-eight years and managing the fear it evoked. Her story illustrates the powerful process of self-observation and self-inquiry for managing emotions and change. Aware of her pain, she inquired of herself, "What am I feeling now? What am I thinking now?" By following her feelings through to the source—fear—she was able to look at what she was afraid of, separate the fiction (the story) from the truth, and free herself from her pain.

> In the beginning I didn't want the divorce. I thought if he had just been more honest with me I could have done something to save our nuclear family. However, we were both growing, but in different ways. We were both quite spiritual, but my path was more traditionally Western and his was more Eastern. Ironically, it was our growth, not our stagnation, that opened us up for divorce. Now, looking back, I can see that our decision was so right. Now I am with a man who is

a better fit, who I am growing with instead of in spite of. And my ex-husband has traveled the world and done things he probably wouldn't have done if we'd stayed married. What felt horrible at the time turned out to be a good decision for both of us. We are probably better friends now than when we were married.

I think our choice was one of courage. The day he left, I remember coming home and all his stuff was gone. I stood in the center of my living room. I was crying a little, shaking and feeling fearful.

A part of me said to myself, "Okay, what are you are feeling? Are you sorry he has left?"

Truthfully, I said, "No, I'm glad."

"Then what are you feeling?"

"Fear."

"Fear of what?"

"Fear of being alone."

"But you have been alone a lot in your marriage, and now you will have a choice to be alone or to be with other people."

Seeing the truth of that, I answered, "Fear of the unknown."

"But you like to go on journeys alone and explore, because life is an adventure to you. Let go of that fear."

Again, the truth helped me release the fear. This time I answered, "And fear of not being able to support myself." But I had a good job and could make enough to eat and keep a roof over my head. My children were old enough to take care of themselves. So I let go of that, too.

I continued, "And a fear that I will never be loved again." Boy, has that turned out to be a joke! So I let go of the fear and began slowly to put one foot in front of the other, and each day it became easier. I rebuilt my life out of courage and love—love for my ex-husband and love for myself. And we are both really proud of ourselves today!

 Love Tip: Don't take anything someone else does personally. Take everything you do personally.

Fear vs. Intuition

Fear and intuition are hard to tell apart. Both are gifts meant to protect us or something we cherish, such as our lives, our families, our relationships. The irony is that we tend to honor fear regardless of its basis in truth, and it often makes our lives more difficult, scary, and unmanageable. Yet we tend not to honor intuition in spite of its truth, which could empower us, strengthen us, and help us to avoid many difficult situations.

The only way I know to tell the two apart is to pay attention to what you are feeling and to inquire whether it makes you feel stronger and more capable (intuition) or weakens you and makes you crazy (fear). Does the image in your head empower you, as if it were meant to help you protect yourself? Or does it paralyze and debilitate you with anxiety, jealousy, or rage? Intuition is generated from your spirit, your heart, your authentic self. Fear is generated from your personality, from ego. When you feel something—fear or intuition—pay attention to whether your need for approval or your need for control is involved. If you are operating from a need to control someone and you "have a feeling" that they are going to get into trouble or are doing something wrong, it is probably fear and is ego-based rather than authentic. If you have a need for approval and "have a feeling" that someone is talking about you behind your back or is having an affair, it is probably ego-based fear rather than truth. If, on the other hand, you really tune in, transcend your ego needs for approval and control, tap into your most authentic self, and find a "knowing," then pay attention.

Although everyone may be different, it is my sense that intuition is proactive and purposeful. Intuition makes us wiser and stronger. It does not make us become unreasonable and judgmental, nor does it make us want to inflict pain or harm others. Intuition offers information that allows us to strengthen and protect ourselves or someone else. Intuition offers the truth, and even if it is painful the truth will make you more authentic and bring you closer to your spouse.

Many years ago I was home alone at my parent's house and I suddenly found myself unconsciously locking all the doors. When I became aware of what I was doing I asked myself, "Why am I locking the doors?" Then, as if watching a movie, I saw in my mind's eye a man approach the house and go door to door to see if any of them were unlocked. I could even see his shadow on the opposite wall as he passed by the windows. I thought it was a weird and unlikely image, but, obedient to the feeling, I made sure every door in the house was locked. I didn't feel fear; I just did what I was guided to do. Within an hour there was a knock at the door. I looked out the peephole, and there stood a man I had dated a few times who was upset because I had told him I was not interested in seeing him again. I didn't open the door, nor did I let him know I was home. Within minutes I could hear him go from door to door to see if he could find one that was unlocked. I even saw his shadow being cast on the opposite wall as he passed by the windows—exactly the way I had seen it in my mind's eye. If I had failed to trust that intuitive image, I honestly can't say what harm could have come to me that day. What I can say is that the message was not wrapped up in judgment, the way ego-based messages are. I did not get the message that a creepy, horrible man who was trying to hurt me was coming to the house. I simply saw what I needed to do to protect myself, and why. The difference is subtle and hard to distinguish—especially when you are new to doing so (and it may work differently for you). A friend of mine describes fear- or ego-based decisions as being accompanied by a sense of "contraction," while following her intuition makes her feel a sense of "expansion." If you practice transcending your ego and tapping into your true self, you will eventually be much more confident in trusting your intuition.

Overcoming overwhelming jealousy

Dear Eve,

I'm in a relationship with a man I believe to be a good and honest person. This is the love of my life, and at forty-nine years old I'm feeling quite overwhelmed by it. I was married once, years ago, and my ex was unfaithful. After that I put myself on the shelf till I met this beautiful soul. We have been together for a little over a year. Every aspect of our relationship is great, except I have overpowering feelings of jealousy that are hard to control. He's never given me reason not to trust him. It's just petty stuff on my part, like when he gets an e-mail from a woman (which he doesn't try to hide from me) or

when I find a piece of paper with a phone number on it. If
I don't get a handle on my feelings, they are going to eat
me alive and destroy this relationship of a lifetime. I
would appreciate any insight you can give. Thank you.

Aloha,

First of all, I applaud you for recognizing your problem
and seeking help.

There are a couple things to consider: Jealousy is just
another word for fear — fear that he is going to leave
you, fear that you aren't good enough, fear that someone
else is better than you. F.E.A.R. stands for Fantasized
Experiences Appearing Real. Since fear is ego-based and
ego is the thing that always blocks love, when we give
energy to our fears we can actually cause what we fear
to happen by blocking the love between us and those whom
we love.

Your feelings are a direct result of what you are thinking
and imagining. "All" you have to do to feel differently is
to choose new thoughts and visualize new images. I put
"all" in quotes because I know I'm making this sound easy,
when in reality it will require some persistent effort on
your part. While it may not be easy, it is simple.

How do you begin to think new thoughts?

First of all, you need to practice self-observation. You
need to pay attention to how you are feeling and what you
are thinking that is causing those feelings. Constantly
ask yourself, "What am I feeling now? What am I thinking
now? What am I doing now?"

Self-observation will lead to self-awareness. When you are
aware of what you are doing, you will realize that you
have a choice about whether or not to continue doing it.
When you make new choices, you will create new experiences. As long as you are unaware of what you are thinking
that is causing you to feel the way you do, you will be
unable to do anything differently.

Self-talk is the constant tape playing in your head. As you observe it, whenever you find yourself thinking a thought that causes you discomfort, stop and ask yourself, "Is this happening to me now? Is this thought real or fantasized? What can I think or imagine instead that would lead to a different, healthier feeling?" For instance, when you find a phone number on a piece of paper, you say you immediately start fantasizing that the number belongs to some beautiful woman whom your boyfriend is having an affair with. Try the following instead:

1. Take a deep breath and bring your attention back to the present moment. Take several deep breaths if you have to—remember, what you fear isn't happening to you now. By constantly bringing your attention back to the present moment (where none of what you are worried about is really happening), you can bring yourself back to a peaceful mindset.

2. You have no evidence of an affair, only a phone number; so for right now the fear is completely imagined. Focus on reality. You have no supporting evidence for your fears.

3. You have a choice at this point either to wait until you can ask him whose number it is or, since you are making up explanations anyhow, to make up a scenario in which you are a winner in the realm of love, not a loser. Imagine that the phone number belongs to a coworker, or to a florist your boyfriend called so he could order flowers for you, or to his sister.

The other issue here is self-esteem. If you truly knew your own value and worth, you would not be so quick to assume that your partner wants to be with someone else. Take this as your golden opportunity to do some serious work on restoring your faith in who you are and what you have to offer, so you will believe that your partner wants to be with you.

With aloha,

Love Tip: When you are afraid of losing someone, either you can make them so miserable by trying to control them that you drive them away, or you can focus on why
you want to save the marriage, grow the love between you, and
give them reasons to stay. The choice is yours.

➤ KRISTIN AND DAN, MARRIED TWENTY-FIVE YEARS

The early years of my and Dan's marriage—when we felt the magic
of wholeness and perfection—were the anchor for all that has come
after. That time, those feelings, that magic was the Truth of our relationship. God served up dessert before the vegetables! Of course, it
was tough when the frosting got replaced with brussels sprouts, but
that's where the work and opportunity, a.k.a. change, come into play.

The real reason we are in the marriage and chose each other is
because we have all the qualities, habits, and button-pushing capa-
bilities to help the other grow. The qualities in the other that irritate
and confound us are merely opportunities to face our wounds, our
demons, and our angels, which is what the magic was showing us.
That sense of wholeness was saying, "You can face it all with this
person."

Most of us don't particularly enjoy brussels sprouts, or facing our
pain. We want it to be happy thoughts and icing, but that is not life
in the real world. People get fat, we get skinny, we fart, we get sick,
we get wrinkles, we yell, we laugh, we cry, we get angry, we get
bored—and always there is change.

The key to loving our marriage and surviving the changes has
been to anchor into the part that is real: the love, the magic, and the
wholeness we experienced in the beginning. Over the years, there
have been times when Dan and I seemed to hate each other, but underneath it all we knew that wasn't real. We were anchored in the
love. Our egos hated each other for bringing up our issues. It's easy to
blame your partner for the feelings you have. "If only he did this." "If
only she did that." "If only my partner would support me in the way I
want to be supported." Several times during the "ebb years" I would
think, "I can't go on like this forever." Then I would remind myself that
I can do it for today. The "one day at a time" philosophy works in

marriage, too. I know the one thing I can count on in life and in marriage is change, so even the bad times pass eventually—especially when we are conscious of moving through them.

As partners, our choices and life experiences send out ripples that affect the other; whether it's a job choice or an illness, we are affected. The marriage is affected. I believe there are three parts to a marriage, the two individuals with their individual life lessons and destinies, plus an entity that is the *we,* the destiny of the couple. The *we* is the place where the ripples meet and roll back. How we perceive the ripples, how we respond to change, is key to loving our marriage. As we've ridden the waves, these are the things that we have discovered are important and can pass on to others:

- Trust the unfolding. Everything is unfolding as it should. You cannot always perceive the perfection at first, so you need to trust.

- Deal in your sphere of influence. Your sphere of influence is your individual response to change, how you deal with it. You cannot change your partner or anyone else, only yourself.

- This too shall pass. The most wonderful moments and the worst moments will eventually pass. Be present with whatever is happening.

- Keep your observer intact. The observer is the wise and objective part of yourself. Your observer can show you what your lessons are in the moment.

- It's all about me! Yep, it's all about you, but not how you think it is. Your feelings, your thoughts, your anger, your pity parties are your work. Your partner agreed on some level to assist you by poking every wound you ever got so that you could do the work and become whole. This is the biggest misunderstanding in the world when it comes to love. We believe it is supposed to always feel wonderful and supportive, but as souls we have work to do, and our partners have agreed to help us do the work. Unfortunately, many people run away as soon as the icing disappears. They move on to the next person who will provide the icing, so they never get any deeper in their process.

- Relationship is the fast track to growth and healing. As mentioned above, your partner has agreed to help you. He or she will relentlessly hold up the mirror for you so you can see your stuff.

There is nothing more wonderful than having someone to walk through my life with—someone to witness all the stages and changes. Dan has seen me at my best and my worst—as a bitch, as an angel, fat, skinny, beautiful, ugly—and he has loved me through it all. I have done the same for him.

There is a deep peace in that, an enormous well of unconditional love that is birthed through the processes of change and bearing witness to another person's life. This is the reward of change. It brings us back to the place where we began. And then, we get to start all over again with the next part that needs healing.

Chapter 8

Managing Emotions and Communicating Clearly

To keep your marriage brimming, with love in the wedding cup,

whenever you're wrong, admit it; whenever you're right, shut up.

OGDEN NASH

Relationships are full of emotions. Our feelings can range in any given moment from one end of the spectrum to the other. They are affected not only by the circumstance that triggered them but also by factors such as how much sleep we've had, how much stress we're under, whether we've eaten, hormone levels, grief, and illness. Healthy relationships depend on our ability to communicate our needs, wishes, and thoughts, and also on our ability to discuss issues of concern and resolve problems. Our emotions affect our ability to communicate, and our ability to communicate can certainly impact our emotions. This chapter addresses both topics—emotions and communication—in an effort to help you unravel the two and utilize them in a way that supports your marriage. Whether you are dealing with anger over past events, are wondering how to connect with an emotionally unavailable spouse, or just want to deepen the intimacy in your communication with your spouse, this chapter provides skills and tools to guide you.

Integrity Agreements

To talk about these issues, a good place to start is with a discussion of integrity agreements. Integrity agreements are unspoken (for the most part) agreements that we humans have with each other that say, "I will not harm you, emotionally or physically." With our spouses, the agreement is spoken out loud and made public. It is implicit in the parent/child relationship. It is even assumed to exist among strangers. Our society operates on the expectation that we can trust each other not to harm one another physically or emotionally.

Unfortunately, people break the integrity agreement with each other in little ways all the time—by failing to do what we say we will do, failing to be on time, being dishonest, being judgmental.... When someone we know and love breaks an integrity agreement with us, big or small, immense emotions can erupt, including anger, betrayal, abandonment, hurt, fear, and insecurity. When this happens it is important that we take a look at how we are feeling, examine our part in the situation (there is that EROS response again!), discuss the situation with the other person, and come to a renewed agreement with each other—before resentment builds up and irreparable damage is done. All this requires the ability to communicate in the middle of a stream of emotions. Few of us are well trained in these skills, and most of us have seldom seen anything modeled during conflict beyond the expression (or the suppression) of anger, which seldom helps in resolving the problem.

If you are the one who broke an integrity agreement and your goal is still to have a loving marriage, you will need to take responsibility for what you have done and accept the consequences, which may include having to endure your partner's pain. When you don't acknowledge what you did that inflicted pain, or don't take responsibility for your actions, but rather defend your ego, you block the ability to resolve the problem by honoring ego instead of truth, love, and compassion. The two of you may both need to work through the full range of your emotions in order to find your way back to love and understanding, reset your intentions, and make a new agreement.

When you feel guilty, you also need to clear up the integrity agreement that you broke with yourself, achieve a sense of forgiveness for yourself, and restore self-love. Otherwise, your guilt and distrust of yourself will contaminate your actions in the future.

 Love Tip: When you trust yourself, you may find that the rest of the world is suddenly more trustworthy.

Remember, ego is what blocks love and compassion. When we are able to transcend issues of the ego and focus instead on the bigger picture of why we are here and what is really important, we are able to clean up broken integrity agreements, even years after the fact, and begin to handle them immediately instead of holding on to the hurt they inflict.

This is obviously easier said than done, but mending any agreements that we have broken is an incredibly freeing thing to do. Even years later, a phone call or e-mail saying, "I realize that I hurt you, and I apologize. I was wrong," is very powerful. Sometimes the "wrong" we have committed is simply to have held on to a grudge for a long time, maybe even years, after someone violated an agreement with us. We may at first justify our lack of compassion and forgiveness by thinking that the other person is the one who broke the agreement. When we contemplate it further, however, sometimes we are able to see that the other person made amends and tried to make it right, and that we held on to anger and hurt without looking at the whole truth, owning our responsibility, and moving back to love.

EXERCISE ∾ *Have you broken any integrity agreements with your spouse? Do you need to clean up your emotions regarding agreements broken with you? How about agreements you have broken with yourself?* ∾

The Mountain of Emotions

Broken integrity agreements evoke a lot of emotions for both people involved. When we become aware of our feelings—particularly the emotions that don't feel good, like anger, hurt, fear, jealousy, frustration, anxiety—and stop to inquire by looking deeper into them, we can use them to guide us back to love.

When we feel *anger* or a variation of anger—frustration, irritation, annoyment, or resentment—it is really like a flag on top of a mountain of other emotions. It doesn't exist all by itself. Several other emotions are also affecting us.

Directly under anger is *hurt*. When we are mad at someone, we also feel hurt in some way by them or the situation. Our feelings are hurt that he or she didn't consider us; we are sad that he or she didn't trust us.

Underneath hurt is *fear*. We are afraid of losing the relationship, afraid of what others will think of us, afraid that we will continue to be hurt, afraid that we will never be able to trust again, afraid that we are being made to look foolish, and on and on. We are afraid of losing control or losing approval. Our need for control is embedded in anger, and our need for approval in hurt. Both are hiding in our fears.

Underneath fear is *responsibility,* recognition of or remorse over our part in the situation. It is rare to encounter a conflict or circumstance for which we do not have some responsibility or remorse, even if it is simply being in the wrong place at the wrong time. When expressing the whole truth of our feelings, it is very empowering to admit to ourselves (and to let our partners know) what we are sorry for and what we could have done differently. Remember, our feelings are the result of something we thought (our response to an event). So if you are feeling angry, hurt, and fearful, taking responsibility for the thoughts that led you to feel that way is very empowering. Again, it is in our response-ability that the power to heal and change exists.

When we let go of blame to the extent that we can recognize our responsibility in a situation, we are then able to have a sense of *understanding and forgiveness.* In other words, when we transcend our egos and drop our guards of defense and resistance for a moment, we can feel some compassion for what the other person is experiencing. From a place of understanding, we may see our partner's perspective and possibly even his or her innocence, or why our partner did what he or she did, or we can see what the misunderstanding was that contributed to the situation. When we take a moment to try to see it from the other person's side and to take in all the information, we become better able to understand the situation. When we achieve a sense of understanding, we are far better equipped to forgive. "Forgiveness" comes from a root word that means "to give." When we forgive out of compassion and understanding, we clear the ego blocks and restore the ability to give and receive love. When we take the time to look at the situation from our hearts, with compassion and understanding, instead of from our egos, what really matters and what does not begins to become clear.

Beneath understanding and forgiveness is what we **want.** We want to be treated fairly, we want a loving relationship—or we may want out. Regardless, when we express our desires, half the battle of achieving them is accomplished. Whenever people come to me for any sort of relationship mediation, the first thing I ask is "What do you want?" We need to know where we are trying to go in order to figure out how to get there.

Underneath what we want is *appreciation and love.* Regardless of the fact that we're feeling all these emotions, there are still things we appreciate about the other person. Underneath the mountain of emotions, love still exists. The love is easier to see when we're dealing with partners or family members than it is with total strangers, but even when we don't know the person we are angry at, on the soul level we care about him or her as a human being. With our loved ones, however, it is much easier to recognize and express what we love and appreciate about them. *The bottom line is love.*

Love Tip: Love and anger exist simultaneously. Be sure when you are expressing the anger that your love is also shining through.

We are often unaware of all these underlying emotions that present obstacles to the expression of our love. Consequently, we express to our partner only our anger or hurt—or we inflict pain and hurt on them. As a defense they then express their anger and hurt to us. Often an argument based on protecting both egos ensues, which is a very difficult place from which to reach an agreement (and love). Anger doesn't cancel out love, but it certainly can block the experience of it. The conflict goes back and forth on the surface of the emotional mountain without getting closer to resolution. Jumping from anger to agreement is a long stretch. When we express our full range of emotions—anger, hurt, fear, responsibility, understanding, forgiveness, want, and love—we can then begin the process of negotiation and agreement. When we take the time to truly self-inquire into all the feelings we are experiencing, we often find that the original event we were reacting to isn't even the real issue that needs addressing. When we dive into the total truth, we often reveal the real truth.

A woman recently told me that she had just informed her husband that she wasn't in love with him any longer. She explained, "I'm just not *in love* with him anymore. I want him to spend more time with the kids and me and less time working." I invited her to reframe the belief that she wasn't in love with him into recognizing that her love for him is blocked right now. (After all, why would she want him to spend more time with her if she didn't love him anymore?) It is much easier to remove blocks that are damming the flow of love than it is to conjure up love where there isn't any.

It would also be much easier for her husband to know what to do about the situation if he knew the total truth of her feelings. Simply hearing that his partner doesn't love him anymore doesn't offer him any concrete information about what he might need to do, nor does it offer him any sense of motivation or hope that the situation can be remedied.

Using this woman's scenario as an example, the total truth might sound like this:

I am really angry that you spend so much time away from home. I feel that you have clearly prioritized work over family, and I feel that I— we—just don't matter that much to you. I get so frustrated having to raise the kids myself and having to explain to them again why their dad isn't home for dinner, or for the weekend, or there for the school play, or why we are going on vacation without you.

I am hurt because I thought that "I do" meant that "you would" be more involved with the kids and me. I ache from loneliness, and it makes me sad to think that I would be so lonely within my marriage.

I am sad that so many other emotions besides love come up when I think of us. I feel like my sadness is drowning out the love.

I am afraid that our marriage is going to fall apart. I am afraid that the damage is going to become so great that we aren't going to be able to rescue it. If I'm really honest, I am afraid that I won't be able to resist when someone else offers me love and attention because I miss being intimate with you. I'm also afraid that you are working so much, and dealing with so much stress, that you are going to damage your health.

Responsibility: I realize that I have not always made our home an emotionally safe place for you to come home to. When I am unhappy or wanting something more from you than you have to give, I can see that I actually make your work a more desirable place to be; even with all the stress there, the stress at home leaves you with no safe place to just let down your guard. I apologize for not expressing my gratitude more for all you do.

I understand that you are working hard to ensure our financial security. Without that, our family would suffer far greater stresses than just missing you. I know you work as hard as you do in part to please me, and it must be really frustrating to you to feel as though I am not appreciative. I know your work is extremely stressful and that adding the stress of my unhappiness only makes everything harder for you. I realize that you are doing the best you can with the current set of circumstances.

What I want is for us to have a loving marriage again. I want us to be a happy family—with both parents present. I want you to schedule family time, and I want you to be committed to our well-being, as though we are just as important as work. I want for the two of us to spend time alone together again, falling back in love, being romantic, laughing together, and enjoying life—like we used to. I miss you. I want us to make our relationship a priority so that it doesn't just slip away unconsciously. I want to feel fully alive and in love with you again. I want to grow old with you, in love.

I deeply appreciate all that you do for our family and how great an effort you put into everything you do. The truth is that I love spending time with you, or this wouldn't even be an issue.

I love you and cherish you as my husband, my friend, and my lover.

Let's agree to pick at least one day a week—or even half a day—
that is sacred family time, with no work. I agree to express my gratitude instead of my displeasure and to make our home a place you
want to come to at the end of your day. Let's take a vacation together, at least once a year, even if only for a weekend.

I'm sure you can see that this is a far cry from "I'm not in love
with you anymore." Once the total truth of this woman's emotions
has been expressed, her husband is far more likely to be able to "hear"
her and to make agreements.

....

EXERCISE ∾ *Share the total truth.* *

*When you encounter a conflict, think through the following sen-
tence stems (or write in a journal), fully expressing the total
truth of your emotions. Sometimes just thinking through your
emotions by yourself will move you to resolution, and you will
have no need to discuss the matter with your spouse. You may be
able to gain understanding, take responsibility, achieve forgiveness, and let go of the anger just by becoming aware of all that
you are feeling. If a discussion and agreement are necessary,
when you are ready, share your feelings with your partner. Ask
him or her to listen to all your feelings before responding, and encourage him or her to use the same format as you listen.*

I felt angry when . . .

I was hurt that . . .

I am afraid that . . .

I am sorry for . . .

I understand that . . .

What I want is . . .

What I appreciate about you is . . .

I love you . . .

*After you have both expressed the full range of your feelings—
and have listened to each other—see if you can come to an
agreement.*

What I'd like to agree to is . . . ∾

....

* Adapted from Jack Canfield's *Self-Esteem in the Classroom Curriculum
Guide.*

Even if you never share your feelings with the other person, the
process of writing them down will help you to release them and return to love. This tool is also great for letting go of emotion that has
built up over past relationships or for clearing up unfinished business
with people who have passed away or with whom you are no longer
in contact.

Love Tip: When you return to your heart—to love—
you can use your head to create a relationship built on
compassion and respect.

When you are angry, if you can't communicate the total truth of
how you are feeling, or at the very minimum you can't align with the
goal of a loving marriage, agree to wait until you have cooled off to
talk about it. Give yourselves time, and then resume your effort to resolve the problem.

Own It with an "I" Statement

Notice that the sentence stems for expressing the total truth of your
feelings are all in "I" statements, rather than "you" statements. People
are far better able to take in what we tell them when we share what is
true for *us,* instead of what we think is true for *them.* This can be
communicated by simply changing the pronoun in our sentences.
Doing so also helps to separate the deed from the doer. With "you"
statements, we are assessing or attacking the other person's character
traits, rather than focusing on his or her words or actions.

For example, if I say to my husband, "You are mean," he will object and defend himself because I am attacking him personally; he

undoubtedlly doesn't see himself that way, and he believes it isn't a true statement (he isn't mean). Even if he were to say something that I perceived as unkind, the core of who he *is* is not *mean*. If instead I say, "I was hurt when you said…," then he is far more likely to explore with me why I was hurt, explain what he meant in order to clear up the misunderstanding, or apologize. People are far better at changing their behavior and words than they are at changing their character.

By the same token, I am far more likely to "hear" him if he says, "I don't see it that way," rather than, "You are wrong." I can't argue with how he sees things, but I can argue with whether or not I am wrong. If I say, "It's cold tonight," my husband may not agree because he may be completely comfortable. If, however, I say, "I'm cold tonight," I am owning what is true for me and it is not disputable. The same holds true with more personal matters. "I'm not happy with certain aspects of our marriage" is a very different statement—and more honest—than, "Our marriage isn't working." Saying, "*I feel like* you are pulling away and distancing from the relationship" is more accurate than telling your spouse, "*You are* pulling away and distancing from the relationship." Your spouse may not see it that way at all, and a statement from you about what is true *for him or her* will likely make your spouse mad, which may in turn *cause* him or her to pull away and become distant.

It takes practice—and self-observation—to begin speaking in "I" statements. In fact, our everyday language has replaced "I" with "you" even when we really are talking about ourselves. People say things like "You get stuck in a rut and you just don't know how to get out," or, "Sometimes you just feel like everything you do is wrong and it is hopeless. You just want to give up." In actuality, they are talking about themselves. They really mean, "*I* get stuck in a rut and *I* just don't know how to get out," or, "Sometimes *I* just feel like everything *I* do is wrong and it is hopeless. *I* just want to give up." Using "you" allows us to distance ourselves from the painful truth, rather than owning it. It is much harder to say, "I feel hopeless," or, "I want to give up," than it is to say, "You feel hopeless," or "You want to give up." Using "I" is a more honest and responsible form of communication. If you find yourself using "you" when what you really mean is "I," simply become aware of what you are doing, and turn it around when you catch yourself doing it. You will find that the more you practice using "I" statements in your everyday communication about yourself, the easier it will be to own your statements and your feelings when you are communicating with your spouse.

Tell the real truth

Dear Eve,

I need your advice. I've been married for eighteen years, and in the last nine years my husband has been very, very verbally abusive to me. I was wondering how much longer I have to take it. His complaint is that we don't spend time together, but we are together just about all of the time that we are not at work — we go bowling, we're together at home, etc. He lectures me all the time. It's always about what he wants and how I "better make changes or else he's going to make changes." He cuts me down by telling me in front of others that I am a lousy mother, lousy house-cleaner, lousy financier, and lousy wife. I feel so hurt that I want to divorce him. Even though I am fifty years old I'm not afraid of starting a new life without him. I would really appreciate your advice on this.

Aloha,

Your story reminds me of a man I saw standing on a corner begging for money. He held a sign saying, "I need some change." To me, nothing seemed closer to the truth, but he was missing his own message by thinking it was money he needed. I wanted to run over with a pen and cross out "some" and write "to" so that the sentence read, "I need to change," in the hopes that he would get the irony of his own sign. You, too, are holding an "I need some change" sign. Your husband is also holding one up with his bla-tant comment, "You need to make some changes or I will." Indeed, one or both of you need to do just that. Unfortu-nately, divorce is often one of the first changes we think of trying before learning new skills and practicing new approaches.

I have a couple of questions for you: What happened nine years ago that instigated this change in the way he treats you? Did something in your attitude or lifestyle change? Is something missing that was there previously? Have you told your husband how you feel? What else does he say to you? Does he ever say nice things? So often we only hear the mean things being said even though there may be just as many positive comments. Be sure to look at the whole picture, not just the negative part. For instance, he must like something about you if he wants to spend more time with you. Do you know what it is? Have you ever asked him why he wants to spend more time with you? It probably isn't "more time" he is looking for so much as a different quality of time. Maybe he misses time alone with you, or time spent having fun instead of working around the house. Another question: What kind of "changes" is he asking you to make? Are they reasonable? Are they changes you can feel good about making?

It is my experience that when there is a problem in a relationship, it can almost always be traced back to not telling your partner the truth about what you are feeling. The "truth" is not simply that you are angry and you want a divorce. If you dig a little deeper into your heart you will find that underneath your anger is hurt and fear. You are hurt that he would say such mean things to you and afraid that you two will never return to loving communication.

Underneath that pain, there is something you want — to feel loved rather than threatened and appreciated rather than ridiculed, for example. Perhaps what you really want is for the relationship to work.

And there is something you understand or need to understand from his perspective. Perhaps you understand that you have pulled away from him emotionally or physically, or that his complaints are his unskilled attempts to make the situation better. From that perspective, you are better able to forgive his unskilled, unkind methods and look at what he is really trying to achieve: a new and improved relationship.

Underneath all of this is something that you love and appreciate about him.

So when you decide to tell him the truth of how you are
feeling and to listen to the truth of how he is feeling,
be sure that you explore everything you are feeling and
not just the negative. Listen not only with your ears but
also with your heart.

How much do you "have to take"? As much as it takes for
you to be inspired to do something different.

With aloha,

 Love Tip: Sometimes we will be happy because of our marriage or relationship; sometimes we need to be happy in spite of it. Find happiness internally, regardless of your external circumstances. Your internal happiness will affect your external circumstances, but your external circumstances should not affect your internal happiness.

Emotional Availability

One of the complaints I often hear is "He (or she) is not emotionally available." What does this really mean, and how do you know if this description fits you?

Emotional *un*availability means that for whatever reason, you are choosing to honor *protection* of your heart instead of love. Protecting your heart is understandable, and sometimes even wise, if you need a period of strength building and rejuvenation between relationships or even while recovering from a life tragedy during a relationship. However, if you're married and are still making yourself unavailable to love and be loved for an extended length of time, take a look at whether this defense mechanism—designed to protect you—is working against you by blocking the flow of love. Think back to the discussion in Chapter 4 on self-esteem. Emotional unavailability is the "glitter" layer (how you show up to other people) that is covering the pain or the fear of pain (the "oil"), which is covering up who you really are (your source of love; the bubbly, pure water).

Being emotionally available means that you are ready, willing, and able to love, regardless of the potential for loss. This may sound simple, but it requires a willingness to take a risk, to open your heart to another, even while knowing full well that in one way or another your heart will experience loss. There is no escaping it; just like life cannot escape death, love cannot escape pain. You will eventually lose or leave your beloved, whether by choice, circumstance, or death. There is no ultimate "happy ending" (from the ego's point of view), but still you know that it is indeed "better to have loved and lost then never to have loved at all." Being emotionally available means that you are going to experience intimacy (in-to-me-see) by sharing yourself with another. You are going to take the risk that the other person may or may not like all that he or she sees, but you are going to let go of your need for approval and control and share yourself anyway. This takes courage.

As I've said elsewhere, courage is not the absence of fear; to do something you are not afraid to do requires no courage at all! Courage is to move forward *in the face of fear*. Since being afraid isn't "cool," and it isn't what we generally want to present to others, a lack of emotional availability shows up instead, as indifference or withholding. When you are only sharing parts of yourself, there is no way the other person can unconditionally love you, because he or she doesn't know you. It is like taking someone on a tour of your home but keeping the door closed and locked on your favorite room. You'll let them into the kitchen, living room, and even the bedroom, but not into your most treasured room; perhaps it is your shrine, perhaps it is your garden. In any case, it is your sacred space. The "heart of your home" is off-limits, leaving others to feel as if they don't really know you completely, or feeling left out of an important part of your life. This leads to mistrust because they don't know for sure what you are withholding, and they begin to feel like you are hiding something. Indeed, you are: your most authentic self.

In order to be fully emotionally available you have to be willing to invite the other in and allow him or her to explore the whole you: the good, the bad, the ugly, the beautiful. You have to be willing to explore all of them, too. This is intimacy, and leads to unconditional love.

Steps for Enhancing Your Emotional Availability

Before you start any of the steps below, utilize the steps you learned in Chapter 6: Remember who you really are, become self-observant, and notice when you are and when you aren't being present or authentic in your emotions. Identify whether your needs for control or approval are interfering with your authenticity. Transcend your ego, reconnect with your heart, and choose thoughts, words, and actions that are in alignment with your goal of having a healthy, loving relationship.

1. **Decide.** The first step is to set the intention of being available to love. If you *don't want to* expand your capacity to love and be loved, the steps won't work. Expansion of the heart begins with the decision to make it so.

2. **Trust.** Trust *yourself* enough to know that no matter what life dishes out to you, you can handle it! Promise yourself that— no matter what—you will not abandon yourself. This means, regardless of your relationship, you will take active steps toward strengthening yourself: doing the things you love to do, staying connected to family and friends, learning new things, expressing your creativity, honoring your spirit, and taking care of yourself physically. You need to agree (with yourself) that you will seek professional assistance if you are unable to do these things by yourself.

   When you master this step, you have greatly diminished the need to trust others, those over whom you have no control. It is great to feel that we can trust other people, but we shouldn't *need* to trust them to be okay. We need to trust ourselves to handle whatever happens regardless of what other people do. Even partners who are typically trustworthy may go astray at the spur of the moment. And since we can't control anyone else, the need to trust others isn't as important as the need to trust oneself. Perhaps most important of all is trusting the divine plan to provide the perfect learning experiences.

3. **Take reasonable risks.** Use both your head and your heart to
assess when it would be wise to move deeper into love and
truth and when it would be wise to pull back. Typically, we
become emotionally unavailable when we believe that the
risk of sharing is likely to yield painful results. What sometimes starts in childhood, perhaps even wisely, as a defense
mechanism designed to protect us turns into a habitual way
of showing up with others that eventually limits our ability
to connect intimately, heart to heart. Indeed, there are times
when it is wise to hold back emotionally. Revealing deeply
emotional feelings to my husband when he is in the middle
of a stressful project or engrossed with something on television would be unlikely to yield the results I want. If his lack
of ability to engage with me could inflict pain, I'm best off
looking for a more appropriate time to open up. By the same
token, if your spouse is under a lot of stress, fatigue, or other
pressures, it may be wise to hold back and not risk opening
up. However, if you are simply stopping yourself because you
are making up stories in your head about what your spouse's
response will be, you are keeping yourself emotionally
trapped and you aren't giving your spouse a fair chance at
engaging with you. Being able to express yourself and share
the truth of your feelings and experiences with your spouse
could set you free. Be self-observant and notice when you are
withholding. By becoming aware of the habit to withhold,
you can then decide whether to make a new choice.

   On an episode of *Friends,* Rachel (Jennifer Aniston)
was dating a guy played by Bruce Willis. Rachel was upset
because he was very reserved and wouldn't open up to her
emotionally. She finally confronted him and begged him to
trust her and share information about himself. Suddenly the
floodgates of a lifetime of trapped emotions came pouring
out. He shared story after heartwrenching story about his
life, sobbing the whole time. Rachel, initially touched, was
consoling and compassionate, but finally, after days of his
continous self-disclosure, she couldn't handle it and told

him he had to stop. Although this was a very funny scene on
TV, in reality it is not. It is important to know when to express deep emotions and when not to, so pay attention to
what is going on around you and watch for the appropriate
times and places for intimate self-expression.

If you feel you are withdrawn because you are holding
back a deluge of pain from previous experiences, you may
want to seek professional assistance in dealing with your
past. The value of processing your feelings is that doing so
allows you to clear the pain out of your system where it is
affecting you—and your relationships—in spite of all of
your best efforts to hide it. If, however, withholding is just a
habit developed over the years out of fear of other people's
reactions to your feelings, begin "coming out" emotionally
by sharing yourself a little at a time with your spouse. Start
by telling him or her how you are feeling, what you are
thinking, what you are afraid of, what you want. Test the
waters, so to speak. Surviving reasonable risks is what grows
our confidence and capability. If you aren't sure whether you
should move forward, pay attention to how you feel. Notice
what you are concerned about and evaluate the risks. Look at
the situation like a "strategic planner" and see if there are
steps you can take to lessen the risks or to think through
them better. We often hold back because we want to avoid
conflict or judgment. *Remember that conflict is often a part of
coming to agreement. If you avoid the conflict, you may also be
avoiding the agreement.*

4. **Learn from your mistakes.** The moral of the story is *never*
"Don't love or trust or open your heart again." If that is what
you "learned," then you missed the real lesson and may have
to endure the experience again and again until you get the
lesson right. A decision to give up, to never love or trust
again, or to close your heart is a decision of the ego, based in
fear. Ego shuts down love and trust. Spirit teaches you how
to love more—more wisely, more responsibly, more healthfully. The lesson may be "pay more attention," or "tell the

truth sooner," or "examine your expectations of others to see if they are unrealistic," or "don't take happily-ever-after for granted," or "honor yourself enough not to allow mistreatment," or "choose more wisely whom to trust," or even "be more trustworthy yourself." *You will know if it is the "real lesson" if it points you* toward *love and trust, not away from it.*

Love Tip: Don't give up on yourself! There is very little that a heavy dose of self-love can't fix! When you know that you are "in it" for life, and that you will not abandon yourself no matter what, there is far less to fear.

Telling Your Partner the Painful Truth

Sometimes our withdrawal of emotions is an attempt to avoid unpleasant moments or to avoid having to face the truth. Maybe you need to talk about issues related to money or the need for budgeting; about your spouse's personal hygiene or (lack of) self-care; or about something wrong or hurtful your spouse has done to someone else. Maybe you need to admit to something you've done that your spouse won't like, such as spending a large amount of money without having discussed it with your spouse; having feelings for (or encounters with) another man or woman; losing a job (or quitting one) in a moment of rage. Maybe you need to share your concern over the way your partner is parenting or interacting with the children, or discuss questions you have regarding your sexuality or sexual preferences. When what you need to communicate is a truth that you know won't feel good, and you are closed down because you don't want to hurt your spouse or cause an emotional reaction, there are things you can do to help your message be heard—if it needs to be.

First, silently pass the information through the "purpose test" before you say it out loud. Ask yourself the following important questions:

Is it honest? Is it true? Let's clarify what we mean by "honest." Sometimes we use honesty as a weapon of destruction rather than a tool for building. We need to be conscious of how we are using the truth, and we need to ask ourselves whether it is "the truth" we are sharing or simply *our perception* of the truth. You can always examine this issue by asking yourself, "Is this true?" Think through whether "the truth" is simply true for you, or if *anyone* examining it would agree to its truth. If it is only "your truth" and not "*the* truth," then be sure you own it as such, and communicate it as your opinion or your experience of the situation. Using "I" statements for expressing your feelings about the situation really helps, but the "I" statement still needs to be based in your truth, instead of in your perception of the other person's truth. The statement "I think you drink too much" may be a true assessment to you, but not to your spouse. Someone who comes from a family or community of heavy drinkers may feel that his or her drinking is moderate compared to those he or she was raised around. If you examine what the really true aspect of this issue is, perhaps you'll discover that you are concerned about your spouse's health, or about decisions being made, or about your welfare due to his or her behavior while under the influence. A more truthful statement would be, "I'm fearful about the effects of alcohol on your health and the impact of your decisions on our lives. I don't like what happens to us when you are drinking." The truth here is your fear and your experience. Ideally, you would be able to move through the total truth of your entire range of emotions, as we discussed earlier in the chapter, and come to an agreement that would help alleviate your fear.

Discussing your partner's habits as they relate to his or her health and to your level of attraction to your partner may be a very sensitive topic. Even if it is honest, it is likely going to be a painful conversation. Whenever possible, share your concern for your partner's well-being, health, and happiness, as well as your concerns about how the issue impacts you. Make sure the love shines through more than the judgment. An expression of concern, based in love, will be easier to hear than an expression that seems selfish in nature. You then need to remember that whether or not your partner chooses to do anything with the information is entirely up to him or her. Also, how you choose to respond to his or her decision is entirely up to you.

Does it matter? What is your desired outcome for sharing the information? Is there a valid purpose for sharing the information beyond simply feeling the need to be honest? While issues of substance abuse obviously matter and thus merit discussion and resolution, other bits of truth may not ultimately matter. For instance, you may notice someone of the opposite sex whom you think is really sexy, but sharing that tidbit of truth with your partner probably serves no purpose as long as your appreciation of the other person remains simply visual and isn't something you act on. This, of course, depends on the levels of security and trust within your relationship. Some couples have no discomfort whatsoever in sharing with each other their positive opinions about attractive members of the opposite sex; ideally, we would all be able to appreciate the beauty of everyone else without feeling jealousy and fear. However, to many people, their partner's noticing a member of the opposite sex feels threatening and disrespectful; being sensitive to how your partner feels will help you make this determination. Bottom line: If it doesn't really matter whether you tell your partner, there may be no valuable purpose in doing so.

Is it your ego speaking or your love? Sometimes we tell someone something simply to exercise our need for control, rather than sharing information that is truly purposeful. We think we know what is best for them, how they should handle a situation, how they should use their free time, how they should manage their friendships; we want them to do it *our* way, on our timeline, regardless of whether it matters or not. I used to date a guy who would tell me how to do things, like how to wash the dishes or where to set things on the table. Even though he presented his suggestions as, "You are doing this wrong; here is the right way," in truth there wasn't a right way or a wrong way; there was my way and his way. Often we get caught up in trying to get our partners (or our children) to do things the way we think they should be done, but if we step back for a moment and take another look at the situation, we can see that as long as it *is* done, *how* it is done usually only matters to our egos. Self-observe to be sure your ego is not the one doing the talking, but rather your authentic self. Remember the EROS equation. Chose your response in alignment with the outcome you want. Keep your goal in mind as you form your words.

Is there anything your partner can do about the information, or will it just hurt them? Telling your spouse that you don't like what they are wearing after you have already left the house for your destination is not purposeful because there is nothing he or she can do about it. Before you say something that may be hurtful, determine whether the timing is right, so that the other person can actually benefit from the information.

Is it something your partner already knows? Telling your partner that he or she needs to get into shape is probably something your partner already knows. Will it motivate them to be told by you, or will it simply add to the hurt? Telling your partner that they made a mistake is unnecessary when they have already figured that out, are suffering the natural consequences, and are beating themselves up for it. It is, however, another issue to let them know how their choices are affecting you.

Love Tip: Communication can heal a lot of wounds— especially the ones that only exist in a person's imagination. When in doubt, ask. If you think what you know will help someone else, tell them.

When we share a painful truth with someone, it is important to support them to the other side of their pain. While there are times when they will want to be alone to process the information, letting them know you are there if they need support is helpful. It is often our natural inclination to "drop the truth bomb" and then run, so we don't get caught in the fallout or have to witness the pain our words may cause. By doing so we avoid the consequences of our words and actions. If your partner gets emotional and you aren't sure how to handle it, refer to the section below titled "Guidelines for Receiving Your Spouse's Emotions." Always remain self-observant. Breathe and let go of your need for approval and control. Simply stay in the present moment.

If the truth that you have shared is an admission of your own wrongdoing, try not to get defensive (which means you're coming from ego). If you wronged your partner in some way, you will have to expect that he or she will be angry, hurt, and fearful. You can use your knowledge of the emotions hiding under anger to anticipate and address your partner's feelings. Acknowledge the pain you've caused, and aim to alleviate any fears that your words or actions may have raised. Without being defensive, give your partner any information you think he or she will need to better understand the situation and what to expect. Have compassion for what your partner is feeling on account of what you have shared.

Be especially careful not to make your partner the "bad guy" if you are the one who hurt him or her. It seems to be human nature to justify our poor decisions or our behavior that harmed someone else by making them at fault. To the best of your ability, own your behavior, take responsibility for what you did, reset your intentions, and work with your spouse to come to agreement again. Then, aligning with your most authentic self, honor your agreements.

Love Tip: If you don't always receive a verbal apology after your spouse has been unkind or particularly reactive, notice instead when your spouse says "I'm sorry" in other ways—by making an unexpected trip to the market, doing a chore without being asked, giving a hug after a disagreement. Learn to listen to more than words.

➤ DINK AND JERRY, MARRIED THIRTY-ONE YEARS

For me, it's almost easier to say *what doesn't work* in a successful relationship than what specifically does work: not talking about problems, hurts, or differences in direction. The only times when things have been really bad for us were when we lived very separate lives and let issues build up. Sometimes it took a counselor to get us talking again. But once we did, we found that there was always a well of love and caring for each other that was deeper than we had even guessed. *We've found that any problem can be resolved if we communicate what's going on for us.*

What works: always laughing together, having meals together as often as possible, appreciating the small things, hugging hello and goodbye when either leaves or enters the house. Nothing grand— just living in appreciation of the great person you happen to be married to.

The Emotionally Unavailable Spouse

If you are in a relationship with a spouse whom you deem emotionally unavailable, begin (as always) with the process of self-inquiry and self-observation. Rather than starting with trying to get your spouse to change, start with seeing what you can do differently that might cause your spouse to respond to you differently.

EXERCISE ∾ *Is it true that your spouse is not available emotionally? Has it always been this way or did something in your relationship change? Are there certain times when your spouse is available emotionally—is there an ebb and flow? Can you start to recognize patterns in when you can look for an emotional connection and when you can't?* ∾

We all have different patterns of energy. I can wake up talking about anything; in fact, due to the time differences between Hawaii and the mainland, I often have to wake up in the middle of the night and within minutes be involved in a radio interview via the telephone or Internet. My husband, on the other hand, prefers an hour or so after he wakes up to start talking. Having learned these things about each other, we respect our differing body clocks and wait until he is available to have a conversation.

Consider not only your own emotional availability but also how emotionally inviting you are. We cannot expect someone to open up to us when we are unwilling to share with them. One-way self-disclosure doesn't usually feel safe. Continue sharing your thoughts and feelings with your spouse and inviting him or her to do the same. Be careful that you don't stop inviting intimate communication just because your spouse hasn't been open to it in the past. So often I have heard people say, "I tried getting him (or her) to open up, and it just didn't work. Now I just don't even try anymore." When you're tempted to give up, always evaluate what it is you are giving up on. If you are giving up on love, trust, communication, compassion, kindness, or respect, then you are giving up on yourself—and on loving your marriage.

You also need to take an honest look at whether you make it safe for your partner (and your children) to talk to you. If they get shut down, criticized, embarrassed, or teased for sharing the truth, you can be sure they will be unlikely to do it again.

EXERCISE ∽ *Are you safe to share with? What is it like to open up to you? Do you invite honest communication and then judge and punish your partner for opening up to you? Does your tone of voice communicate judgment even when your words don't?* ∽

Love Tip: When you give others the space to be upset, you will often find yourself feeling more at peace. If you try to force others to be happy, you will make yourself—and them—crazy.

Guidelines for Receiving Your Spouse's Emotions

Being able to receive someone else's feelings is a bit of an art. As a relationship advisor, I hear people's deepest secrets, fears, truths, and troubles all the time. I realize that hearing these things from strangers and friends is not the same as hearing them from someone whom you are married to and whose life choices impact you personally; however, there are some guidelines that will help you be a safe person with whom to open up.

Self-observe and let go of your needs for approval and control so that you are listening from your authentic self, not your ego. In essence this means that you have to get all your judgments and opinions out of the way so that you can listen with your heart instead of your head. Even if your response would be exactly the same, when you say something from your ego it blocks the love and communication. When you say it from heart, from authentic truth, people are far better able to receive it.

Don't try to fix it; just listen. Only offer advice if the other person asks for it. When people complain, share a story, or confide their feelings in you, they usually aren't looking for you to fix the problem. Rather, they just want you to be a witness to what they are going through, empathize with their frustration, and provide a safe place to express their feelings. When you tell them what to do or not to feel the way they do, they usually become frustrated with you as well. Trust their self-healing process. Don't make their emotions wrong; just allow them. When people are told not to feel the way they feel, resistance flares up and their emotions usually dig in deeper. When they are allowed to simply feel what they feel, observe it, and do some self-inquiry, they are usually able to move through their emotions and resolve the issue. Your job is simply to be a mirror so they can reflect on their own feelings, with you. If you want to do something to help, simply listen. Then ask, "How can I support you through this?"

This does not mean you need to agree with their version of things if you think they are off base, making up false stories, or obsessing about something that doesn't seem right to you. If this is the case, before sharing your thoughts you can ask if they want your input or just want to vent, or you can simply ask questions to help them reflect on the situation; for example, "Are you saying that he didn't have a right to be mad at you?" "What are you basing that thought on; what is your evidence?" "What would you do if your ego were not feeling bruised?" Or simply guide them by saying, "Remember what your goal is," so they can make decisions that will lead to where they really want to go. When you feel it is important to point out an opposing perspective to theirs, it is often helpful to validate their feelings first, and then offer an alternative viewpoint. In my advice column I often start my response with, "I empathize with how difficult this time is for you," or something similar, before I launch into giving my advice.

Watch your but! Pay attention to your use of "but" in communication with your spouse. "But" tends to cancel out whatever came before it. When you say, "I love you, but. . . ," know that whatever is said after that little three-letter word will take away the power of the little three-word phrase that came before it. Instead, see if you can word what you want to say in a way that adds to the first phrase instead of emotionally erasing it. For instance, "I love you *and* I need some time alone to get my thoughts together." Watching your buts also helps when offering an alternative viewpoint after your partner has shared an emotional assessment of an event with you that you don't necessarily agree with. When you say something like, "I understand how you are feeling, *but* I think you are wrong," the "but" eliminates much chance that your partner will feel understood. Instead, try saying something validating like, "I understand why you feel that way, *and* yet I wonder if you have considered the possibility that he didn't mean to hurt you."

Love Tip: Sometimes those we are involved with need our help rather than our evaluation. Just offering to help and showing consideration may be all that is needed to turn things around.

Trust in the other person's ability to resolve issues. If necessary, communicate your faith in them with comments like, "I know you will figure out just the right way of handling this," or, "I know it seems overwhelming, but I am certain you will do the right thing." Empathize while still offering confidence. It is our ego at play when we think the other person needs us to solve their problems. We serve others' highest good when we support them in handling what is theirs to handle.

If a response is necessary, use "I" statements. If you do use "you" statements, do so to reflect back what you think you heard, check for understanding, and gain clarity, for example, "You sound really frustrated with your work." This opens the door for the other person to say, "I'm not frustrated; I'm hurt that my boss would treat me that way," or maybe, "Yes, I really am frustrated."

Don't take it personally. Just because the person sharing feelings is your spouse doesn't mean you have to take on what he or she is going through. Practice letting your spouse feel what he or she feels without letting it impact your emotions, too. Your spouse's problem doesn't necessarily have anything to do with you.

Look for the truth. The hardest time to receive your partner's emotions is when it *is* personal and your partner has something to tell you that is about you or that will affect you. Try not to get hooked by your ego. Keep breathing. Self-observe and let go of any ego needs that may surface. Self-inquire and determine if what your partner is saying about you is true. If it is true, take the feedback as valuable information and see what you can do to amend the situation. If it is not true, listen with your heart instead of just your ears. What is the truth under the false accusation? Sometimes the complaint is about one thing when it is voiced as something entirely different. Sometimes the complaint is about a dirty house when the issue is really about respect. Aim to communicate the complete truth of what you are feeling and to listen for the real truth of what your partner is feeling so that you can get to the bottom line of love and come to an agreement. If your spouse is making up stories about you, or is expressing fear over what he or she thinks is going to happen next rather than staying focused on the present, aim to bring the focus back to truth using the truth. You can say, "I understand why you would be afraid of that, but I don't see it that way." It is very helpful if you have agreed to fair-fighting rules before issues arise (see Chapter 3). Remember, your response is what is going to make or break the outcome and lead to (or not lead to) the potential solution. You have the power to escalate the problem or defuse it. Remember to keep your goal of having a loving, healthy relationship, and choose words, thoughts, and actions that will most likely lead you closer to your goal instead of farther from it.

Love Tip: When you are going through pain over someone else's words or actions, try to separate the part of the pain that arises out of your bruised ego's desire for ap-

proval and control from true pain over the situation. Transcend
your ego and you will find peace.

It may be hard for us to imagine ourselves or our loved ones experiencing serious health issues or dying. When we do imagine it, we
often don't think we can handle the loss (or the fear of the loss).
However, statistically speaking, we *will* have to handle serious health
issues or deaths during the course of a marriage—either our own,
our spouse's, our children's, or those of other family members. When
one partner becomes ill or hurt, mentally or physically, or when a
child does, a series of difficult decisions must be made. Coming to
agreement on such issues isn't usually easy. The challenge is amplified
by the potentially serious consequences of a wrong decision, the possible impact on a spouse or caretaker, and the expense involved in
health care. The stress of health issues is even greater when one partner is suddenly responsible for every aspect of the family and home,
especially if they've had no previous experience with making or managing the income, cooking, doing laundry, taking care of the children—or all of the above.

Although the tendency for many of us at times like these is to
withdraw emotionally or toughen up and put on a strong front, it is
important to allow yourself to feel and express your feelings rather
than sweeping them under the carpet. Communication between
partners or family members becomes even more important during
trying times. Utilize the skills offered in this chapter to help you share
your emotions and to receive the emotions of your loved one when
you are going through difficulties. You may find that the two of you
alternate between being strong and falling apart. Use these differences
in timing to support each other. (More on grieving can be found in
Chapter 10.)

➤ BOBBI AND RON, MARRIED FORTY YEARS

Being asked "How does it work?" many times over the years has
caused me to try to define the consistent factor. Since it's so simple
and so obvious, it might have been easy to overlook. We each must
have known on some deep level—without ever having had to speak

the words to one another or even consciously to oneself—that never would we both "leave" at the same time. By "leave" I mean fall out of love, emotionally or physically check out, give up, not care, go crazy, have huge personal or career growth spurts (or disasters), or get sick. We somehow always managed to take turns. Somehow you need to agree that you will never both leave at the same time, however you define "leaving."

Also—and this is no small thing—upon entering into marriage the word "divorce" wasn't on the option list. It was a nonissue.

Mastery over emotions and over handling changes is essential when working on loving your marriage. Always remember who you really are and what you are trying to create. Let love, rather than ego, do the talking and the listening.

Don't Underestimate the Power of Communication for Growing Love

We've looked closely at communication as the means for resolving problems and expressing challenging emotions. It is equally important to remember the value of communication for building your relationship and deepening your friendship. *Intellectual Foreplay: Questions for Lovers and Lovers-to-Be* is the provocative title of a practical book I wrote to help people enhance their communication skills and make conscious decisions both about the partner they were *choosing* and the kind of partner they were *being*. The book was originally written for people who were dating, in order to provide them with tools they could use to get to know each other. However, asking questions, sharing visions and dreams, and discussing feelings, thoughts, and ideas on an ongoing basis has proven to be an invaluable aspect of marriages that work. It seems like a no-brainer that married people talk to each other! Unfortunately that isn't always the case.

There was a study done several years ago in which researchers asked a thousand single people what their number-one complaint was. The overwhelming majority said loneliness. The researchers then asked a thousand married people what their number-one complaint was. Remarkably, they, too, answered loneliness! A certain proportion of those responses is due to people's poor sense of self-esteem; when people don't feel worthy of love, they don't feel love and connection to others, even when these things are there all along. The other significant proportion of lonely feelings is due to a lack of communication skills. Many spouses stop talking to each other about anything that is fun to talk about and instead spend the majority of their time arguing, engaging in ego and control battles, or just handling the business of living.

When new couples are getting to know each other, they generally participate in long, involved conversations. They look forward to phone calls, e-mails, and time together. They talk. The process of discovery is a fun one. Equally fun is the process of sharing yourself with another and enjoying his or her attention. The challenge is that we get complacent in marriage. We think we know what the other person thinks. We think we know all there is to know about our partner, and, worse yet, we stop asking questions or listening with the pure intent of learning about the other. We begin turning on the television instead of conversing or touching. We get lazy, and we risk losing our spouse because of it.

After many years of being an online relationship advisor and listening to the stories of people who had lost their partner to an Internet romance, I had to ask why someone would leave his or her spouse of many years for a complete stranger—especially one they had never met. I've come to the conclusion that it is simply because the new person talks to them, listens to them, shows interest in them, and instills hope in the future. The new interest appears to care. Since the two haven't yet met in person, you can't even blame the tryst on sexual chemistry or attraction. At this point the attraction is entirely in their heads. Although sexuality may be part of the promise (because it may be lacking in the marriage), the truth is that the two don't even know if they are really attracted to each other. The "hook and sinker" are the shared conversations and the dreams of what may come. It is fun to have someone ask you questions when he or she isn't giving you the third degree or judging you. It is fun to share your stories with someone who wants to hear them. It is stimulating to feel that you have something in common with someone. It is arousing to have someone care and pay attention. These types of conversations are literally the intellectual foreplay to what is perceived as a more fulfilling relationship.

The good news is that you can reinstate or introduce this level of communication into your marriage. Intellectual foreplay begins with being curious and asking questions; it also begins with sharing of yourself. Giving your spouse your undivided attention when he or she is speaking is very powerful. Often, after years of being married, we only half listen to what our spouses are saying. Actively listening and engaging in the conversation, no matter how short or even trivial, will create a stronger sense of connection between you.

Love Tip: Words are very powerful. Sometimes the most romantic thing you can do is to simply tell your spouse that you love him or her.

Guidelines for Engaging in Intellectual Foreplay

There is a difference between intellectual foreplay and regular communication. Intellectual foreplay may at first sound similar to everyday conversation, but the intention is different. Regular communication may be about daily chores or activities. Intellectual foreplay isn't undertaken in an effort to get a task done; it is a task in and of itself. Intellectual foreplay is communcation for the pupose of deepening your relationship, expanding your understanding of each other, stretching your communication beyond that needed for day-to-day living, and deepening your intimacy.

Here are some guidelines to help make communication between you and your spouse more successful:

Engage in the conversation with an open mind. Avoid contradicting your spouse by saying what you believe is true for him or her. When your spouse tells you that his or her favorite ice cream is blueberry, for example, don't repond with, "That isn't true, your favorite is chocolate." Allow your spouse the space to change and grow, and enjoy the process of rediscovery with your spouse. Don't assume; ask. Ask questions not to find fault in your partner, but to *learn about* your partner.

When you ask your partner a question, be sure to also answer it yourself. Sometimes you may find it appropriate to provide your answer only after your partner has had ample time to offer (and elaborate upon) his or her own answer to the question. At other times, you will find that if you pose the question and then answer it yourself first, it takes some of the pressure off your partner and helps to keep the conversation a dialogue rather than an interview. As appropriate, keep it playful—like you did when you were dating.

Stay in the present moment. Sometimes your partner may share an idea or a hope for the future that scares you because it means potential change. Avoid getting freaked out over anything that isn't happening now. My husband once told me he wanted to go work in Antarctica for several months. Rather than worrying about what that might be like or offended that he wanted to be away for so long, I just listened and empathized. It wasn't happening to us at the time and, so far, it still has not happened. However, it is important to know about your partner's hopes and dreams, because they may come up again. Pay attention to topics that may need further discussion, and take advantage of the opportunity to think before responding so you can create a supportive, win/win strategy.

> *Love Tip:* When you are overwhelmed by or afraid of the future, take a deep breath and remember that you only have to handle the present moment. Focus on the here and now, and the "then" and "when" will be handled automatically, or with much greater ease.

Simply listen, discover, and avoid judging. To help your partner feel safe sharing with you, keep in mind the guidelines for receiving your partner's emotions (provided above). And remember to breathe!

Remain self-observant. Notice what you are feeling, both as you answer and as you listen. Pay attention if certain questions or answers cause you fear—and notice what intrigues you, entices you, and fills you with curiosity.

Only ask what you want to know or are willing to answer yourself. At the same time, pay attention to what you avoid discussing. Important issues tend to hide themselves, including self-esteem issues of shame, self-acceptance, and forgiveness.

> *Love Tip:* Often we pretend not to notice that we are avoiding issues or that we are afraid to talk about certain topics. By paying attention to what you are pretending not to notice, you'll discover some very important issues that need to be handled.

Be mindful of what you say and how you say it, and know when to stop talking. Some people are "natural talkers"; others are more frugal with what they say and when they say it. Those who talk a lot often overpower those who talk less. Notice if one or the other of you is "filling the space" with words, and if it is you, stop. Let there be silent spaces so the other person has time to think and then speak. When I went through teacher training, they taught us to pose a question to the class and then to give "wait time." People need time to think of *what* they want to say, and they often need time to think about *whether* they want to say it. Hopefully, they are also putting some thought into *how* to say it, so that it stands the best chance of being heard. Be careful also to avoid rambling unconsciously and without meaning, or bombarding your listener with negativity; either pattern tends to make the other person simply stop listening. We have one friend who refers to his wife's talking as "white noise." Be sure your communication is more than merely "static" to your partner.

> *Love Tip:* We have one mouth and two ears...so maybe we should listen twice as much as we speak. Whenever you find yourself feeling disconnected from another human being, try listening to him or her. Remember to listen not only with your ears but also with your heart, because often the words don't adequately reflect the message.

EXERCISE ∾ *Begin simply noticing the quantity and quality of your communication. Notice the tone of voice you use with your partner. Notice the topics you discuss. Notice the topics you avoid. How many minutes a day do you spend in dialogue, and on what subjects? How much of your conversation is geared toward appreciation? How much is spent on nurturing your relationship and discovering deeper facets of your partner's soul? What is the quality of your communication? Simply begin to notice. A huge part of doing something differently is becoming aware of what you are doing in the first place.* ∾

What to Ask and How to Ask It

Since you are most likely married or in a long-term relationship, I am assuming there are many things you and your partner already know about each other. Still, it is always amazing how much we base on assumption rather than actual conversation. When you engage in intellectual foreplay with your spouse, someone you have probably known for at least several years, it is important to remember that people are constantly changing, growing, and learning. If we expect someone to remain the same as he or she once was, or if we think we really know the person, we may well be in for a surprise.

Simply begin to notice what you are naturally curious about, and make a mental note of these topics. When the time is right, ask your spouse about one of them. If doing so would be helpful to you, start writing down things to talk to your spouse about. Think about your spouse's interests, and pay more attention to what you don't know. Allow your spouse to teach you. Generate questions based on what your partner shares with you. Develop your natural curiosity. Show your interest. Start with your list of values from Chapter 3; see if questions or topics can be generated from it. In the book *Intellectual Foreplay,* suggested topics of conversation include values, health, religion, morals, communication, the past, the future, children, family, household concerns, dreams, vacations, romance, and sex. With just a bit of thought you can generate a lengthy list of wonderful things to discuss with your partner that go far beyond daily tasks, chores, and responsibilities.

You may need to introduce intellectual foreplay into your marriage slowly, if it isn't something you've done much of before. Some people have never been asked about themselves unless they were being questioned in a search for blame. Follow the guidelines presented above, and make sure the attitude you bring to the occasion will promote the aim of growing closer to your spouse. Remember to check your ego at the door if you want to get to the heart of the matter.

As you think about questions you want to explore with your spouse, you'll find that certain ones are more likely to lead to a romantic, stimulating conversation than others. Here are a few types of questions and some things to consider regarding each:

Interrogation questions. *Who were you with? What did you do? Where did you go? Why did you do it?* Some questions seek to discover who, what, when, where, and why. Although such questions certainly have a place in conversation, they seldom lead to a closer, more intimate connection because they can be intimidating. Be watchful of whether your questions are designed to assign blame rather than to achieve a more purposeful outcome.

Quiz questions. *Guess what Aunt Sue said! Do you know what today is? Don't you remember when I told you. . . ?* These sorts of questions generally imply, "I know something you don't know." They are great when you are playing a game, but when trying to have an intimate, heart-to-heart conversation they can be a bit challenging. Quiz questions generally have a "right" or "wrong" answer, according to the person doing the asking, and they have the potential to make the other person feel stupid or inferior because either they *don't* know the answer or they have to try to guess what you are thinking. Neither scenario is likely to make the other person feel confident, loved, trusting, and safe.

"Tell me more" questions. *Tell me more about your camping trip in the Sierras. Tell me more about your promotion. Tell me again about the time when you won that award.* These questions are great for friendship building and relationship enhancement because they invite the other person to be a storyteller and they show your genuine interest and concern about him or her.

Consultation questions. *What do you think about this situation? Can I have your opinion on something?* These questions can be very honoring because they indicate your respect for your partner's opinions and judgments.

Personal questions. *How do you feel about...? What are your favorite...? What are you enjoying in the book you are reading?* These types of questions are wonderful forms of intellectual foreplay, as they show your desire to get to know your partner better. Your personal interest and care can go a long way toward nurturing the relationship.

The whole point of asking and answering questions—especially when you are already married—is to increase the depth of your intimacy and make your discovery of each other an ongoing, lifelong journey. Not only are you learning *about* your partner and sharing yourself *with* your partner, but even more importantly you are expressing your interest *in* your partner. This can go a long way toward enhancing the love between you.

Love Tip: When in doubt about what to say, tell the truth. In fact, make it a point to tell the truth sooner rather than later. People are often more compassionate and more capable of hearing the truth than we give them credit for; the challenge is not as much about their ability to hear the truth as it is about our ability to own the truth.

Long-Distance Marriage

I would be remiss in this era if I didn't speak about the issue of long-distance marriages. Some couples choose to live apart for business reasons or because of different lifestyle choices, but for many others living apart has been forced upon them due to war, incarceration, or family illness. My husband and I have had to endure quite a bit of time apart. Our first five months of dating took place while we were living three thousand miles apart. When my mom got ill many years into our marriage, I went back to my parents' home to care for her. This time we were three thousand miles apart for a year, during which I commuted home to Maui once a month or so.

On my flights back and forth I met several other people who had long-distance marriages. Some managed to see each other every weekend, others every month or two. One woman was a newlywed. She and her husband were both in the military, stationed in two different places. She told me that the longest time they had spent in each other's company during the course of their two-year relationship was the three weeks they were together for their honeymoon. Another man explained that he was on his way to Hawaii to see his wife of over thirty years. He lived in California, where his job was, and she lived on Maui. Every Saturday he flew to Hawaii to see her; every Sunday he flew back to Los Angeles for work. Marriages have taken on many new forms, requiring different skills and a much higher level of communication.

Marriages that are long distance by choice are easier to manage than those that aren't. Especially challenging are long-distance marriages that include a fear of physical loss, added difficulty in communicating with each other, and much greater time spans between visits, such as military families endure. However, all long-distance marriages face a greater fear of loss than traditional marriages. Trust and honesty are essential. Trust must often extend beyond simply trusting your spouse into trusting that you will be able to handle whatever happens. Long-distance relationships—actually *all* relationships—require that you let go of your need for control, and simply trust. Trust your partner. Trust God. Trust yourself. If you're participating in a long-distance relationship and you don't feel strong enough to handle the possible consequences, go back to Chapter 6, "Steps for Turning It All Around," and do the work on self-strengthening.

In addition to being trusting, it is important to be trustworthy. Keeping an already difficult situation as simple as possible will really help. Stick to your normal routine, and go out of our way to reassure your spouse of your love while he or she, or you, is away.

Love Tip: Whether you and your partner are far apart or close together, every ounce of extra attention you devote to showing your love, sending romantic notes, and reassuring your partner of your presence will be worth the effort.

Communication is a critical ingredient in keeping the love alive while living apart. We've all heard the saying "Absence makes the heart grow fonder," but we've also heard "Out of sight, out of mind." So which is it? My personal beliefs are that *communication* makes the heart grow fonder and that being out of touch is slow torture when you are trying to keep a relationship together.

A long distance between partners leaves a tremendous amount of room for insecurity, jealousy, and fear to breed. The only way to combat these very human emotions is to reassure and communicate with each other *a lot*. What may seem like "abnormal" amounts of contact in a face-to-face relationship are actually *required* amounts for a long-distance love. Communicate as much as you can while apart, and share as many details about your life as you can. Whereas in a close-distance relationship you may not need to recite whom you went out with, where you went, and when you got home, in a long-distance one you may. In order for your sweetheart to feel that he or she is a part of your life, that you aren't hiding anything, and that you are aware of how he or she may be feeling, your partner may need the vicarious experience of hearing the details you may not otherwise be compelled to share. The more information you provide about what you are doing and how you are feeling, the more your partner will feel as though the two of you are sharing your lives and the less he or she will fill in the blanks with imagination.

If you are in a situation in which you can't enjoy the immediate gratification of e-mail, instant messages, and cell phones, write good old-fashioned letters. Knowing what to say can be challenging when the communication is only one way due to your partner's inability to communicate regularly (when on deployment, at war, or in jail, for instance) or when, over the course of time, you simply feel as though you have exhausted your list of topics. Remember, though, when someone is away due to extreme situations like these, even the smallest, most everyday pieces of news are treasured. Share from your heart as often as you can. When decisions need to be made while a partner is away, whenever possible include your partner in the decision-making process to keep him or her connected to his or her role in the family and the relationship.

If you have children, be sure to help keep the child's relationship with the absent parent alive. Talk about your spouse to your children every day, share letters, look at pictures, and encourage your children to draw pictures for Mom or Dad. Depending on your children's ages, keep them informed about what is going on, and be sure they truly understand. Watch for signs of stress in your children, and talk to them about how they are feeling.

Long times between visits and limited communication are obviously not the only things that impact the marriages of military personnel and of those who are incarcerated. In addition to the high levels of stress and fear involved, the dynamics at home must change significantly to accommodate the absence of a spouse. While one is away, the other has to become head of the household, handling all the issues that the other spouse previously handled. In the case of traditional male/female roles, when the man returns to a home where he was once in charge and where the woman has by necessity stepped up to the plate, a major clash of control issues can arise while the two renegotiate household and parental roles.

> **Did you know?** According to an article prepared by the Army News Service, divorces among military officers have tripled since the beginning of Operation Iraqi Freedom.

In addition, especially in the case of war or incarceration, the partner who has been away has undoubtedly endured circumstances that affect his or her emotions. He or she may even suffer from post-traumatic stress disorder, which can cause emotional withdrawl, depression, and an ongoing sense of danger or distrust. In the meantime, the stay-at-home partner has had to endure life as a single parent and to mentally prepare for the possibility that this may become a permanent reality. In such cases, a person's natural defense mechanism often leads them to become totally independent and to withdraw emotionally in an attempt to feel the loss less deeply. When the partner returns, it can take a while to allow the emotions to flow back into the void created by the absence and to break down the walls that both partners built to protect their hearts.

Remember, attachment to *what was* interferes with embracing *what is*. When managing the re-entry of a spouse who has been away for an extended period of time, it is helpful to imagine that you are starting a new relationship with each other, rather than trying to re-create the old one exactly as it was. Both partners have had significant life experiences that have brought them new growth and insight. Even though you're married, this is an opportunity to "date" again and to get reacquainted. It is an excellent time for utilizing intellectual foreplay—asking questions and exploring deeper levels of communication and discovery.

At the same time, it is important to remember that someone returning from extreme conditions and high levels of stress and fear may become emotionally unavailable for a period of time during recovery. They may not want to talk about their experiences but may simultaneously be unable to get certain images out of their mind. Revisit the tips on handling an emotionally unavailable partner and the guidelines for receiving your spouse's emotions (discussed earlier in this chapter). Tread slowly, gently, and compassionately as you navigate the new terrain of your and your partner's emotions. Remember, it is more likely that the love is simply blocked rather than gone. Your job is to break through the obstacles to allow the love to flow again.

Did you know? In a recent study of over five hundred California parolees, researchers discovered that the number-one factor affecting whether an inmate returned to prison after his or her release—more significant than drug use, race, or any other demographic category—was whether the inmate was part of a stable family relationship.

If you have children, prepare them for the possible changes they may encounter when a parent returns home. If necessary, seek professional help. Many community services, private therapists, and support groups are available. In addition, the military has implemented several programs specifically designed to assist military families and marriages. Many states' prison systems also have programs available that recognize the value and importance of marriage counseling for inmates.

Long-distance marriages usually involve a high level of written or verbal communication to fill in the gaps for face-to-face time. This depth of intellectual foreplay is intimate and can be addicting (in a good way!). The challenge is that you may experience withdrawal when you get together, unless you keep some semblance of stimulating communication going. When my husband and I were dating long distance, we spent several hours a day on the phone. Once we finally were able to be together, I wanted to continue that level of communication, but unless we set aside specific time for deeper conversations, daily life interfered. There were times when we were navigating the transition from long distance to up close during which I felt as though I should leave home for an hour or two and call him on the phone so that we could reconnect verbally, in the same way we had built our relationship. Engaging in intellectual foreplay on an ongoing basis and utilizing the romantic tips presented in the next chapter can assist you in keeping the love alive, or in rekindling it after an extended period apart.

Love Tip: Be creative in discovering ways to engage in long-distance romance. Send pictures, talk about "someday" dreams, explore your hopes and wishes. Then, when you get together, act them all out!

PART III

PLAYING TOGETHER

The real test of friendship is:

Can you literally do nothing with the other person?

*Can you enjoy together those moments of life
that are utterly simple?*

*They are the moments people look back on at the
end of life and number as their most sacred
experiences.*

EUGENE KENNEDY

CHAPTER 9

Love and Romance

A successful marriage requires falling in love
many times,

always with the same person.

MIGNON McLAUGHLIN

S
o far we have taken a detailed look at the "work" involved in
loving your marriage. Loving your marriage is work in the
sense that it requires you to be diligent about paying attention
to what you are doing, saying, and thinking. It calls for you to keep
your eye on the prize, continuously reset your intentions, and take
action in alignment with what you want to create. What's involved is
less about working on the marriage than it is about working on yourself.

In Part III of the book we turn our attention to the marriage itself. Playing together is the reward. A loving marriage, the prize we
have been working for, consists of stimulating conversations, the exploration of who we are and what we want to become, and companionship through challenges, joys, and successes, both everyday and
momentous. A loving marriage is where we go to rest, to rejoice, to
cry, to consult, to be authentic, to let go, to forgive, to be forgiving, to
hug, to kiss, to make love, to learn, to teach, to give, to receive, to pray,
and to love. We are going to look at things you can do either to
reignite the love, romance, and passion in your relationship or to
keep that fire burning. Ironically, the action step and the prize are
usually one and the same. This is truly the meaning of the adage "It is
in giving that we receive."

234

Attraction, romance, and physical touch are what separate a friend from a romantic partner. Without those elements, a relationship is just a friendship, and a spouse becomes a roommate. And although there are many reasons beyond love and attraction why people get married—pregnancy, a means for citizenship, parental pressure, social pressure, arranged marriages—once two people are married we can probably assume that in most cases they would prefer to grow their love and become true sweethearts, which means evoking romantic love. Few of us would prefer to cohabitate with a spouse whom we do not feel connected to or physically and emotionally intimate with. This chapter takes a look at how to reignite romantic love, which is an inside job. Although it takes two to tango, it only requires one to invite the other to dance.

The Key to Your Heart

All around us and within us is a never-ending source of love that we can access at any time. Because our souls *are* love, we usually don't need an object for our affection in order to feel love. Our natural state *is* love; however, most of us learn to close our hearts, which prevents love from streaming in, or out, freely. The saying "You hold the key to my heart" recognizes that sometimes people are able, through their words, touch, smile, or chemistry, to help us unlock that door, allowing the love of our own soul to flood us and fill our being. That person then becomes the object of our love because we're so grateful that he or she has helped us to experience our soul's capacity.

Relationships have the potential to be a beautiful flow of love between two open hearts. We help our beloved to feel the love within himself or herself, our beloved helps us to feel the love within us, and the two of us share our love with each other. Our love runs over and spills onto everything around us. The experience transforms us. When we are in love, we feel love for everything more easily. The access to our ever-present (but sometimes blocked) well of love is open.

Mistakenly, we often entirely credit the other person (the "event") for the way we feel, when we actually had that capacity for love all along. The problem with giving the credit away occurs if that person leaves or changes his or her behavior; when this happens, we think we no longer have the key to our source of love. We close the door to our heart and feel cut off from love. So often we give our power away, thinking that someone else holds the only set of keys, and feeling empty or powerless without him or her. This mindset makes us emotional yo-yos, dependent on our spouse's behavior for our experience of love. Since you are already familiar with the EROS equation, you know this means we are putting the power on the event instead of on our own response, where it belongs.

> *Love Tip:* Love exists within our hearts all the time. Different experiences and people serve as keys to unlock the door and allow us to feel the love. Don't mistake the key for the room where the love dwells (your heart) or for the source of that love (your soul essence). When you know this, you realize that no one can take away your love.

We can open the door ourselves by taking back our power over our responses, and therefore over our outcomes and solutions. We can access the source of love all the time, within our spouses and elsewhere. We can love God, we can love life, we can love nature, we can love our Selves, and we can love love. By raising our self-esteem, that is, by accessing the well of love within ourselves, we can live in alignment with our souls—*in love all the time.* By doing so we will have much more love to share with others, and, perhaps even more importantly, we will not have to cling to others like energy vampires in search of what they really can't give us. When two people are together who already feel love—for themselves and for life—they have more love to share and don't need the other person in order to feel complete. Being together simply amplifies the joy.

Here is the kicker: It is possible to love someone who doesn't love you in return; indeed, most of us have been in that situation. *The other person's participation is not required for us to feel love.* In fact, the other person doesn't even really need to know you exist for you to feel love for him or her. The love is within us; it is who we are. Other people just help us *access* it. When people say to us loving, kind, comforting, or romantic things, regardless of whether they are even telling the truth—or sometimes if they simply look at us in a certain way—we begin to open the door to our hearts and let our love flow. *The feeling of love is our own; someone else does not give it to us.*

Recognizing that it wasn't the other person who brought you the feelings of love but rather that you simply accessed your own source of love can help you to see that love doesn't go away when that person is gone or behaves differently. You just closed the door to love. The other person never held the key in the first place; he or she just activated your *choice to love*. This is important to recognize because it allows us to make life a treasure hunt for the multitude of keys that can open our hearts, helping us to be more loving and to feel more love throughout our lives, regardless of what the people around us (including our spouses) choose to do. *Love is generated from within and shared; it is not harvested from others.*

On the flip side, your spouse can shower you with appreciation, romance, kindness, and love, but if you have put up a wall of ego—full of distrust, fear, or judgment—the love simply won't be felt. *Love is also blocked from within.*

How you and your spouse each give and receive love can also impact whether you feel the love being offered. Perhaps the two of you show and respond to love differently. Some people respond best to visual stimulation; they feel most loved when someone takes the time to present concrete, visible signs of affection. Other people are kinesthetic and need to be touched to feel loved. Others are auditory and need to hear how their partner feels about them. Which are you? Which is your spouse?

One woman, being visual and auditory, spent hours cleaning house, set a beautiful table, and prepared a special meal to let her husband know how much she loved him. She anxiously waited for him to come home so he could *see* what she had done and so she could *hear* his appreciation and love. When he arrived, however, her husband (being kinesthetic) said nothing about the house or table but immediately wanted to sweep her off her feet, take her upstairs, and make love with her to show her how much he cared. She was upset that he hadn't noticed anything she had done and consequently was less than receptive to his attempts at lovemaking. He thought he was trying to *give* something to her, while she thought he was trying to *get* something from her. She felt unappreciated, and he was totally baffled. Instead of either partner feeling honored, both felt rejected. Although you and your spouse don't have to have the same means of experiencing love, knowing each partner's style of giving and receiving love can help tremendously so you can speak and hear your partner's language when communicating love and appreciation.

As is the case with everything else we have talked about so far, igniting the romance and evoking the love will require that you become aware of what is happening in your marriage, aware of how you respond to your spouse, and aware of how your spouse responds to you. You'll need to let go of your ego needs for approval and control and align your actions, words, and thoughts with what you want to create.

> *Love Tip:* There is nothing more romantic than someone who sees the real you and loves you anyway, regardless of whether you stutter and stumble or are suave and sophisticated. The key to love like this is showing the other person the real you. Be authentic. (Here is a hint: You'll have to let down your ego shield to do it.)

What Are You Thinking?

Let's talk about thoughts for a minute. In the realm of intimacy, thoughts are critical in terms of what you are thinking *about,* what you are thinking *about your partner,* what you are thinking *about yourself,* and what you are thinking *your partner is thinking about you.* It sounds confusing because it can be. Our thoughts have the power to turn a beautiful moment into a horrendous one, or vice versa.

Imagine that your spouse is preparing for a romantic evening and lights a candle. The candle causes you to think about whether you have paid the electrical bill yet. Suddenly you are totally preoccupied with paying bills, and the romantic mood quickly disappears. What you were thinking *about* totally changed the mood, and undoubtedly the outcome, of the evening.

Imagine that your spouse is preparing for a romantic evening and you start thinking, "Again? He only acts this way when he wants sex. I'm sick and tired of having to respond every time he...." The romantic opportunity is completely contaminated with what you are thinking *about your partner.*

Imagine that your spouse is preparing for a romantic evening and places his (or her) hand around your waist. You start wondering if he or she can feel how much weight you've gained. You start to be uncomfortable with your partner's touches and attention because now you are thinking about having to get naked in front of him or her. Then you start thinking about how out of shape you have become and how uncomfortable you are with your body. The romantic mood is severely damaged because of what you are thinking *about yourself.*

Imagine that your spouse is preparing for a romantic evening and glances over at you and smiles sweetly. Then you notice that his eyes pass over the pile of clothes in the corner of the room, which haven't yet made it to the wash. You start thinking that he is wondering what you did all day. You guess, "Does he think I was watching TV? He must think I'm lazy. Doesn't he know how much I do? How dare he!" Suddenly you are mad and fighting with your spouse instead of sharing a romantic evening—all because of a story you made up in your head about *what you thought your spouse was thinking about you.* All he was *really* thinking was how much he was looking forward to what he thought was about to come next.

Notice that in every one of these scenarios the event was the same: Your spouse was preparing for a romantic evening. In terms of the EROS equation, your response to the event—in this case in the form of thoughts—is what created the different outcomes, none of which were in alignment with the goal of having a healthy, loving relationship.

The good news is that you can change what you think, but to do so you have to become aware of your thoughts and of what they are doing to you (instead of blaming your spouse). This requires practicing self-observation, noticing your self-talk, and refocusing your attention on your goal for that moment (or evening). We discussed self-talk and its impact on self-esteem in Chapter 4, but, as you can see, self-talk can also critically impact your relationship.

Romance happens hugely inside our own heads—somewhat regardless of what our partner does. We can make or break a romantic moment all in the flash of a thought. Consciously choose thoughts that empower your relationship and serve the romantic quality. When in the middle of a potentially romantic moment you catch yourself thinking negative things about yourself, your spouse, or sexuality, call upon a different aspect of yourself to come forth. We all have "subpersonalities" that emerge at different times, and just as it is inappropriate to have your inner child show up at work, it is equally inappropriate for your inner child to show up during physical intimacy with your spouse (baby talk probably isn't what turns your partner on). Equally inappropriate is to have your angry self show up at a love fest. We all have a subpersonality that loves sex, intimacy, and romance, and I would venture to guess that many of us also have a subpersonality that hates it, fears it, or judges it, based on preconceived beliefs or past experiences. There is a time and place for everything. A romantic interlude with your spouse is the time to invite your inner lover to emerge instead of your inner critic or inner judge or inner nun/monk. (Of course, if you are being intuitively warned about an unsafe situation or resist doing something that will cause you pain or harm or that goes against your values, pay attention. Sexuality is supposed to be a fun aspect of your marriage, not a frightening one.)

> *Love Tip:* Self-respect is critical to relationship respect. When you do something that doesn't feel right to you, even if you do it at someone else's urging, in the other person's heart it won't feel right either.

The Romantic Touch

One of the definitions of "romance" that is listed in my dictionary is "a tendency of mind toward the wonderful and mysterious; something belonging to fiction rather than to everyday life." Romance is the stuff that makes your relationship seem special rather than mundane. It is the juice that makes you feel that you are the prince and princess in a fairy tale, but the "spell" is easily broken if you don't both pay attention to honoring the "royalty" in the other. No one wants to wake up one day and realize that the loving relationship they yearned for is finally here and all it really boils down to is slave labor. It is each partner's responsibility to keep the essence alive, to let the other know that you honor him or her as a sweetheart—not just as parent to your children or housekeeper or handyman, but as your beloved, someone wonderful and mysterious. This really isn't hard to do and it is actually the fun part of being in a relationship. It just requires some conscious thought—and thoughtfulness. In fact, often the simplest and littlest gestures mean the most.

About a month before my husband and I got married, he was busy with something in the backyard that he wouldn't let me see. A short while later he came in with a scruffy but cute teddy bear that some dog had unceremoniously deposited in the yard. When he found the bear it was filthy and had been torn apart. He rescued it, scrubbed it clean, and sewed it back together, and then gave it to me as a gift. My husband is a very masculine kind of guy: boat captain, scuba diver. Thus, his doing something so tender—something I would have thought rather out of character—was one of the more romantic moments in the early years of our relationship.

➤ **SUE AND MACE, MARRIED OVER FORTY YEARS**

Dancing—whether it is slow dancing cheek to cheek or enjoying some fast-dancing moves—is still one way to fall in love again and again even after forty-plus years! There's something about music and movement that revives the soul and rekindles love. A dance in the kitchen while the pasta bubbles is the best prelude to dinner.

Keeping the romance going over the course of time may come naturally to some, but for others it requires conscious effort. It is easy to slip into a day-to-day routine that doesn't include spending a moment to watch the sun set or asking your partner to climb up on the roof to watch a meteor shower with you at two in the morning or kissing under the full moon. To me, honoring all that is wonderful and mysterious in life *is* romantic. Spending moments together in nature, sharing the silence of a canyon, cuddling next to a campfire in the backyard, watching waves break by moonlight, seeing fireflies dance in the trees, witnessing your child learn a new skill, making time to honor the magical things and to share them with your sweet-heart—these are moments to live for! To you, romance may mean taking a moment to do that special thing for your partner that he or she likes so much. Perhaps you could take it or leave it, but you do it anyway because you know it matters to your sweetheart. People ex-perience romance in different ways, so it is important to learn what is romantic to your spouse and to let him or her know what you con-sider romantic.

Love Tip: Turn off the radio, TV, and computer, and just sit outside together listening to nature, watching a crackling fire, or taking in the sunset. When you become com-fortable in silence together, you will discover a sacred place.

Don't Be a Victim

If your partner doesn't create romantic moments for you, be the one to initiate. Ask for what you want or create it yourself. Your ego will tell you, "He (or she) should be the one to buy me flowers and bring home a bottle of champagne," but your ego will keep you feeling lonely, unloved, and disconnected. If need be, buy the flowers and bring home the champagne yourself, and invite your spouse to a ro-mantic moment of your making. Or ask him or her to pick up some flowers and champagne on the way home from work. Remember the goal; how you get there is not as important.

The same holds true for remembering anniversaries and special occasions. When I hear people get upset with their spouse about fail-ing to remember a birthday or anniversary and feeling that they have been wronged or that their partner doesn't care about them, I always want to remind them to rethink the conclusion they have come to and to take responsibility for their part in the situation. First of all, forgetting an anniversary doesn't equal a lack of love—only a lack of momentary consciousness, perhaps. Second, you can avoid this problem by reminding your spouse. When your birthday or anniversary is coming, start the countdown a month in advance. Say things like, "One month till our anniversary!" Your enthusiasm about the upcoming event will be contagious. At the very least it will be hard to ignore.

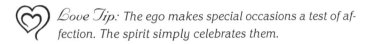 *Love Tip:* The ego makes special occasions a test of affection. The spirit simply celebrates them.

Falling in Love Again . . . and Again

When thinking about reigniting or evoking the elation in your *relation*ship, recreation cannot be underestimated. In essence, recreation means to re-create, and it has the power to do exactly that—to re-create a relationship. The *American Heritage Dictionary* definition of "recreation" is "refreshment of one's mind or body after work, through activity that amuses or stimulates; play." Household duties and job responsibilities have a way of taking over our lives, leaving little room for anything else. If you want to re-create your love or stimulate your relationship, give your relationship time away from the stresses of everyday life, cell phones, pagers, bills, and duties—and occasionally away from the children. Don't wait for a vacation once a year. Take mini-vacations regularly, whether they last two hours or two days. Although recreation can serve the whole family, it is important that you find ways and take time to feed your relationship *aside* from being parents. Otherwise, when the children grow up and move out, you are going to be looking across the table at a total stranger. Focus on keeping your primary relationship primary. Your kids will definitely benefit from your solidarity and demonstration of love and partnership.

Figuring out how to re-create your marriage may require that you become creative problem-solvers. Consider the interactions and activities that caused you to become interested in each other in the first place. Did you fall in love while you were sharing your hearts in communication? Did you fall in love doing things you both enjoy, such as camping, bike riding, traveling, or reading? Pay special attention to incorporating the things that initially drew you together.

Love Tip: A little forethought goes a long way. Think ahead. Don't wait until the special day to buy the flowers, make the reservation, or buy the card or gift. Do it now! The thoughtfulness and consideration will be noticed even more than the present.

➤ PHYLLIS AND ROGER, MARRIED FIFTY-THREE YEARS

The most important things, besides love and devotion, are being attentive, helpful, and respectful, and having fun with one another. We only come this way once, and it behooves us to make it a joyful journey.

While certainly love is evoked and grows naturally as we let down our ego walls of defense, certain behaviors can stimulate that process. Practice the behaviors of people falling in love. Here are some suggestions:

....

EXERCISE ⤳ *Look into each other's eyes. Eyes are the windows to the soul, as they say. It is almost impossible not to feel love from and for another person when looking deeply into his or her eyes. Take a moment every day to consciously share a glance across the table, to simply gaze into each other's eyes, or to establish eye contact when proposing a toast or saying "I love you." Or make a practice of spending one minute a day silently looking into each other's eyes.* ⤳

Communicate your love. New lovers go out of their way to contact each other. They regularly send each other messages via e-mail or instant messaging. They call each other several times throughout the day just to check in and say hi. They send letters and cards. They let the other person know that they are thinking about them. They take advantage of the opportunity to say "I love you," directly and indirectly, throughout the day. Continue this practice (or reinstate it) in your married life. ⤳

Talk to each other. *Whether you use as your starting point questions chosen from Intellectual Foreplay, a communication game (there are a lot of games available for spouses and families to inspire communication), or just a natural conversation, spend an hour walking and talking. Or just turn off the TV and spend an hour together exploring hopes, dreams, plans for the house—whatever. Develop your natural curiosity. Play "show and tell" like you did in school. Share your day with each other. Make time to talk—and listen.* ∾

Celebrate the silence. *An equally important form of communication is the comfort that derives from enjoying total silence together. Enjoy the sounds of nature. Enjoy just being together with nothing needing to be said.* ∾

Do silly little things. *Romance can have a silly edge to it. Life can get so serious, and the reminder to lighten up and be playful is invaluable. As you explore falling in love with your spouse again and again, enjoy being playful together.* ∾

> **Did you know?** By the time a child reaches nursery school, he or she will laugh about three hundred times a day. Adults laugh an average of seventeen times a day.

Laugh! *Maintaining a sense of humor is critical to keeping the joy alive in a marriage. Seek out opportunities to laugh together. One couple shared with me that whenever they get into an argument, one of them will put their underwear on their head like a hat to remind both partners not to take any part of the conflict too seriously.* ∾

Spend time together. *Make a point of going on "dates." Even if you can't get away from the kids, do romantic things with them. Go on picnics, go to the movies, walk on the beach, watch the sunset.* ∾

Touch. *Couples who are falling in love touch each other. They hold hands. They put their arms around each other. They hug and they kiss. They connect physically regardless of whether it is sexual. (More about this in the next chapter.) Amazingly, couples who have been together for a long time can manage to go through an entire day without touching. Make a conscious point to touch your spouse in a loving way daily.* ∾

Put it in writing. *Poetry and love letters have been sweet expressions of love throughout the ages. They are time-proven symbols of romance.* ∾

Enjoy simple expressions of care. *New couples don't need big, monumental expressions of love to feel the connection. They revel in a glance. They rejoice from a phone call. Strive to allow the simple things to fuel your relationship.* ∾

Communicate your appreciation. *Catching your spouse (or your kids) doing something right and letting them know you appreciate it goes a lot farther than always (and only) focusing on what they do wrong and reminding them of it. Being appreciated is motivating. The people who love us want to live up to our expectations and to the level of our appreciation. The great news is that being appreciative is good for you, too! You will notice the difference in the way you feel as you adopt an attitude of gratitude for your spouse and family. As cliché as it sounds, this means not taking for granted all that your spouse does. Rather, thank your spouse for his or her efforts, no matter how small.* ∾

Focus your attention on what you love about the other person. *New couples tend to see only what they love in the other, often to the exclusion of seeing anything else. This is the joy of the truth that "love is blind." When a relationship is faltering, each partner is typically focusing on what the other person is doing wrong, and thus that is all they see. When you want to fall in love again and again with your spouse, switch what you are focusing on to what you love about him or her. Simply set your intention to see your partner's goodness. As Benjamin Franklin said, "Keep your eyes wide open before marriage, half shut afterwards."* ∾

Keep learning. *My parents were together for fifty-five years. As I watched them interact, I realized that one of the things that kept them interesting to each other was their continuous growth.*

They were constantly learning, reading, taking classes, and exploring new concepts. They had spent over five decades together, and yet they continued to discuss new topics, teach each other what they learned, and have fascinating conversations with each other. As my mom said, "Spirituality, sexuality, education, communication, and humor. What more do you need?" ↷

More Romantic Notions

What follows are romantic ideas from several couples:

After a long romantic weekend, my sweetheart had to go on a trip. After she left, I found a wonderful love note in my wallet. Throughout the next week I found lovely little notes tucked into dresser drawers, kitchen spaces, and clothing. Then I received several beautiful, lo-o-o-ong letters illustrated with hand-drawn pictures and stuffed with fragrant plant clippings. That kind of care lets you know you are loved.

My husband and I play Tickle. We just get really goofy and roll around the living room floor like two little kids, tickling each other and giggling. A bout of Tickle can come on when we least expect it, and as silly as it is, it is one of our more treasured moments.

One of my favorite romantic moments was when my sweetheart climbed into the shower with me and stood there naked playing the flute while I bathed.

When the kids were little, since we didn't want them to have to go to a babysitter all day, I worked nights and Dan worked days. It was the right thing for our family, but it seemed like we were two ships passing several nights a week. One year on Valentine's Day, I came home at about 11:00 P.M. The front door was cracked open a little, which was odd. I couldn't find Dan. I went to our bedroom and saw that the bathroom door was closed. I said, "Hi, I'm home."

Dan opened the door, wearing nothing more than a strategically placed construction-paper heart, and said, "I've got a heart-on for you!" I was floored. I cracked up and felt touched, all at the same time. He had also written some erotic poetry for me. The surprise and creativity of his gesture meant a lot to me.

In our hectic lives one of the things my husband does that makes me feel special and loved is simply to place his hand on my shoulder or neck while I am working as he passes by, or to give me a fifteen-second back rub while I'm at the computer. It takes no time; it takes no words. It's just a simple gesture communicating his love and appreciation.

One Valentine's Day I came home from work and my wife had made me a "heart beet casserole." She had carved all the sliced beets into heart shapes.

One way my husband could be assured of putting a smile on my face was to bring me gladiolas every week. As soon as he saw me empty the vase, he came home with more. Since I never expected him to do it, it always made me smile and appreciate him. He loved that—and so did I.

Sometimes when I'm working on something, my husband will come over, take my hand, and say, "Come here, you have to see this." Then he'll lead me outside and point at a rainbow or a cloud, at a flower that has just bloomed or the sunset. I am so honored that he takes the time to simply share beautiful moments with me.

I went outside one morning planning to wash my car and discovered that my wife had done it for me, before I got up, just as a gift to me.

One year we were really broke, but it was our anniversary and we wanted to celebrate. I had a two-for-one coupon from an upscale take-out restaurant. We packed a basket with utensils, a bottle of wine, glasses, and cloth napkins, picked up the food, and drove to the beach. We spread out the blanket and had our feast while the sun set. Afterward we walked on the beach and sat quietly together. It was great to celebrate our anniversary in such a simple but satisfying and romantic way—and it only cost ten dollars!

I will never forget when Tim was trying to win my love from another fellow who had sent me a huge bouquet of flowers (he had tons of money to waste on me). Tim, being a humble soul, knew he could not outdo this floral show of wealth. Instead, he went into the woods, handpicked a bouquet of fresh wildflowers, tied a pretty ribbon around them, and hand delivered them to my front door with a kiss. He won my heart. I knew, at age sixteen, that this was the guy I was going to marry, and we are now celebrating our twentieth wedding anniversary. Through the years Tim has continued with sweet surprises to keep the love alive. I am truly lucky to be blessed with a gentle, loving, and supportive man!

On our honeymoon in Costa Rica we got stuck indoors due to a day-long rainstorm. We found a corny novel in the hotel room, and I began to read it out loud to my new husband. It ended up being one of the trip's more memorable days and began a long tradition of reading aloud to each other. It makes reading a shared and romantic activity instead of an isolated, individual one.

Eddie is not the most conventional romantic. He won't buy flowers because they die; he figures what's the point? But he surprises me on occasion. Once, I went to Australia for three weeks, and when I got back he had planted a flower bed of impatiens that spelled out "I love U," with a heart!

We spoon in bed every night and every morning. It makes us feel close. We kiss and hug frequently. I am pretty average looking, but my husband makes me feel like the most desirable women on earth, and when you feel that good about yourself it makes you feel sexy.

EXERCISE ◌ *What does romance mean to you? What have the most romantic moments been in your marriage? What romantic thing have you done for your spouse recently? What can you do today?* ◌

Romance is usually as simple as a surprise in the form of a thoughtful gesture. It doesn't have to be expensive; a flower picked in the yard is just as sweet, if not sweeter, than, a dozen long-stem roses. It doesn't have to be monumental; sharing the sunset only takes a few minutes. What makes something romantic seems to be the element of the unexpected. In your efforts to be romantic, pay attention to your partner's temperament and honor your own. Some people are not impressed with sugary words and love notes, but would be over-whelmed by coffee taken to them at work or a thoughtfully placed phone call to see how their day is going. The most romantic thing you can do is to authentically express your love.

Love Tip: Recreation has the capacity to re-create. To re-create your sense of self, strength, and well-being, or to rejuvenate your relationship, take some time for recreation.

CHAPTER 10

The physical touch

Marriage has many pains, but celibacy has no pleasures.

SAMUEL JOHNSON

S ex is always a touchy subject, if you'll pardon the pun. People have so many different sexual attitudes, interests, and beliefs. Identity, ego, judgment, expectations, religion, and morality are all wrapped up in sexuality. It can be the beauty or the beast in a relationship, the glue or the wedge. It is my hope that the material in this chapter, and the conversations it generates, will help to heal, inspire, and deepen the physical intimacy between you and your spouse. The chapter is not a sex manual offering tips for how to have sex (well, maybe a few). It does, however, provide tips for how to change your attitude about sex. It also discusses what typically goes astray in couples' sex lives and offers guidance for how to remedy these problems using all we have discussed so far, and more. Of course, if your sex life is already satisfying, this material may be unnecessary—for now. However, the more you know, the better equipped you will be to maintain an active and healthy sexual relationship with your spouse for the long term.

First of all, let's look at semantics. We commonly hear the term "making love *to*. . . ." It is my contention that you do not make love *to* your spouse, just like you don't make cookies *to* someone. You make love *with* your spouse or you make love *for* your spouse. This subtle shift in wording actually carries a large psychological difference. Making love is something two people do together, for each other; it is not something we do *to* someone else or they do *to* us. It is not inflicted; it is given and shared. Ideally, sex is a mutual activity for mutual enjoyment. I invite you to shift the way you use this expression and the way you think about it to more accurately reflect the truth—and the beauty—of the experience.

> **Consider this:** Contrary to the popular belief that married sex is boring and infrequent, married people report higher levels of sexual satisfaction than both sexually active singles and cohabiting couples, according to a comprehensive survey of sexuality as reported by the National Marriage Project. Forty-two percent of wives said they found sex to be extremely emotionally and physically satisfying, compared to just 31 percent of single women who had a sex partner. And 48 percent of husbands said sex was extremely satisfying emotionally, compared to just 37 percent of cohabiting men. Hmmm—that leaves 58 percent of wives and 52 percent of husbands who must have said they could be more satisfied. That is why this chapter is important!

Second, let us consider the meaning of the term "making love." People call it that because it does—or at least it can. When your relationship is experiencing an ebb in the expression of love, it is undoubtedly also experiencing an ebb in the bedroom. There are two ways to remedy this situation. One is to wait until you feel the love again and then have sex. The other is to have sex and reignite the love. Since we talked pretty extensively in the last chapter about reigniting the love, let's take a look now at reigniting the sex. The key point is that you have to do *something* to get back into the flow.

Let's Start with Foreplay — Always

Foreplay is physical preparation or stimulation before interecourse. There tends to be a significant difference between foreplay for a man and foreplay for a woman that is important to understand and work with. In general, foreplay for most guys is relatively quick and easy; direct touching of the genitals typically does the trick. Visuals are usually appreciated; lingerie is a nice touch. Initiating sex, breaking routine, exploration, new places, new positions, and letting him know you want him sexually are what turn him on. In fact, most men can be really angry about something yet can still be swayed relatively easily into having sex. All it usually requires is direct touching.

Foreplay for women it is a bit more complicated. For women, foreplay starts long before the couple gets into bed. Generally speaking, and particularly in a marriage, for most women, the setup or preparation for sexual activity is a sense of feeling loved and cared for—outside of the bedroom as well as within. In fact, for most women, foreplay really starts in the realm of topics we covered in the last few chapters: romance and communication. If she is angry about something, you better attend to that first (go back to Chapter 8). Touch her heart; then touch her body.

Ideally, physical foreplay for women begins well *before* direct genital touching. Making her feel that you want her for more than sex—that she is cared about as a person—is what turns her on. When she knows that you are interested specifically in her, she is far more likely to be interested in you sexually. Kissing, at least for most women, is usually a must. Exactly opposite of men, for a woman, the genital area is typically the *last* place that should be touched during foreplay.

> **Did you know?** Men can become aroused in two to three minutes (or quicker!)—but women can take up to *ten times* as long. That's twenty to thirty minutes for a woman to become as aroused as her man.

Just about everywhere else on her body should be considered a good place to touch, massage, and kiss before going "there." The idea is to make her *want* to be touched there. *Wanting* sex is part of the turn-on for a woman. When insufficient time is allowed for foreplay before intercourse, the experience is less enticing.

Foreplay is almost more important to a woman than "the real thing." In addition to its romantic qualities, foreplay has some really important physiological effects that make sex much more pleasurable for a woman. Simply put, a woman's physical response of lubrication is as important as a man's erection for creating satisfying intercourse.

A hint for guys: You've got to think like a mechanic. You need to lubricate the parts, or the friction will damage the machinery. You've got to warm the motor before you run it, and you've got to watch the gauges to be sure everything is operating smoothly, that nothing is overheating, out of "oil," or making abnormal sounds. In other words, if she doesn't sound like it feels good, looks to be in more pain than pleasure, or glances at her watch rather than gazing into your eyes, consider these to be warning lights flashing! In the same way that a machine which isn't well maintained eventually stops running, if you bypass the foreplay, your partner's engine won't start.

A hint for women: Don't be lazy when it comes to love, foreplay, and sex in your marriage. Chances are, if you and your spouse are not having sex regularly, one or both of you is likely to be unhappy. If your spouse is unfulfilled sexually and you are unwilling to participate in turning things around, don't be surprised when he feels pushed away.

Did you know? For men, the top complaint is low sexual frequency—not getting enough lovemaking (although many women share this concern). For women, the top complaint is poor sexual quality. Seems like a direct correlation between cause and effect. Improve the quality; improve the quantity!

If sex doesn't feel good to you or your partner, get creative. See if you can discover ways that do feel good or find remedies for the reasons it doesn't. Talk about it. Try new things. Touch each other. Find ways of pleasing each other. Remember, ego is what blocks love every time. When your control and approval issues loom large in your sexuality, your marriage is going to diminish in quality. Take it seriously while at the same time becoming more playful. Much like a fuel gauge, sexuality can be an indicator of how much mileage a marriage has left in it. The good news is that there are definitely steps you can take to rev things up. I share many of them here.

Love Tip: Instead of "just saying no," just say know. The biggest obstacle to good sex is silence. Know what your partner wants and what you want, and work to find a way to satisy each other. When you let go of your ego needs for control and approval you will be much better equipped to see options that will serve you both.

Overcoming the Obstacles

One of the stereotypical complaints about marriage is that the sex diminishes in frequency over time and the spark of passion goes out. The classic assumption is that the woman stops wanting it and the man is deprived, but it also happens the other way around. From my discussions with couples I've concluded that there are a variety of reasons why this occurs and determined some definite things that can be done about it. Here is a list of some of the most frequently cited relationship-related reasons couples shut down sexually:

- A lack of adequate foreplay

- A lack of communication or a lack of respect regarding what feels good and what doesn't

- Unresolved anger, resentment, or insecurity over other aspects of the relationship

- A lack of time or too much stress, which depletes energy; also, a lack of empathy regarding stress and exhaustion

- Confusion regarding sexual orientation

- Sexual attitudes triggered by previous experiences or religious beliefs or an unwillingness to experiment

Self-esteem also comes into play in terms of body image as it relates to managing weight and dealing with age-related changes in appearance. Not feeling sexy is an issue that interferes with sexuality, and so is diminished attraction to one's spouse due to physical changes. The good news is that if restoring your relationship and reigniting your sexuality are important to you, all of these things are manageable. In fact, most of these topics have already been addressed; now you just need to put into practice what you've learned.

Physiological issues can also contribute to a decrease in sexuality. These issues include

- ill health or a lack of physical fitness

- recent childbirth/current breastfeeding

- hormonal changes (in both men and women)

- side effects from prescription medications

- inability to "perform"

It is important to consult with a physician to control, minimize, or at the very least understand these issues. What you should *not* do, if a healthy relationship with your spouse is your goal, is simply ignore what is going on with your body.

This includes paying attention to your level of fitness and health. I know firsthand the challenges of getting and staying fit and feeling comfortable with one's body. I also know firsthand what being out of shape does to one's self-esteem and how that impacts a relationship. While it may be unrealistic to expect to get super fit, it is possible to take a walk daily or do sit-ups or squats or jump rope with the kids. It is possible to choose foods that make you feel good and give you energy instead of making you feel sluggish. Every step, literally, that you take toward caring for your body's health and fitness will have a positive impact on your relationship (unless you are obsessed with being thin or fit and prioritize that over being healthy and living a balanced life). Only you know the truth for you (and only your spouse knows the truth for him- or herself), but the impact of your fitness (or lack thereof) on your self-esteem and your sexuality cannot be overestimated.

By the same token, if your spouse struggles with their weight (too much or too little) or has body-image issues for any reason, the more reassuring, complimentary, and encouraging you can be, the better. Remember the discussions on the EROS equation (Chapter 2) and on self-esteem development (Chapter 4). Any criticism, judgment, or sarcasm you bring to these issues will only block the love in the relationship and contribute to blockages in your spouse's self-esteem. If you need to talk to your spouse about his or her current situation and how it impacts you, be sure to review the tips on communicating emotions found in Chapter 8, particularly those in the section "Telling Your Partner the Painful Truth."

If you struggle with being physically attracted to your spouse due to changes in his or her health or fitness, see if you can focus on turning your attitude around. Remember the EROS equation. Your lack of attraction is simply your response to an event. Pay attention to what you are thinking, focus on what is really important to you and on what you love and appreciate about your spouse, and see if you can reignite the flame. You may find that your demonstration of acceptance—no matter what—actually serves as motivation and inspiration for your spouse to improve (when improvement is within the scope of possibility).

EXERCISE ∽ *Look back at the list of values you generated in Chapter 3 and notice if fitness and health are on your list. If so, where did they rank in your priorities? Does sexuality rank anywhere on your list? If either fitness and health or sexuality are missing from the list, or if you find that the list needs amending, take time to make those changes now. Then start with baby steps, and work your way up to giant strides. Remember, you are walking (or running or swimming...) toward love, health, and greater well-being.* ∽

Appreciate your body

Dear Eve,

I really want to have a relationship with somebody, but I am insecure about my body. I am at least fifty pounds overweight and can't imagine anyone being attracted to me. I have been dieting and exercising and I feel much better, but I have such a long way to go. Is there love out there for me, or will I have to wait until I'm perfect?

Aloha,

First, start by imagining people being attracted to you. It all starts with your attitude! If you can't imagine someone being attracted to you, you won't even realize (or believe it) when someone is trying to get your attention. One of the wonderful things about humans (contrary to what the media have told us) is that people are attracted to all kinds of other people and body types. Love is not reserved for the young, thin, tall, or fit — guaranteed. People also fall in love with personalities. Sometimes we unexpectedly experience attraction to people who don't fit our "type" or, surprisingly, we do not feel attracted to a handsome man or beautiful woman. There is just no explaining attraction; it is one of life's great mysteries.

Certain Internet dating sites are dedicated to helping people find the "large and lovely" mate of their dreams, so don't convince yourself that there is no one out there who will be attracted to you. Once, when I was twenty-four, lived on Kauai, paddled outrigger canoes daily, and was at my all-time fittest, a local man said to my then-boyfriend, "Eve is pretty, but Claire is beautiful!" Claire was his three-hundred-plus-pound wife. That was when I realized (thankfully) that our perception of beauty is not only cultural but also personal — and unique to each individual.

The real challenge you face here is not other people's perceptions of you, but your own self-perception. If you really want to have a relationship with somebody, you must start having a healthy relationship with your body. Start taking active steps toward appreciating your body now for what it does for you, how it serves you, and what you are able to do on account of it. Don't wait until your thighs look a certain way to appreciate the fact that they allow you to walk, run, stand, and dance.

I cared for my mom prior to her death from A.L.S. (Lou Gehrig's disease). I watched her lose her ability to use one body part after the next, to the point where she could no longer talk, eat, walk, stand, or move her arms. Witnessing her physical deterioration forced me to ask myself whether I was taking my own body for granted or whether I adequately appreciated my tongue, arms, legs, voice, and other "normal" bodily functions. I share this with you to encourage you to start actively practicing appreciation of your body. You say that watching what you eat and exercising make you feel better. Rather than worrying so much about what you look like, focus on "feeling better" as your inspiration to continue your healthy new habits — one day at a time. By doing so, you'll be able to appreciate your body all along, not just when you reach your goal weight. Keep moving, and keep loving every minute of it! Even people with perfect bodies who exercise daily often do so out of insecurity. We would all benefit from loving our bodies more for what they do rather than concerning ourselves so much with how they look.

Do the following mirror exercise: Stand naked in front of
the mirror, and observe the thoughts that you automatically pummel your body with. Then replace any negative
thoughts with positive statements, appreciating your body
and how it serves you. For instance, rather than berating
your thighs because they may have cellulite, thank them
for serving their purposes of dancing, jogging, walking,
and supporting you. Rather than focusing on the extra flab
on your arms, send love to your arms for allowing you to
carry a child or hug a loved one. Spend a moment acknowledging and thanking the aspects of your body that work
miraculously without your even thinking about it: your
tongue for helping you speak and swallow food, your heart
for pumping blood day in and day out, your other internal
organs for processing everything efficiently, your brain
for helping you think things through.... As you look in
the mirror, train yourself to notice the aspects of your
body that you do appreciate rather than the ones you
don't. Appreciate your beautiful eyes, the texture of your
hair, the color of your skin. Do this every day until you
have switched your automatic self-talk from negative to
positive.

Until you fully love yourself — and your body — you won't
believe that someone else can love you. "Happily ever
after" always begins within! I wish you the best.

With aloha,

Eve

Of course, some bodily issues aren't as easily remedied as improving diet and exercise habits. I get many letters from people asking
me how to deal with a physical challenge as it relates to their intimate
partnership. Perhaps they are enduring the long-term effects of an
accident or surgery, or their bodies are aging less gracefully than they
would like, or they are dealing with an illness that is causing major
physical changes. These are, of course, very difficult situations. All
you can really do is take a deep breath (or several), transcend your
ego, align with your authentic self, practice acceptance, and know
that your value is not based upon your body.

It is important to take the time to emotionally grieve the loss of good health if you or your spouse has been struck with a serious chronic condition or the loss of faculties. Cry, journal, talk with your spouse and family, seek professional assistance—do whatever you need to do to process your emotions around the major life changes you are encountering. Creative self-expression is often a great way to express your feelings in a constructive way. Even if what you face is not terminal but just a major life change, you may find yourself experiencing the five stages of dying identified by Swiss-born psychiatrist Elisabeth Kübler-Ross: denial, anger, bargaining, depression, and acceptance. Remember to utilize the total-truth process presented in Chapter 8. Focus your attention on what you have gained from the experience, what you have learned, and how dealing with these particular challenges has made you stronger, wiser, or more compassionate. These mindsets will help you move toward acceptance. Obviously, this is all easier said than done, but it can be done.

This is why the concept of honoring your partnership "in sickness and in health" is so important. If your spouse is going through any of these changes or challenges, showing him or her love, tenderness, and compassion will go a long way. When serious heath issues impact your sex life, do your best to keep touching your partner as often as possible; if nothing else, touch him or her in nonsexual ways. The power of touch, both in healing the body and in healing relationships—or in keeping them healthy—cannot be overestimated. Rather than focusing on what you can no longer do, see if you can find new things that you love to do together that are manageable with the health limitations. One woman shared with me that when her husband got ill the doctors said, "No more wine and no more sex," at least for a period of time. So, instead of indulging in their quest for the perfect glass of wine, they began exploring the many virtues of fruit and vegetable juices—a healthy and delicious alternative. This became their new "taste-testing" passion, and a daily wine glass full of fresh tangerine juice soon became a new favorite. Replacing sex was a little trickier, but when they let go of their resistance to their new circumstances, new opportunites emerged. Since, in her opinion, foreplay and nonsexual physical affection had already been a bit lacking in their marriage, this period of healing provided a time for them to develop new ways of physically loving each other. Things they did before they got married—holding hands, foot massages, snuggling, and cuddling—were reintroduced, bringing a more conscious focus to the way they expressed their love physically.

Another couple reported that when the woman became ill and could not physically engage in a sexual encounter, she could still snuggle with her partner and share the experience while he masturbated. This allowed her to feel involved in their sex life and kept them feeling bonded, even though she couldn't actively participate. Of course, each couple's particular set of circumstances is different, allowing for varying degrees of interaction. If one partner is able to enjoy sexuality and the other is not, it is important that the nurturing touch still continue to be two-sided, even if it isn't sexual for both partners.

> **Did you know?** According to Kathleen VanKirk, author of *Orgasms: Good for Body, Mind and Soul,* those who have sex once or twice a week show 30 percent higher levels of an antibody called immunoglobulin A (IgA), which is known to boost the immune system. Individuals who have sex three or more times a week reduce their risk of heart attack or stroke by half. And sexual intercourse burns approximately 150 calories per half hour.

Dealing with major health issues is challenging, and yet it is an excellent time to "think outside of the box" and come up with new ways to express your sexuality or establish new forms of physical intimacy.

> *Love Tip:* When health issues get in the way of having sex, it is helpful to redefine "making love." Recognize that your spouse is making love with you in every action of caring for your well-being and in every utterance of "thank you." While it is certainly not the same as sex, in some ways it can be even more gratifying.

As needed, practice the skills covered in Chapter 8, "Managing Emotions and Communicating Clearly." Life includes misfortune, so the better we get at accepting what is rather than resisting, the greater our chances of experiencing well-being in the midst of challenges. Once again, keep the EROS equation in mind; rather than focusing on the event, focus on your response.

Dreading sex

Dear Eve,

I've been married for several years. My husband and I have
an excellent relationship. We love each other dearly, and
we both find each other very physically attractive. We are
best friends and spend as much time together as we can.
When we first met we had fantastic sex. Then our relationship went through a rocky period for about nine months.
During this time he was verbally abusive to me. I started
dreading sex because I was hurt and felt unloved and
disrespected. He'd pressure me into sex even though I
didn't want to. We eventually worked out the verbal abuse
thing, and for the last two years he has been a wonderful
and loving husband. Yet I still dread sex, which he wants
all the time. I've been trying really hard to give it to
him every other day, although I'm not an enthusiastic
participant.

My husband and I are so very much in love, and yet I know
the sex issue is going to build up and damage us very
soon. He wants me to want it and be into it. I want to
want that too, but something about the way he approaches
me just turns me off. Sometimes I think it might be a
control/power issue. Can you please help me? Thanks!

Aloha,

We humans are a bit complex. In addition to our rational
adult self, we have a whole host of subpersonalities,
for example, our inner child, inner teenager, and inner
critic. We have sexual subpersonalities as well. Imagine
for a moment that we are like a school bus. Our rational
self is the driver and our subpersonalities are in the
seats behind us giving us their two cents' worth on the
direction our lives should take. When we are mentally
healthy we can listen to the input of our subpersonalities
but remain in the driver's seat as we make decisions. When
we are mentally unstable (and here I'm referring to the
"instability" caused by everyday reactions such as sleep
deprivation, the need for food, stress, etc., rather than
clinical mental illness), we let the subpersonalities
drive the bus.

Although your rational self has made peace with your husband, there is likely a subpersonality that remains deeply hurt. Perhaps that part of you was reinjured because your husband's actions triggered old pain from something else. In my experience, ongoing resentment and hurt have to do with unexpressed or unheard feelings. Since you and your husband have made peace, my sense is that this isn't stuff you need to express to your husband so much as it is stuff your rational self needs to listen to from your injured subpersonality. Then that injured part of you needs to heal. There may be things left unsaid between you and your husband, but the issue sounds like it is more internal than external. When your subpersonalities don't feel heard, they self-sabotage. Then you find that you "cut off your nose to spite your face."

I recommend that you do some journaling in which you dialogue between your rational self and your subpersonalities to find out what is going on. Lucia Capacchione has written a great book called *The Power of Your Other Hand* that explains how you can dialogue between your rational self (with a pen in your dominant hand) and your subpersonality (with a pen in your nondominant hand).

It may be that a subpersonality is mad at you (rather than at your husband) for choices you have made and thus does not feel safe. Allow your subpersonality to express to you what it is angry about, how it is hurt, what it is afraid of, what part it plays in your situation, what it wants, and what it appreciates about you, your marriage, your husband, and sex. Then, just like you would with another person, go about problem solving and coming to agreement so that you and your subpersonalities are on the same team and share the goal of creating a dynamic and healthy sexual relationship with your husband.

Here is the good news: In addition to your injured subpersonality, you also have a sexual self that still finds your husband attractive and who enjoys sharing intimate time with him. Your sexual self didn't go away; she just got sent to the backseat of the bus. Your job is to invite her into the driver's seat when opportunities for intimacy arrive. If you don't like the way your husband approaches you, try approaching him and thus beating him to the punch.

```
I am quite certain that you can restore the sexual health
in your relationship as you learn to manage the internal
power struggle between different aspects of yourself.
```

```
With aloha,
```

Eve

Respectfully Yours

As a relationship specialist, I am approached by many people who ask my opinion about what sorts of sexual expression are right and wrong as they try to define their own levels of willingness and acceptance. I always explain that there is no clear definition when it comes to consensual sex. "Right" and "wrong" are defined by the morals of the people participating, not by experts, ministers, or friends. Sexuality isn't a "right-and-wrong" issue; it is a *respect* issue. If something is right for you but wrong for the other person, then trying to push or impose your way on him or her is not respectful and, therefore, not right.

A beautiful woman in her early thirties once told me, "I am still a virgin waiting for marriage, but my boyfriend is not. He is trying to be respectful of my pace, but it is hard for him." Any of us can empathize with the challenges presented by two such different levels of sexual readiness or experience, but this wasn't their real problem. She said, "He told me that if we got married, he would want me to do all this kinky stuff." She described a variety of sexual practices that are more the extreme than the norm. He wanted her to get breast implants and acrylic nails, dress in revealing clothing, and occasionally act as dominatrix in some sadomasochistic play. I looked at this sweet, innocent, churchgoing woman in amazement as she described what her boyfriend was asking her to do. I thought of all the women who already matched what he was looking for and wondered why he would want to transform his girlfriend into something so far from her natural self. Searching for understanding, she asked me, "Is that normal?" I took a deep breath and resisted my temptation to tell her to run as fast as she could away from a man who seemed to show her no respect and caused her to doubt her own beauty, style, sexual desires, and morals. Instead, I said to her, "It is normal *for him,* but it isn't normal *for you*—and *that* is what is relevant."

♡ *Love Tip:* Rather than worrying about what may be right or wrong for someone else to do, simply gauge your choices by what is right or wrong for you to do.

Sexuality is a matter of honor and respect. The goal is to share feeling wonderful, beautiful, celebrated, loved, touched, adored, ecstatic, and fulfilled. If only one person is feeling any of these things and the other is not, then respect and honor are missing. One of the biggest disservices the pornography industry has done is that porn often serves as a young man's introduction to sex and provides his ongoing primary sex education. Unfortunately, in porn there is little or no attention paid to foreplay, communication, or satisfying the woman. Pornography, for the most part, is all about what women can do for men, not about men loving women and mutual satisfaction. When this model is used by a man with a real woman, though, it doesn't generally work for the long-term. In the beginning she may comply with simply satisfying her man, but over time if she is not being satisfied too, the sex act will begin to feel empty, her resentment will build, and her interest will wane.

As I've pointed out, even the nature of our language of love has contributed to these problems. If we simply change our language and the mindset that accompanies the words, a whole shift in the way we make love could take place. By exploring each other's desires, interests, and boundaries, and honoring them in the process, we truly make love *together,* rather than doing it *to* someone else or having it done *to* us.

EXERCISE ∼ *Pay attention to the language you use when thinking or talking about sex and marriage. Do your words carry the meaning you want to convey? If not, shift your words to align with your heart.* ∼

If at First You Don't Succeed, Experiment!

Experimenting and stretching your sexual interests and activities can be wonderful, but when you get out of bed in the morning your self-respect must still be intact. Even in a marriage you need to know, honor, and communicate your personal boundaries. At the same time, hopefully, marriage is a safe realm in which you can safely experiment with each other and stretch your preconceived boundaries to discover the full range of what you and your partner enjoy.

If your partner is requesting sexual experimentation and you are unwilling to participate, examine what is stopping you. Is it religious beliefs, fear, body-image issues? What are you feeling? What are you thinking? Pay attention to whether you are allowing your need for control or approval to interfere with a deepening of your intimacy with your spouse—and with the full enjoyment of your body. If you discover that this is the case, take a deep breath—or two or three—and rather than "just saying no," see if you can break the suggested experience into baby steps that you *are* willing to try. For instance, if your partner wants to share sexual fantasies but it feels too vulnerable to you to do so, rather than allowing this to become a control issue of right or wrong, get a bit more creative. Rather than revealing your *own* fantasies—which may feel threatening and too real—try reading aloud to each other erotica describing other people's sexual fantasies or experiences. If your partner wants to try a position you are uncomfortable with, see if you can alter it into a position you are willing to try. If you are concerned about body-image issues, see if you feel more comfortable wearing certain articles of clothing or lingerie or dimming the lights or using candles. If your partner wants to have a threesome and you don't want to open that door, consider the use of pornography as a "virtual" experience while you still maintain the safety of your twosome. I'm not advocating pornography; I'm advocating finding nonthreatening ways to satisfy your and your partner's sexual interests.

Often one of the things that stops people from experimenting with a spouse is a fear that they won't do it right or a fear of being judged. Revisit our discussion on fear in Chapter 7; ask yourself whether you're allowing fear to stop you from experiencing life's fullness. Then educate yourself; make learning and teaching part of the fun. Numerous sex-training videos are available that you can watch in the privacy of your own home. Many books are on the market that provide instruction in just about every sexual activity a person can do with another person. Teach each other; tell each other what you like and don't like. Although you may feel uncomfortable telling your spouse that you need an adjustment in the way things are being done, there is a good chance that he or she would prefer making an adjustment over no longer sharing the experience. At the very least, your partner will know why you aren't interested in participating in a particular activity instead of leaving the reason to his or her imagination.

If your spouse is the one who is unwilling to experiment, before jumping to the conclusion that something is wrong with him or her, put the EROS equation to work. First explore whether you are a safe person to experiment with. When a spouse approaches sex solely from an attitude of wanting to be satisfied rather than wanting to satisfy the other, it can be a turn-off. When a partner is judgmental outside of the bedroom, it is hard to trust him or her to be kind and encouraging in the bedroom. Revisit the self-observation and self-inquiry exercises from Chapter 6, and use those processes to evaluate yourself as a sexual partner. Are you kind, encouraging, and complimentary, or do you tend to put your spouse down? Do you invite and encourage sexual play, or do you demand and expect it? Do you compare your spouse to previous partners and thus contribute to a sense of inferiority? Do you express your love and caring for your partner outside of the bedroom? What do think it is like to have sex with you?

The next section lists questions that will encourage you and your spouse to talk about issues related to sexuality. After that you will find sex tips from a female perspective (mine) and then from a male perspective (that of sex expert Bob Berkowitz). Even if you or your spouse has been unwilling to be an eager participant or adventurer in the bedroom, as you read through these "talking points" and suggestions, see if you can begin stretching your sexual personality one small step at a time. All that may be required is a little communication or a slightly different approach.

When in Doubt, Ask for Directions

Ironically, although you may have been having sex with your spouse for many, many years, when asked to *talk* to him or her about sex, you may suddenly become very shy and uncomfortable. In reality, however, almost all of the relationship-related issues listed earlier as reasons why someone's sexual interest might dwindle can be addressed through honest conversation, communicating your feelings, working together to come to an agreement or resolution, and taking responsibility for your part in the problem.

If you feel uncomfortable jumping into these questions with your spouse, start by answering them alone. Either just think your answers through, or, better yet, write your answers in a journal. Answering them on your own first will give you the luxury of thinking about how you really feel, and it will also help you become more comfortable with the topic. Be sure to give your spouse the same head start if he or she isn't ready or willing to discuss the questions off the cuff.

The following questions, from my book *Intellectual Foreplay,* are geared to helping you and your spouse get to know each other better sexually. Even if you have lived with your spouse for many years, don't assume that you know his or her answers to these questions. You may not even know some of your own answers. Or you may find that you only *think* you know the answer because of the way it has always been. In fact, since we have established that people change with time, you may find that your assumptions based upon past experiences are no longer accurate. You may also find that you don't want to know your spouse's answers to some of the questions. Pick and choose questions that will help you be more intimate with your spouse, both physically and through communication, and ignore the ones that don't apply to you. Just because a question is listed here doesn't mean that you should explore these particular aspects of sexuality in your marriage or that you haven't already done so. This is not a list of suggestions; it is a list of questions to explore as a couple to deepen your intimacy, knowledge, and understanding of each other.

If during this discussion you get plugged into anger, hurt, or fear, take a deep breath, release your ego, and return to your authentic self—the one that is strong, has faith, trusts, and can handle anything. Share the total truth (see Chapter 8). If you are hurt, look underneath the hurt to see what you are afraid of and what you are thinking of that is causing the pain. Then look beneath the fear to see what you want and what you treasure. Avoid getting stuck in one emotion when slightly deeper inquiry will bring you back to truth, love, and greater understanding. Keep your focus on arriving at a solution, so that you and your spouse can come to agreement on any areas of difference.

Review the section in Chapter 8 titled "Guidelines for Engaging in Intellectual Foreplay." Share your concerns with an open mind; don't just ask questions but also answer them yourself; stay in the present;

Something to consider: One woman shared that she got married in part to be free of the constant pressure for sex that she experienced from men she dated. Her spouse got married in part so that he could have sex whenever he wanted it. That made for a disconnect of intention right from the start.

Although most people nowadays think that the concept of waiting to get married before having sex is outdated and unrealistic, you do have to wonder how sex between spouses would be different if marriage were the place where all of your introductions and experiments took place, rather than (falsely) serving as a respite from or a taming of your sex life.

don't get jealous over the past or start worrying about the future; listen without judgment; be observant of what you are thinking and how it is making you feel; only ask what you want to know and are willing to share about yourself; be mindful of what you say and how you say it. And by all means, if you feel so inclined, stop the conversation and engage in some foreplay of the nonintellectual kind! This discussion can definitely be a round of show and tell. It is not an interview, so if you only want to discuss one or two questions at a time, that is fine. Do what feels right for you and your spouse.

EXERCISE ∾ *On a scale of one to ten, rate your sex drive.*

- *How often do you want sex?*

- *When is your sex drive the highest (night, morning, afternoon)?*

- *Does your sex drive vary throughout the month?*

- *Are you comfortable with the type of birth control, if any, you are using? Does using birth control, or not using it, affect your sexuality?*

- *How do you engage your partner in a sexual experience?*

- *Do you think both people should initiate sex, or should only one or the other?*

- *Do you want your partner to be sexually aggressive or passive?*

- *What were you expecting sex after marriage to be like?*

- *How do you like to be kissed? How important is kissing to you?*

- *How much or what kind of foreplay do you prefer? Is there anything you don't like in the foreplay stage of lovemaking (direct genital touching, kissing on the ear, etc.)?*

- *Is there anything that must be included in foreplay or lovemaking for you to be really aroused (e.g., kissing, talking, direct genital touching, ear kissing, eye gazing, etc.)?*

- *Do you prefer the lights on or off while you make love?*

- *Do you have a favorite place for making love? Or a place where you've always wanted to make love? If so, where?*

- *Are you interested in or willing to have sex in different or unusual places (outside, in the vehicle, etc.)?*

- *What are your feelings and levels of desire or objection concerning the following sexual experiences, from the perspective of both giving and receiving?*

    – *Oral sex*
    – *Masturbation*
    – *Verbally sharing fantasies*
    – *Acting out fantasies*
    – *Anal sex*
    – *Sex toys*
    – *Porn movies/magazines/websites*
    – *Bondage*
    – *Voyeurism*
    – *Threesomes or orgies*

- *How much are you willing to experiment? Is there a difference between what you like to fantasize about and what you actually want to do?*

- *Are there things you're unwilling to do?*

- *Are there certain positions that you prefer or dislike?*

- *Do you want or expect your partner to wear sexy garments? How do you feel about wearing sexy clothing or lingerie?*

- *Do you tend to like spontaneous lovemaking? How do you feel about prearranged sexual encounters (e.g., reserving Saturday mornings for lovemaking)?*
  As a follow-up question: What times/days do you want to reserve for lovemaking?

- *Is it okay for the other person to say no to sex? How does that make you feel?*

- *If you want to have sex and your partner doesn't, how do you think this should be handled? Would you insist? Do you think your partner should do it anyway?*

- *If your partner wants sex and you don't, do you feel obligated? Would you say something or just go ahead and make love? If so, do you make the best of it or feel resentful?*

- *Is it okay with you to cuddle and be intimate without having it lead to sex?*

- *When you don't feel like sex but just want to cuddle, how do you negotiate that?*

- *Are there times when you don't want to be touched? How do you express that to your partner?*

- *How do you like to be touched?*

- *For women: Does your monthly cycle affect your desire to be touched?*

- *In general, how do you feel about your partner's masturbating? How do you feel about your partner's masturbating when he or she is alone? During lovemaking? In front of you? Are you comfortable masturbating in front of your partner?*

- *Do you ask for what you want sexually? How do you let your partner know what you want?*

- *How do you respond when you don't get what you want?*

- *Are you able to have orgasms? Do you have any difficulty having orgasms? Do you have multiple orgasms?*

- *Are you currently satisfied sexually? Do you pay attention to each other's needs? Is satisfaction equal? Does it need to be?*

- *Do you expect an orgasm every time you have sex?*

- *Is it okay with you if your partner doesn't achieve an orgasm every time? If it bothers you, do you think this is because your ego is involved, or is it simply your desire to please your partner?*

- *Can you give pleasure to your partner without expecting anything in return?*

- *How do you feel about receiving pleasure without reciprocating to your partner?*

- *Are there ways you'd like to improve in bed or things you'd like to learn more about?*

- *Do either of you tend to use sex as a bargaining tool for get-ting your partner to do something for you? Do either of you withhold sex to "punish" your partner? How do you feel about that? When is it legitimate negotiation, and when is it manipulation?*

- *Does your perception of yourself (your appearance, weight, etc.) affect your sexuality? If so, what are you willing to do about it?*

- *Are you comfortable with the way your partner requests sex or speaks about it?*

- *How do you feel about your partner talking "dirty"? Do you like it, or does it offend you?*

- *Are you satisfied with the level of intimacy you share during lovemaking?*

- *What is your level of interest or understanding about sacred sex or sex as a spiritual experience, e.g., tantra? What are your thoughts about sex being sacred? Is it some-thing you are willing to explore?*

- *What are your spiritual beliefs concerning the topic of sex? Do you have beliefs that make you feel guilty about shar-ing sex with your spouse?*

- *Are emotions from previous relationships or experiences contaminating your current relationship?* ⟳

We get along great, but we don't have sex

Dear Eve,

I live with a woman with whom I've been compatible for many years. The only problem is that she has cut me off from sex, but I manage to take care of myself. How hard should I try to extricate myself from the relationship? How much money and effort should I put into dating others?

Aloha,

You raise two questions that are directly related to each other. How you handle one dictates how you should handle the other. However, there are other questions that you need to answer first: (1) Are you willing to continue living in a "compatible" situation with no sexual involvement? (2) What is the verbal agreement between you and this woman regarding your sex lives, monogamy, and your relationship? How does she feel about your dating other women? Is she negotiable? (3) Do you know why she has cut you off from sex, and is there anything you can do to resolve it? (4) Do you want to end this relationship?

You should also take into consideration the age and stage of life you are in and assess how easy you think it would be for you to meet someone with whom you get along better.

If you are unwilling to continue living as is, you have two choices: either rekindling the relationship you are in or getting out. Unless the two of you have explicitly agreed that it is acceptable to date other people, you should put no time and money into dating other women until you have finalized your current relationship. If you think getting out of the relationship is too complicated now, just wait until you bring a third party into it!

Since you are implying that you want out of the relationship, you should not have to "try hard" to extricate yourself; you should just do it. Breaking up with someone isn't something you attempt (which implies that you may not succeed). It is something you either do or don't do. Granted, doing so may be both emotionally and financially challenging, but it is still possible.

If you have reservations about breaking up, then I suggest you try to make the relationship work, as your hesitation may mean that you have not done all you need to do to make the relationship vital. If you want to save your relationship, I suggest you pretend (just for the sake of the exercise) that all the problems in the relationship are your doing. Then take 100 percent responsibility for transforming the situation. This doesn't mean trying to get her to have sex with you; it means amending whatever it is that made her stop wanting to have sex with you. When you change how you are showing up in the relationship, she will change the way she responds to you.

Keep in mind that if the reasons she cut you off from sex have something to do with you — the quality of your sexual interaction, your attention to foreplay, your ability to make her feel cared for outside of the bedroom, your hygiene, your willingness to communicate and resolve issues totally unrelated to sex (but from which emotions still flow into the bedroom) — you will bring those same issues into the next relationship. So you may as well address them now.

My feeling is that if you are in a compatible, long-term relationship with someone, you would be well served to "try hard" and to invest your "time and money" into healing that relationship and restoring its health before you try hard to get out and spend your time and money on dating other people.

With aloha,

Eve

Love Tip: Did you ever put a house up for sale, clean it, put on new paint, and do the yardwork only to find yourself thinking, "This looks pretty good! Why didn't I do this while I lived here?" The same holds true in relationships. Take the money, time, and effort you would spend on finding and courting someone new and invest it in the love you already have, and you may be amazed at how good it can look—and feel.

Tips for Improving Your Sex Life, Part 1: A Woman's Perspective

One definition of insanity is to keep doing the exact same thing over and over while expecting different results. The bottom line for everything we have talked about so far is that if your marriage isn't what you want it to be, you need to do something different. Apathy is guaranteed to kill the love in your marriage. Make changing things a priority. Take a deep breath. Wake up, look at what is really going on in your marriage, and determine what you truly want. Transcend your ego. Align with your goal. Let down your guard and grab your spouse. It is time to make your marriage more fun!

Below are several ideas for reigniting the passion between you and your spouse. Remember, these aren't things you do once and call it done. Just like you need to reaffirm your love for each other daily, you also need to reaffirm your sex life regularly. On one of my favorite episodes of *Friends,* Monica educated Chandler about seven different erogenous zones. She numbered them and put them on a body map. She explained to him that most men go to "number one" and stay there, with maybe some "number two" mixed in. (The locations of the different numbers were left completely to the imaginations of the viewers.) She suggested he try mixing up the order and adding the other erogenous zones. With great orgasmic emphasis she said, "Try a little two, then a four, some six, more six, move to three, then five, then three some more, then one, one, one...." I recommend that you try mixing up the suggestions below in much the same way. Try a little of this, some of that, one of these, and two of those.

> **Did you know?** Studies have shown that frequent hugging has a positive impact on our health; it even serves to release stress and to lower blood pressure and heart rate.

> **EXERCISE** ∾ *Touch with no agenda. When reigniting both the love and the passion in your marriage, a little nonsexual touch can go a long way. Make sure you touch your spouse at various times and in ways that convey no sexual overtures. When a woman feels affection beyond the bedroom, she is more likely to share her affection in the bedroom. If every touch or every kiss translates to "it is time to have sex," the result could be a withdrawal of all affection. Holding hands, neck rubs, hugs, kissing, back rubs, foot rubs—all of these sweet gestures feel good; they are like the foreplay to the foreplay. Nonsexual physical touch serves as emotional touch.* ∾

> *Explore and honor your partner's whole body. As singer/songwriter John Mayer so aptly puts it, consider your bodies a "wonderland" and relish the process of discovery. There are many*

parts of the body that enjoy being touched besides the genitals. Hmmm, come to think of it, every part of the body enjoys being touched! ∾

Show each other what you like and exactly how you like to be touched. If done playfully, the teaching—and the watching—can be almost as much fun as the doing. ∾

Add an element of surprise. Remember that what is considered "romantic" is the unexpected thoughtful gesture. An unexpected sexual encounter or experiment—when based in thoughtfulness—will likely have the same effect. This is not "Surprise, this is what you can do for me," but rather "Surprise, look what I am going to do for you!" It is in giving that we receive. ∾

Don't wait; initiate. Instead of wondering why the two of you are not having sex, initiate the experience. There is no time like the present. ∾

Schedule sex dates. If time is limited, take the initiative to schedule a weekly encounter with your spouse by writing it into your day planner. This can take some of the pressure off attempts to find time for sex and also can ensure that you have intimate encounters. One couple I spoke with got tired of trying (unsuccessfully) to squeeze sex into their busy lives, so they began scheduling a "sex date" every week. If between dates they managed to find an opportunity for lovemaking, great, but if not, they knew they had something to look forward to. They anticipated the date, planned for it, and enjoyed it. If your spouse requests sex and you say no, give him or her a time when it would work better for you—and then stick to your word. "Not tonight, honey, but definitely in the morning" is far easier to receive than "Not tonight." ∾

Shake it up. If you are bored with your sex life, stop being boring. If the lights are always on, turn them off and make love in the pitch dark. Or try having sex with the lights on and your eyes open, maintaining eye contact the whole time. If you always *have sex when getting up or going to bed, try it in the middle of the afternoon. Always in the bedroom? Try the shower, the kitchen, the closet...anywhere else. If you always have sex naked, try it with some clothes or lingerie on—or vice versa.*

Compromise when need be. One couple found that he was most aroused when he first woke up in the morning, and she was most aroused at night. Their solution was to take a nap in the afternoon on the weekends and make love right after he woke up—a delight for both of them. ∾

Did you know? According to Mitchell Tepper, Ph.D., in a sample of men and women in the United States, 61 percent of women who engaged in self-pleasuring always or usually experienced an orgasm, versus 82 percent of men. Yet only 29 percent of women reported always having an orgasm during sex with a partner, versus 75 percent of men.

Self-observe. Use your newly developed skill of self-observation to pay attention to your wandering mind during sex. Constantly bring your attention from the past or the future to the present moment, where you can engage with your partner now. While you are at it, monitor your self-talk and make sure it is working for you, rather than against you. ∾

Enjoy "mini-sex." If you are too tired or don't have time for intercourse or oral sex, try a quicker, mutually satisfying interlude of masturbation, sex-toy play, or a "teaser" for later. The key is staying sexually connected. ∾

If it doesn't feel good, do something different. Pain blocks pleasure (for most people). If you are in pain, tell your spouse, and immediately switch to something different. Sex is supposed to feel good! ∾

Make it safe. Expressing your sexuality can be a vulnerable experience. Keep ego, judgment, teasing, sarcasm, and criticism out of the bedroom. One critical comment about your spouse's body, technique, or sexuality can trigger years of limited, inhibited sex or none at all. Instead, for years of mutual enjoyment, guide your partner by telling him or her what you do like. Be sure to use "I" statements instead of "you" statements. ∾

Try it; you'll like it! *Desires to experiment should be explored with a "what is in it for my partner" approach—not just from the angle of what is in it for you. Make sure both of you are likely to benefit; make mutual pleasure your selling point. On that same note, sometimes you just won't know if you like it until you try it. Aim to keep an open mind regarding your spouse's requests to see if you can discover what is in it for you. It may be that a slight alteration in strategy does the trick. A little creativity can go a long way.* ∾

Express your appreciation and enjoyment. *The reason why cats are fun to pet is because they purr. Make sure you let your partner know that you like what he or she is doing, and thank your partner for his or her gift to you. When your partner knows what you love, he or she is likely to do it again.* ∾

Compliment your spouse. *Tell your spouse that he or she is beautiful, handsome, sexy, and good in bed. Your spouse is more likely to be sexy when he or she feels sexy. Reassuring your spouse that you find him or her attractive will help your spouse to overcome (or temporarily forget about) any insecurities he or she may harbor.* ∾

 Love Tip: Think sexy and you'll be amazed at how your body responds.

Give, just for the sake of giving. *Every now and then, treat your spouse to an orgasmic encounter, with no expectation of reciprocation.* ∾

Take advantage of technology. *There must be something to online communication since so many are finding their sweethearts this way. Engage in an online tryst—with your spouse. Instant message each other. Send each other love letters. Ask questions. Share fantasies. "Pick up" on each other. Flirt. Use the Internet to engage in intellectual foreplay as practice for when you get home. You may find that a different aspect of your personality emerges in writing.* ∾

Do unto your spouse as your spouse would have you do unto him or her. Touch your spouse in the way he or she wants to be touched. Often the only way to learn how to do this is to ask. ∽

Tips for Improving Your Sex Life, Part 2: A Man's Perspective

For a man's perspective, below you will find some excellent tips from Dr. Bob Berkowitz, one of America's leading authorities on sex. He has a Ph.D. in clinical sexology and is also a certified hypnotherapist. He is the author of the best-selling books *What Men Won't Tell You but Women Need to Know* and *His Secret Life: Male Sexual Fantasies.*

EXERCISE ∽ *The five-minute massage. This is a great technique if you need a little help getting in the mood. Alternate giving and receiving front or back massages with your partner. For example, you start off massaging your partner's front for five minutes. Your partner returns the favor. Then you each do the same thing for the other's back. It's the best investment of twenty minutes you can ever make in your love life.* ∽

Show and tell. None of us are mind readers. You need to show your partner exactly what you like, how you like it, and at what speed and intensity. Simply put: Masturbate in front of each other. Plus, for many people it's a great turn on to watch or be watched. Which reminds me. . . . ∽

Make sex a whole-body experience. Sometimes we make a beeline for the genitals and never leave. Not that there's anything wrong with paying lots of attention to and spending lots of time with that part of the body. But it's also a great idea to spread the sexual energy all around. Explore every part of your partner's body. Leave nothing to chance. During or right after orgasm you may even want to run your hands from your partner's genitals all over the surface of his or her body to spread the sexual energy. And speaking of other parts of the body. . . . ∽

Oral sex: A full-body experience. Let your tongue wander. Again, don't let the genitals be the sole target of attention. ∾

Who's in charge? Alternate who initiates sex. One of the top male sexual fantasies is for a woman to be sexually assertive or confident. In other words, she's in charge. Done all the time, however, this can get old, so take turns. ∾

Fantasy exchange. Have the courage to reveal your innermost fantasies. And while you're at it, encourage your partner to reveal his or hers. This can be an exciting and erotic addition to your love life. But remember, sometimes a fantasy is just that; it doesn't mean you have to or even want to act it out. Some people don't want to enact their fantasies. Can the reality match your sexual dream? After all, you are the star, writer, and director of your fantasy. Reality can rarely match that. In addition, your fantasy might be frightening to you partner. If so, keep reading. . . . ∾

Virtual fantasies. Let's say your favorite fantasy is to have sex with a third person in bed with you and your partner, but your partner finds that notion uncomfortable. Well, use your imagination. Pretend there's a third person with you. You and your partner can describe the way that person would look and what he or she would do and what you would do. This creates much of the fun without the complications. Remember, fantasies are a wonderful dress (or undress) rehearsal for lovemaking. ∾

The eyes have it. Try keeping your eyes open during lovemaking. It might intensify your connection—emotionally, physically, and spiritually—with your partner. Which leads me to. . . . ∾

Keep your attention on your partner. Try to keep your focus on the person you're being intimate with. You might find that it makes all the difference in the world to how you and your partner feel about sex. ∾

His secret erogenous zone. Did you know that at least 30 percent of all men find their nipples an erogenous zone? Same thing *with that area between the anus and scrotum. Unfortunately, some men feel nervous about being touched there, as if it were a threat to their masculinity. Gently touch these areas, gauge the reaction, and proceed from there.* ∾

The joys of toys. *Traditionally, sex toys (vibrators, dildos, feathers) have been the domain of women. But men are beginning to see that what stimulates her clitoris, for example, could just as easily pleasure his penis. Some men feel threatened by a woman who seemingly falls in love with her vibrator. They fear they could easily be replaced by that electric gadget. There's nothing wrong with a woman coming to orgasm with a vibrator, but she should make sure that her partner is part of the process, perhaps by asking him to caress her, kiss her, or hold the vibrator for her.* ∾

Bored in bed? Get out of bed! *We can get into a rut by always making love in the same way and in the same place. Try any room in the house—or the backyard for that matter. But if the bedroom is your principal place for lovemaking, make it a special, sacred space. Enhance the ambience with flowers, oils, and other accoutrements.* ∾

Having trouble expressing your feelings? Hit the road. *Dr. June Reinisch has a great idea for talking to your partner about sensitive issues. Do it while driving. After all, you're both looking ahead (without eye contact, it's often easier to express your feelings), and since you're in the car, it's unlikely that one of you is going to run away easily. A safety precaution: If the discussion starts to get heated, pull over and stop the car. Don't resume driving until tempers have cooled.* ∾

Lights on. *Since so much of sex is about visual stimulation, why do it in the dark? Studies show, for example, that men love watching oral sex being performed on them.* ∾

Intercourse: It's not the only game in town. *I sometimes think we're too intercourse oriented. It's a wonderful way of expressing* *your sexuality, but let's face it; it takes a lot of effort and time. Some people work so hard and have so many responsibilities that they skip sex because of the time and energy involved. So let's broaden the definition of sex to include things like mutual masturbation or solo sex with your partner holding you or caressing you. And if we're too intercourse oriented....* ∾

We're too orgasm-oriented. *Don't get me wrong; there's nothing wrong with orgasms. But we seem to make them the end-all and be-all of sex, as if somehow we've failed if we don't climax. It seems we may need to focus more on the journey than on the destination.* ∾

Sex is a voluntary sport. *Never coerce, force, or pressure anyone to do something they don't want to do. That being said, take a risk in trying something you've never done that is mutually agreeable.* ∾

How to criticize someone in bed? *Don't! Let's face it, we all feel a little (maybe a lot) vulnerable when it comes to sex. Positive reinforcement will go a long way in getting your lover to do what you need. Say something like, "I love it when you do that to me." Instead of complaining about what your partner is doing (unless you're being hurt or abused), tell him or her what you do like.* ∾

Reach out and touch someone. *Have phone or computer sex with someone you love. You might find it's easier to say what turns you on when you're not face to face.* ∾

Have fun. *Sometimes I think we get so clinical about sex that we forget it's supposed to be fun. It's adult playtime. Do whatever you and your partner think is okay to put some joy into your lovemaking. Dress up, dress down, use restraints, whatever. Just enjoy!* ∾

As I mentioned earlier, sexuality and romance are what make your spouse your lover rather than just your roommate. You can pretend that physical touch is not important, but you probably won't be fooling your spouse. If you want to rekindle your marriage, you will find rekindling your sex life to be a useful—and pleasurable—step in the right direction.

PART IV

THE BIGGER PICTURE

Your life and my life flow into each other as wave flows into wave, and unless there is peace and joy and freedom for you, there can be no real peace or joy or freedom for me. To see reality—not as we expect it to be but as it is—is to see that unless we live for each other and in and through each other, we do not really live very satisfactorily; that there can really be life only where there really is, in just this sense, love.

FREDERICK BUECHNER

CHAPTER 11

Family Matters

*You don't choose your family. They are God's
gift to you, as you are to them.*

DESMOND TUTU

So far in this book I've spoken fairly little about children, not as a matter of neglect but intentionally. My hope and intention are that the stronger the marriage, the healthier the family. Because children are a huge aspect of most marriages, relating to them is a topic that deserves a book of its own, and, of course, zillions of such books are available. Furthermore, I am guessing that many who are reading this book are past the child-rearing stage or may have chosen not to have children. For these reasons, my focus so far has been on the marriage itself rather than on the family. If you are a parent, or are planning to become one, the good news is that every skill and tool offered in this book can be applied to parenting. Still, I would feel remiss if I didn't dedicate at least a chapter to this critically important subject. If you don't have children, perhaps this material will serve you in interacting with nieces or nephews. If your own children are already grown and out of the house, consider this chapter as it relates to the grandchildren who may be a part of your life.

As I mentioned in the Introduction, my work in the arena of personal growth began with my interest in helping children to raise their self-esteem and make empowering life choices. Soon after working with the students in my classroom, I realized that I also needed to teach their parents these concepts if I really wanted to help the kids; thus, I began teaching relationship and parenting skills. Several years later I worked as a school counselor for sixth, seventh, and eighth graders. I received an amazing perspective from those young people about the importance of family and the changing face of families in the era of stepfamilies and blended families.

Even the best relationship faces entirely new dynamics when children are brought into the picture. Besides the obvious issues involved in figuring out how to juggle time, attention, and resources, dynamics of power and control enter into the picture. My father and I have always gotten along well, but when my mom got ill and I moved home to help him care for her, she virtually became "our child." Suddenly he and I had a much more challenging relationship. Since both of us loved her more than anyone in the entire world, we each had very strong feelings about the importance of her proper care, but we didn't always envision it the same way. We are talking here about a "mama bear" and a "papa bear," both with strong opinions about what was safer and better treatment, vying over the proper care of the beloved cub. On issues where neither of us believed there was a lot of room for negotiation, finding common ground was particularly difficult. I was once again faced with a golden opportunity to put into practice the EROS equation I teach to make sure that love and harmony remained at the forefront. It was not always easy—especially when I hadn't had enough sleep and was feeling steeped in grief—but it is the critical life lesson we are all here to master.

If you already have children, I'm guessing you can relate to the struggles inherent in managing different perspectives on childcare. If you don't yet have children, be advised that every moment of discussion you can engage in and every agreement you can reach beforehand will help you when the children arrive. In any case, if children are still a part of your marriage dynamics, or if you plan that they will be, go back to Chapter 3 and really focus on the guideposts for your marriage: your code of ethics, your values, your vision, and your rules for handling disagreements. Do your homework proactively.

Love Tip: Aim to have your marriage—and your home—be your sanctuary, the safe place your family retreats to in order to rejuvenate and better face the world.

Most of this chapter consists of a brief review of the issues dealt with in earlier chapters as they relate to the raising of children and the creation of a healthy family.

The Relationship Principles

We'll start with a review of the ten relationship principles we discussed in Chapter 1.

Principle number one: Relationships are a process, not a product

The experience of raising kids isn't just eighteen years long. It is truly a relationship that lasts "till death do us part"—and beyond. You don't get it right once and then finish. Raising healthy children and maintaining a healthy relationship with them is an ongoing process. Every new situation and circumstance—every new moment—provides a new opportunity to exercise your skills and make wiser choices.

Principle number two: Every effort you make will benefit you and your family

Every effort you make toward creating a healthy marriage and a healthy family will not only impact and benefit them but will also contribute to your own sense of well-being, trust, faith, health, and happiness. Since you must strengthen yourself in order to strengthen your family, the results for you personally will be tangible regardless of, or possibly even in spite of, what your loved ones choose to do. In the end, you need to know that you did all you could to serve your marriage and your family; regardless of the result, making that effort will serve you.

Principle number three: Your values act as guideposts for your decisions

The clearer you are about the values you live by, the clearer your children will be about the values you are instilling in them. Values act as guideposts for making healthy decisions and solving problems creatively. Not only will your children benefit from your example, but also you will find that resolving your own problems and making decisions related to the children's upbringing will be much easier if you and your spouse are clear about and committed to your values.

Principle number four: Ego is *always* what blocks love and joy

There is nothing like combining intense love and total responsibility for others to bring all your ego needs for control and approval to the surface. By remembering that ego is always what gets in the way of healthy communication and the experience of love, you will be in a powerful position to transform the family dynamics. Every ounce of mastery you achieve will be modeled for your kids.

Principle number five: You are the common denominator in all of your relationships

As Buckaroo Banzai says, "No matter where you go, there you are." (Did I just date myself?!) Teaching this concept to your children can be a huge source of wisdom throughout their lives. When kids would come in my office and complain about a specific relationship, I would try to help them gain understanding and compassion for the other person and teach them skills for managing the person's impact on them. But when a student would come in and complain about his or her friends, teachers, parents, and siblings, I would hold up a mirror and say, "What is the common denominator in all of these relationships?" This goes back to taking responsibility for your part in your experience rather than blaming others. The earlier we learn this skill, the better.

Love Tip: As you know, whenever you point a finger at someone or something else as the cause of your problems, three of your fingers are pointing back at you. One part may indeed be another person's doing, but be sure to take responsibility for the three parts over which you have control.

Principle number six: You can only change
yourself, but doing so influences others

You cannot change your children or your spouse, but everything you do will influence their behavior. One of my favorite book titles (I've never read the book, but the title says it all!) is *How to Behave So Your Children Will Too*. As the title implies, if you want your family to do things differently, *you* need to do things differently. They will change due to your influence, or at the very least they will automatically alter their behavior in response to yours. It is helpful to recognize that the root for the word "parent" is akin to the Latin word *parare*, which means "to prepare." The root word of "discipline" means "to learn" or "to teach." Remembering that your job is to prepare and teach your children may help you to make decisions about how to respond to them.

Principle number seven: You are responsible
for your experience in your relationships

When you stop playing the "blame game" and recognize that what you think, say, and do has an immediate impact on how you feel, you are empowered to do something different and thus to create different results. As a parent, having this awareness will broaden your range of options for dealing with your children. It will also enable you to empower your kids by helping them to take responsibility for the quality of their relationships.

Principle number eight: Self-observation
is the key to change

If you gain nothing else from this book besides the habit of paying attention to what you are doing, thinking, and saying, and you become aware of the impact of these factors on you and on your family, then you've gained a life-changing tool. When you are self-observant, you become self-aware. When you are self-aware, you have the ability to evaluate whether or not your choices are serving you. If they are not serving you, you are able to make new choices.

This skill can assist you in becoming aware of how you are treating your children, how you are speaking to them, and what you are teaching them. You can develop your children's ability to be self-observant by periodically asking them, "How are you feeling right now?" or, "What is going on with you right now?" or, "What were you thinking about when you started to feel that way?" Then help them to explore the thoughts that are creating their feelings. Teaching them to self-inquire and to check their self-talk for accuracy will help them to take control of their experiences. Teaching them to become self-aware will be giving them a tool they can use forever.

Principle number nine: Change can (only) happen in a moment

When you try to transform yourself or your marriage or your life or your family all at once, it may seem overwhelming and impossible. Instead, recognize that you cannot alter anything other than the moment, but you do have the power to do that. In altering the moment, you alter the future. Every time you transform a moment by realigning with your goal of creating healthy communication and joyful relationships based in love, you create a ripple effect that touches the next moment and the next. Once you have repeatedly turned bad moments into positive ones until the bad ones are few and far between, you will have changed your children's lives.

Teaching your children to be powerful over the moment will serve them in managing their emotions, relationships, career, and health, that is, every aspect of their lives.

Principle number ten: Relationships are a spiritual journey

Spiritual qualities are the same qualities that foster healthy relationships. As we help kids to identify which qualities they appreciate in others, and to identify, evoke, and develop those qualities in themselves, we assist them in a very important spiritual process: nurturing and enhancing who they really are. How they get along with others, their sense of belonging, and their belief in their abilities and in their inherent value will hugely impact how they feel about themselves and their lives. As I mentioned early in the book, the three R's of education don't include teaching relationship skills—or spiritual ones. Thus, children need our help with these concepts, which are the subject matter of the next chapter.

The EROS Equation

The understanding you have gained of the EROS equation will help you tremendously in being effective with your children. Improving your ability to change outcomes and find solutions is the key to your empowerment as a parent.

We have learned that what other people say and do falls into the category of an event. As your children say and do things that challenge you, rather than trying to change them, examine your responses. Choose responses that are in alignment with both who you really are and what you are trying to create. Even if you don't apply anything else from this book, learning to tap into the powerful combination of self-observation and the EROS equation can transform your marriage, your children, and your level of happiness. This is truly your power tool.

When I was counseling in an intermediate school, one student had mental and developmental disabilities that prevented him from being able to speak or hear well. He was very loving and kind, but he had a tendency to run away, so an aide was required to be with him at all times. One day I saw him "on the loose," all by himself. He was moving very quickly toward the edge of campus. Being the only one around, I tried to detain him, but he slipped past me and began to run. I started after him in hot pursuit. Since my efforts to control him had failed, I resorted to following him around the campus in an attempt to be sure he remained safe and to keep an eye on his whereabouts until he could be caught. We went around a corner and came upon the special-education teacher engaged in an activity with his students. When the teacher saw us he simply turned toward the student, smiled, and held his arms open wide. Much to my surprise, the boy whom I had been chasing ran to the teacher and embraced him in a hug. Humbled, to say the least, I was reminded that love and respect have much greater qualities of attraction than control and ego do. My responses to the event were not in alignment with who I really was or with who the student really was, and consequently they failed to create the results I desired.

You can teach your children to use the EROS equation by helping them learn to separate the event from their response to the event. You can help them see how their responses lead to the outcomes they experience and the solutions they create. They can begin to see that it isn't the event (friends, parents, school, what someone said) that makes them feel the way they do, but rather how they respond to the event. With this understanding they will begin to see how all of their actions have consequences, and how, if they want to participate in certain behaviors or actions, they are also *choosing* the associated consequences, as opposed to believing that consequences happen *to* them. This is an important concept to remember and teach your children, since you, as the parent, are often the one who must enforce the consequences. When you are fair and consistent in the way you respond to their behavior, they will begin to really see how the principle of cause and effect works in their lives, an understanding that will serve them well.

The Guideposts

Most families have guideposts—values, rules, and beliefs by which they operate—but for most these are vague, undefined, unspoken, and often inconsistent. We have discussed how it can be valuable to your marriage to identify your values, determine what you want, develop your code of ethics, and become clear about what you are committed to. Establishing these guideposts will definitely also help you as parents. Go back and take a look at the guideposts you (and hopefully your spouse) identified in Chapter 3. Amend or add to them as necessary to clarify guideposts for your entire family. First, and most important, the guideposts you identified will help shape your and your spouse's behavior when interacting with the kids and making family decisions, but the impact can be considerably greater than that. Imagine a home in which all the family members knew what the family values were and agreed to live in alignment with them. Imagine a home in which the family had developed a code of ethics and posted it on the refrigerator, along with rules for how to handle disagreements. Anyone could refer to or remind each other of the agreements at any time. Imagine if the family developed a set of vows that each person agreed to uphold, not just the parents. Imagine a healthy, strong family. . . .

One of the funnest workshops I ever offered was on developing family values. After a discussion of the importance of values, I explained the concept of symbols and talked about the symbolism in the American flag. I assigned the task of developing a family flag. Each family member decided on a symbol that represented him or her. Some used animals, some used shapes, and some used words. Each family then decided together which values they wanted to include on their flag, and they came up with symbols for those values. Some used religious symbols; some used hearts to remind them to prioritize love. They determined how the symbols should be laid out on their flag, utilizing repetition, borders, colors, and variations in size. At the end of the evening, each family displayed and explained its flag to the rest of the group. The experience itself was fun and insightful, and I like to imagine that each family posted its flag in a prominent place at home, where it could remind members of the values they stood for and of their individual strengths and contributions to the household.

EXERCISE ∾ *Make a family flag. Use symbols, colors, and different sizes to incorporate your family values. If you are really industrious, you can turn this activity into a social studies lesson by first examining and discussing flags from around the world. As a variation to enhance self-esteem, you can have each family member make an individual flag based upon his or her own good qualities and talents.* ∾

Understanding the Role of Self-Esteem

The awareness you have gained of how self-esteem gets damaged as children grow up and how to turn this process around will prove invaluable in enhancing the self-esteem of your children. Of course, understanding alone won't do the trick. Since your own self-esteem impacts every aspect of your life—and your children's—you have to do the work to transform it. As you raise your own level of self-esteem, you will find that your resources for helping your children improve.

To enhance the self-esteem of your children, you have to model healthy self-esteem, say esteeming things to them, let them know they are appreciated and important, and acknowledge them. Guide them to understand that who they really are is not the weak, scared self or the controlling, defiant self, but rather the strong, wise, capable self that is artistic, creative, expressive, loving, and fun. As they get older, you will need to show them the difference between spirit and ego. If your children are still small (generally under the age of six), observe them closely because they will be the ones teaching *you* about spirit.

The key here is to remember the layers. The behavior you see in others is usually the "glitter," that is, how they want the world to see them. The glitter is generally their defense mechanism, designed to keep out pain, but it is not their authentic self. The glitter covers the "oil," which is how they see themselves—generally as insufficient and "not enough." Under all of this is who they really are, their authentic self, the pure, sparkling "water," the source. The authentic self is loving, thoughtful, creative, wise, and has a great sense of humor. As parents, or as partners, the secret is to see past the ego-driven behaviors that stem from anger, hurt, and fear, past the glitter and the oil, to who the person really is, to his or her heart and soul. When you speak from your spirit instead of your ego, and to a loved one's spirit instead of to his or her ego, your relationships and your loved ones' self-esteem will be elevated to a whole new level.

A common misconception is the belief that building self-esteem in children means that we overlook what they do wrong and only focus on what they do right. This is not accurate. Rather, building self-esteem in the face of poor behavior requires separating the deed from the doer, focusing on the *behavior* that is unacceptable or bad rather than implying that the *child* is unacceptable or bad. For instance, notice the difference between these two statements: "You are a bad child for writing on the walls" versus "Writing on the walls is unacceptable behavior." One comment is based in ego and judgment, and the other is based in education. Both may have the exact same consequence in terms of a time-out, a privilege taken away, or having to clean off the walls, but your response will determine the outcome in terms of the way the child feels about himself (and you). Providing fair and consistent discipline when necessary is also an important part of developing emotionally healthy individuals. Erratic or unjust discipline can do just the opposite.

Sometimes adults think they *want* the child to feel bad about him- or herself when he or she does something wrong, but this thinking is problematic. (This is how limiting beliefs are formed.) When a child begins to think that who they really are is a bad kid, they are going to align their behavior with that belief. If, instead, when they misbehave, you say things to them like, "Wow, it isn't like you to be mean to

> **Did you know?** From the ages of one to twelve, the single most important determinant of children's self-esteem is their perception of how much they are valued by their parents.

your little brother; you are usually so kind and considerate," you have reinforced the reality that acting poorly is not the child's natural behavior, and you have reinforced the idea that his or her true nature is to be good. When we think (or know) that who we really are is a powerful, kind, loving, spiritual, wise, capable, caring being, we are far more likely to behave that way. It is our responsibility as parents to teach this message.

In listening to kids and teenagers I have learned the following:

- They are watching you, more than listening to you, for their example.

- They want you to love them, to let them know you do, and to show them that love.

- They want to please you; they thrive on acknowledgment.

- They want you to appreciate and notice them; they need your attention. If they don't get it from the positive things they do, they will get it in other ways.

- They want you to notice what they are doing and what is going on in their lives and to guide them with love when they are off track.

- They want you to guide them and warn them, and then trust them to act responsibly.

- They want you to let them learn from the natural consequences of their mistakes.

- They want you to be fair and consistent—not wishy-washy and lenient, nor strict and controlling.

- They want you to reprimand or correct them privately and praise them publicly.

- They want you to stay in the present moment instead of reminding them of their past mistakes. This allows them to learn from and move beyond errors of the past.

- They want you to be responsible and to encourage them to be responsible. They want you to show them, not just tell them, how to be good people.

- They want you to take care of yourselves. It is painful to them when they hear about the dangers of smoking and drinking at school, and then come home to a house full of those behaviors. They are afraid of losing you when they know that your choices aren't healthy.

- They want and need some semblance of spiritual life. Whether the family is religious or not, kids need to have a sense of the sacred, powerful aspect of themselves and of all that is around them.

- They want you to separate the deed from the doer. They want you to remember that they are good children who sometimes do bad things.

- They want you to spend time with them. They want to have fun and play with you so that chores and homework aren't the only things they spend time doing when they are with you. Recreation re-creates families as well as relationships.

Sounds a bit like what your spouse wants, and like what you probably want from your marriage, doesn't it?

Creativity is an important characteristic of the esteemed child. Developing and nurturing your children's creativity will go a long way toward helping them to solve problems and bring forth their authentic, capable, and powerful selves. Creativity is a quality that empowers and frees us. When we are stuck—whether personally, professionally, or in relationships—we are generally unable to see our options. When we can tap into our creative self, we become able to see solutions, make discoveries, express ourselves, and fuel our goals and dreams; we become resourceful, able to tap into our own true source. This source is full of unlimited ideas, wisdom, ability, and, of course, love. Part of our human purpose is to learn to express our creative spirit in all we do.

For many of us, creativity is one of those qualities that gets seriously blocked. Somewhere along the line we start to believe that we can't sing, act, draw, or write. This happens either because our creative spirit was never nurtured in the first place or because someone teased us, put us down, or criticized our creative expression. Since this creative aspect is precious to us and is a core part of our authentic self, we immediately put it into hiding to protect it. For many of us, it still remains hidden.

Parents play a critical role in developing children's creativity and in encouraging them to express it. Since creativity is part of their (our) core nature, just like love, it is more a matter of clearing the obstacles blocking its expression than it is an issue of developing something that isn't already there. Kids need ample opportunities to develop their imaginations and artistic selves. They need to color on blank pages, rather than just between the lines. They need to sing and dance and playact. They need to be encouraged to write or recite stories and poems from their imaginations and their worlds of make-believe. They need to simply play and create without criticism.

When I was a little girl, I was lying on my bed coloring on my sheets. My mom came in the room and caught me drawing. Of course, she made me stop immediately. She exclaimed, "Stop that! Wait until I get you permanent markers so that your art doesn't wash out!" She knew what was really important.

 Love Tip: As your self-esteem improves, you will find that your relationships do, too!

The Self-Esteem Self-Assessment

By assessing your own self-esteem and seeing where you have gaps between how you see yourself and how you think you should be, you become better equipped to do the work necessary to bridge the gaps. Simply gaining the perspective that the gaps in your self-esteem are measurable and that there are usually concrete steps you can take toward bridging them is powerful.

You can also use this concept to help your kids identify the areas of their lives that may need work, and you can help them set goals for their own self-esteem enhancement. Remember, though, that the power of the assessment tool is that it is a *self*-assessment, not someone else's assessment of you. If you share this tool with your spouse or children, be sure to let them assess themselves and determine their own areas of desired change rather than telling them where you think they have gaps.

Once your children identify potential areas of improvement for themselves, you can help them see how they can make changes one baby-step at a time. For instance, let's say you want them to begin cleaning their room. To move one step closer toward a clean room would require, say, making the bed every morning. Work with your child to master the step, perhaps creating a chart so that he or she can see progress, and acknowledge your child's success when he or she has mastered the task. Then move on to putting the dirty clothes away. As you break tasks into manageable steps and acknowledge success at each phase, your children will be strengthened to tackle the next step. You may also notice a much greater level of harmony in the household than when you expect them to achieve the whole task of having a clean room all at once. Remember, change only happens moment to moment. Be sure to celebrate small successes!

When I taught school, I used to mark what the kids got right on a test or homework instead of what they got wrong. I wanted my students to look at a graded spelling test with ten questions and think, "I got seven right!" instead of thinking, "I got three wrong." I wanted their work to affirm what they *could* do instead of emphasizing what they couldn't. I wanted them to walk away with the belief and attitude that they could spell. What I didn't expect when I made the switch to catching them doing it right was the shift in *me*, as the teacher. When I was spending my weekends and evenings grading what they did wrong, I almost felt like I was wasting my time when they got all the answers right. If there were no marks on the page, my job of grading wasn't really necessary. I imagine firemen feel kind of the same way when no one calls in a fire. The "bad news" validates our jobs. But making the switch to marking what my students did right emphasized the validity of my job. Suddenly I was rooting for them to do well instead of looking for what they did wrong so that I could "make my mark." Unexpectedly, both my students' attitudes and my own shifted as a result.

Steps for Turning It All Around

The steps are as follows:

- **Wake up and remember who you really are, who you are capable of being, and what you want.** At the same time, remember who your spouse and children really are, too.

- **Self-observe.** Notice where you are now; what is happening in your marriage, your life, and your family; and what needs your attention.

- **Let go of your ego and reconnect with your authentic self.** By clearing away ego obstacles you will reestablish access to your authentic self in any given moment. Look past the egos of your spouse and children to help them see their authentic selves, too.

- **Take action in alignment with who you really are and what you want to create.**

The more you consciously apply these steps, the more automatic they become. As is the case with the self-esteem self-assessment, the first step, waking up, requires taking a serious look at who you want to be and what you want for your family. Step two involves paying attention to what is actually happening. When you wake up to who you really are and what is really happening in your family and in your life, many of the changes start to come automatically, simply because you noticed what was going on. Allow your discoveries to motivate you.

 *Love Tip:* Things seldom improve from neglect.

Imagine driving on a freeway and realizing that you are unconsciously drifting into the next lane. When this happens you automatically self-adjust. Likewise, when you realize that your children are depressed instead of alive and vital, it is time to self-adjust. When you realize you've gained ten pounds and the scale is still climbing, it is time to self-adjust. When you notice that you and your spouse haven't made love in a month, it is time to do something about it.

EXERCISE *What have you been pretending not to notice? Consciously assess what is going on with your kids and with the atmosphere of your household.*

Letting go of ego when dealing with your children is not always easy, but it is always important. We adults may find it tricky to notice when we are being responsible guides versus when we are being control freaks, or when we are being loving versus when we are being needy. One of these responses comes from our authentic self and the other comes from ego. Ego tells the kids to do something and when they ask "Why," it answers, "Because I told you to," without giving an explanation, or perhaps even without reason. Of course children need to be taught to obey their parents' directions without question, but parents need to be taught to question their directions. Controlling for the sake of controlling only creates rebellion. Guiding with reason and responsibility creates respect—and wise children.

I was once leading a walking meditation on the labyrinth and had just finished telling the participants that there were no rules for right or wrong ways to walk. I encouraged them to be self-observant and to notice if they found themselves unconsciously following "rules," and to recognize that the rules were of their own making. I told them to notice whether the rules they followed were serving them or not, and, if not, to consciously choose rules that did serve them. One little girl began running joyfully, weaving her way among the very serious adults, who were walking slowly. I pulled the little girl aside and asked her to walk quietly in prayer. I suddenly became self-observant and realized I had just told the adults that there was no right or wrong way to experience the labyrinth. For some reason I wasn't applying my own rules to children. I had to stop and realign my words and actions to make them congruent and authentic. I took a deep breath, let go of my ego need to control the experience, and released the child to run again.

The power of the steps listed above is that they will guide you to making conscious choices about how you treat yourself, how you treat your spouse, and how you treat your kids. The more conscious you become and the more aligned your words, thoughts, and actions are with love, the more powerful you will be at manifesting the kind of marriage, family, and life you desire. You will be raising your kids with the voice and words of your most authentic self; you will be calmer, clearer, and more effective.

Our words are incredibly powerful. In prayers and chants we combine words and symbols in a certain order and with a certain intention to bring about a sense of peace and spirituality. If you want to create a certain effect in the magical world of Harry Potter, you cast a "spell," which is simply a specific, intentional combination of words or symbols. In the everyday world, when we want to affect things or people in a certain way, we use words, which are simply letters (symbols) arranged with intention into a certain order. When we position letters into words we call it "spelling."

When we string words into a sentence, we can literally "sentence" others to a life of loving themselves or a life of hating themselves. This is particularly true of young children, who are so open that their defenses—especially toward those whom they love the most—are not built up yet. As loving, responsible adults, we must be extra conscious of the words we use around our children. Likewise, we must be aware of the impact of the words we use about our relationships and ourselves when we are in the presence of children. They are always learning from us. Be sure you consciously choose words that are in line with what you want to create. When speaking to your spouse and family, aligning your words with who you really are and with your goals will make a huge difference. Again, this is where being conscious of your self-talk and teaching your kids to be conscious of their self-talk is really important. All it takes to feel bad is to think bad things about yourself. All it takes to feel good is to think good things about yourself. Amazingly, our thoughts about each other carry some weight, too. When you want to turn any relationship around, start with your thoughts and words.

Love Tip: "Sticks and stones may break my bones, but words can break my heart." Words have an amazing ability to hurt or heal, and the effects can last a lifetime. Be careful not to inflict wounds on the hearts of others—or on your own heart.

While often easier said than done, it is critically important to take care of yourself by allowing yourself time to strengthen and rejuvenate so that you have the patience, tolerance, and consciousness to take care of your family. When you're flying, the flight attendants instruct you to respond to a change in cabin pressure by first putting the oxygen mask on yourself and *then* assisting your children. Similarly, in response to life's pressures you have to take care of yourself to be able to assist your family. You have to manage your emotions to be able to help your loved ones manage theirs. If you pay attention to when you are getting out of alignment with your authentic self and with your goals, you will know it is time to take a break. You can go for a walk, get together with a friend, write in a journal, get a facial or body massage, play golf, go to the gym, meditate, go to church— whatever strengthens and restores you. We all aim to do the best we can with the resources we have, but when our resources diminish, doing our best becomes more difficult. Resources for dealing with stress include sleep, health, food, exercise, fellowship with loved ones, meditation, prayer, and time in silence. We must allow ourselves to rejuvenate. To be "re-source-ful" means to be "once again full of Source." When you find your resources getting low and your abilities being stretched, reconnect to Source.

He bugs me, he bugs me not

Dear Eve,

I work with this guy a couple of days a week who I just don't like. He kind of bugs me — nothing really bad. He doesn't seem to have common sense, so he'll talk too loud, ask things that are none of his business, and just gener- ally be annoying. He is good at his work, so he isn't going anywhere. I dread it every time I have to work with him. Any suggestions?

Aloha,

One of the best lessons I've ever learned revolves around the concept that you can't step into the same river twice (meaning that the river is always flowing, so by the time you step into it again everything about it has changed). The same holds true for people; we never encounter the exact same person twice. This is a good reminder that in any given moment the people in our lives can change, improve, or evolve, if we allow them to. Between the last time you worked with this guy and the next time, he could have had new ideas, made new friends, lost old friends, read a book, seen a movie or documentary, fallen in love, fallen out of love.... He could have had a life-changing experience.

What I mean by "if we allow them to" is that we tend to label people as "bad" or "annoying" or whatever, and then to hold them in a box labeled with our expectations. We expect them to be the way they were last time we saw them, and we either look for evidence that matches our expectations or we never give them another chance. We tend to treat them in a way that evokes what we expect to see. This is not to say it is our fault that they show up the way they do; rather, it is to point out that we may have a part in the play without realizing it.

For instance, there is almost no chance that your "dread" doesn't affect your attitude and the way you treat your coworker. Maybe it manifests as a withdrawal of your energy, a rolling of the eyes, or a sarcastic "good morning," but however your dread shows up in your behavior, it is likely affecting his behavior, too. When we shift our attitudes and expectations, we open the door for the possibility that the other person will change. We may even find ways to bring out the best in others if we shift our energy in that direction.

I once had a student who was particularly challenging. He was in my class for several periods each day. When I dreaded having him come to class, my attitude was not welcoming, and he played off my (bad) attitude beautifully. He was obnoxious, disrespectful, and annoying. When he came in late, if I gave him a hard time, I set up his attitude for the rest of the period. When, instead, I welcomed him into the classroom with a smile and acknowledged his effort to get there, we stood a fifty-fifty chance that the period would go well rather than a 100-percent chance that it would not. He often then revealed his funny, clever side. This is not to say that consequences shouldn't be given for coming late, but a consequence works much better if it comes from a desire to educate rather than punish the other person. (It is interesting to note that the root word for "punish" is related to the root word for "pain," while the root of "discipline" means "learn" or "teach.")

If you make working with your colleague a "game" in which you see if you can bring out the best in him by bringing out the best in yourself when you're around him, although you may not succeed in changing him, you will definitely change the situation into something more fun for you. You

may find that in the process you shift into acceptance of
who and how he is and that his behaviors simply don't
bother you anymore.

With aloha,

Eve

Embracing Change, Managing Emotions, and Communicating Clearly

As children and teenagers learn to deal with their ever-changing emotions, they will evoke all of yours. Taking advantage of the tools provided in Chapters 7 and 8 of this book will prove immensely valuable to you in working with your kids.

Whenever your emotions arise, notice whether they come from the present moment or from the past. I have always maintained that we have to heal the child/teenager on the inside in order to work with the child/teenager on the outside. Otherwise, we end up projecting our stuff on to the kids when it isn't really about them. You can do a quick check to see where your own issues may be by simply answering this question: If you could have your kids skip over any ages, which ages would they be? Your answer is likely a reflection of the age at which you still have unfinished business from your own childhood. We tend to avoid that which we don't want to face.

When I was teaching school I clearly stated, "I'll teach kindergarten through fifth grade, but I don't want to teach sixth grade or above." When I looked back on my own education, I loved school until just before sixth grade, and then my experience went downhill. My teenage years were full of poor choices arising from low self-esteem. In spite of a wonderful, loving, and spiritual family, as a teenager I began "looking for love in all the wrong places." Of course, the universe has a way of putting us into situations that allow us to learn what we need to learn in order to heal the past, so I immediately got assigned the task of being a middle-school counselor to sixth-, seventh-, and eighth-grade students. Later I ended up working with teenagers.

I remember the first time a girl came to me and told me she was having sex. To the dismay of my new husband, I went home and sat on the couch and cried for hours. Quite worried, my husband said, "Eve, you can't bring the kids' problems home with you like this." I honestly replied, "I'm not crying for her, I'm crying for me." Hearing about her poor choices made me relive and look at all of my own poor choices as a teenager. It was obvious that in order to help the students I was working with, I needed to clean up my own emotions regarding my past choices. Otherwise I would be counseling "me" instead of truly seeing and guiding them.

When things your children do or say plug you into your emotions, remember who you really are and what you want to create. Self-observe and notice what is going on with you. Are your emotions about you or them? If they are about you, you have a couple of options. You can either put your awareness about your unresolved issues aside to handle later, or you can instead choose to do some work on yourself now. Notice whether your ego needs for approval or control are flaring up. If so, take a deep breath, transcend your ego, and realign with your authentic self. Choose words that are in alignment with what you want to create. Always remember that the bottom line is love. Utilize the total-truth exercise in Chapter 8 for expressing your anger, hurt, or fear. Use it also when new integrity agreements need to be made or old ones need to be repaired.

I have used the process of expressing the mountain of emotions hiding under anger with kids in my classroom with great results. Once, when a student wasn't doing his assignment, I went over to talk to him. He explained to me that his friends had kicked him off the football team and he was so upset that he couldn't work. He provided a great reminder to me that until students' emotions are managed they are going to have a tough time getting to work. I knew a "teachable moment" when I saw one. I explained the stages of anger to him, and instead of forcing him to do the assignment I encouraged him to write a letter to his team describing the total truth of how he felt, complete with an account of his part in the situation and what he agreed to do differently. When the next recess bell rang, he ran outside with letter in hand. I held my breath, not knowing what a bunch of fifth-grade boys would do or say upon hearing a letter about another boy's feelings. I was worried that I may have set him up to be ridiculed, which was obviously not my intent. When recess was over he ran back in, smiled broadly, and said, "It worked! I'm back on the team!" He went straight to work while I said a prayer of gratitude and gave a sigh of relief.

Pay special attention to the guidelines for receiving your spouse's emotions (Chapter 8) and apply them here, to your children. Your children need to know that it is safe to talk to you. If telling you the truth about mistakes they have made or concerns they have is only going to get them into trouble, they are going to be far less willing to be honest with you or to talk to you at all. When they know that you will love them unconditionally while simultaneously guiding them and holding them accountable, they will learn to trust you.

The more you communicate your faith in your children to do the right thing and make the right choices, the more they will believe in their own ability to do so. When a person knows that his or her authentic self is honest, good, capable, trustworthy, and loving, it feels uncomfortable to do anything that is out of alignment with those qualities. When your kids tell you about mistakes they have made, help them identify what they could have done differently that would be more in alignment with who they really are—and with how you expect them to behave.

As we have established, communication is critical both to building relationships and to maintaining them. This is just as true for families as it is for marriages. Studies have shown that mothers spend an average of fourteen and a half minutes a day in dialogue with their children, and fathers an average of twelve and a half minutes. Eight and a half of those minutes are spent arguing about what needs to be done or what has been done, that is, directing and correcting. That leaves only four to six minutes a day for creating, maintaining, and building the relationship, developing self-esteem, sharing feelings, solving problems, deepening values and spirituality, sharing family stories and history, exploring the world of wonder, and educating.

Obviously, this isn't enough time. We need to make sure we give time to the things—and people—that matter most.

The process of intellectual foreplay can definitely be applied to communicating with children and teens (albeit with a different name). After my book *Intellectual Foreplay* was first published, a family wrote and told me that they used it around their table every night with their teenagers. They would pick one question a night and discuss each person's answers. Another couple reported that they used it in the car with their kids when they were on long drives. Obviously, choosing or modifying questions so they are appropriate for kids is important. It doesn't require a lot of extra thought to generate "table topics" for families to discuss. A search on the Internet for "family table topics" or "sentence stems" will yield you enough to talk about for a century! You can also generate your own list based on your family's values and interests. Sentence stems are incomplete sentences that each family member completes. Sometimes kids find it easier to work with sentence stems than with open-ended questions. So instead of asking, "When are you happiest?" ask your kids to complete the sentence, "I'm happiest when I. . . ." Here are some other examples that would be good for kids and families:

My best moment today was . . .

My favorite place to be alone is . . .

The things I like about my best friend are . . .

The things I like best about myself are . . .

What I want most for my birthday is . . .

My strengths are . . .

I want to learn how to . . .

I'm proud of myself when . . .

Truly, the topics are endless. Think back to the list of values you generated in Chapter 3 and form sentence stems related to them. That way, in addition to communicating with each other you are also developing and deepening family values. For instance, if the value is "service," the sentence stem for discussion might be, "The service I plan to provide this week is. . . ." Or if the value is "friendship," the sentence stem could be, "I am a good friend because I. . . ."

Although questions about hypothetical situations can be good for simple entertainment value, keeping the topics related to things like self-esteem, spirituality, values, and relationships can serve the additional purpose of strengthening your family members' sense of who they are. By utilizing sentence stems or questions related to emotions, you can help your kids grow up to be emotionally available and expressive. Here are some examples:

I'm saddest when . . .

I get angry when . . .

Sometimes I feel . . .

I get scared when . . .

What I really hope is . . .

Someday I look forward to . . .

Set up family guidelines before you start talking. Utilize the guidelines for engaging in intellectual foreplay outlined in Chapter 8, and monitor the discussion so that no one gets laughed at or criticized when they share. It is very important that your kids feel listened to, safe, and respected, or the whole experience will backfire.

Romance and Love

What a wonderful experience it would be to have a whole family planning "romantic" little surprises for each other based in love. Refer to the suggestions in Chapter 9 for reigniting love, and use them to keep the love aflame in the whole family. Write each other notes, affirm your love for each other, compliment each other, write love poetry about your family.

One of the biggest complaints from married people is that when children arrive, romance and sexuality go out the door. This is certainly understandable, but it is generally not acceptable. One man shared with me, "It just didn't make sense. Our child was conceived from our love and sexuality, and then the minute he was born our love and sexuality began to diminish until it just disappeared and we got divorced." Make the commitment to yourself and to your spouse to keep the love, romance, and sexuality alive between you. Show your kids how loving spouses treat each other.

My mom, as a young mother of four, used to say, "Babies are our only business, and your spouse is just your oldest child." She meant this in terms of the love and nurturing required to care for a spouse, not in a belittling way.

Just as recreation can re-create a marriage, it is also vital to the family. Make sure that you take time away from phones, computers, bills, and responsibilities to play together. It is so easy to get caught up in the busy-ness of our lives that we forget to do the very things that make life—and families—fun. In addition to potentially serving the purpose of rest and relaxation, recreation is a building block for your relationships with each other.

Playtime is also important because it tends to evoke laughter. Laughter is one of life's great joys. Maintaining a sense of humor can make the worst situations manageable. Remember, though, that ego laughs *at* each other, but spirit laughs *with* each other.

The Physical Touch

While obviously the sexual suggestions provided in Chapter 10 are strictly for you and your spouse, there is no doubt that your kids will benefit from the shift in attitude and mood when you and your spouse create ways to revitalize your sexual intimacy. Since kids learn from your example, they will benefit from the display of loving behavior that results when you and your spouse make love behind closed doors.

Since the value of touch is so great for health, well-being, and a sense of connection to others, modeling nonsexual, nonthreatening touch and providing it to your children will help develop their sense of belonging. Hugs, hand and foot massages, shoulder rubs, back rubs, and holding hands are all wonderful ways to express your nurturing and love. When your kids or teenagers receive appropriate nonsexual touch at home, hopefully they will be less desperate to seek any physical touch they can get outside of the home.

Each day at the beginning of class I used to stand at my classroom door for "H-and-H," which stood for "hug or handshake." The students got to choose which one they wanted. My goal was to make contact with each of my children every day because I had discovered that there were some who were masters at disappearing. They would do what they were told and keep really quiet while those who were desperate for attention stole the show. I realized that a day or two could easily go by without my ever talking to certain students one-on-one. Once I instituted H-and-H, that all changed. The kids—boys and girls alike—loved it. They would run back to the end of the line so they could have another hug. Unlike all the other kids in the class, one boy chose a handshake each day throughout the whole year. Although there was nothing wrong with his choice, I assumed that H-and-H wasn't working for him. During parent conferences at the end of the year, however, his mom told me what a difference H-and-H had made to her son. She said he had become much more loving and that he came home every day and hugged her. I was thrilled to hear this. Having the student hug me wasn't the point of the exercise. Having him seek out other appropriate people and family members to hug was a great result.

EXERCISE ⌇ *Make a point of connecting heart to heart with each child (and your spouse) every day. The older your children are, the more conscious on your part this action will need to become.* ⌇

CHAPTER 12

marriage as a
spiritual journey

To love another person is to help them love God.

SØREN KIERKEGAARD

A seeker once asked a holy man, "How do I measure my spiritual progress?" The holy man replied, "Look to your relationships."

Our relationships are the barometer of how spiritually we are living. How spiritually we live is obviously different from how religious we are. You can be devout, go to church, say prayers, read scriptures, and meditate, but *living* spiritually is another issue. Living spiritually requires unconditional love and acceptance of both yourself and others. Living spiritually requires compassion and forgiveness. Living spiritually means that you have integrity; your words and actions are aligned with your authentic self, or you take responsibility when they are not. Living spiritually means that you recognize and honor the fact that your life is a spiritual journey and thus requires you to step back and look at the "big picture," knowing that every moment, every interaction, every person on your path offers you an opportunity to reveal your authentic, spiritual self. The very same skills required for us to live spiritually are required for us to maintain healthy, loving marriages.

Relationships: We Can't Grow
Without Them

In Chapter 1, I raised the question of why you should do all this work to transform your marriage. The answer is because you are here to

313

learn, to love, to laugh, and to serve. The entire reason for our existence is to love and be loved. It isn't necessary to be married or in a romantic relationship to learn to love, but love is our soul essence, and we are here to reveal and share that essence in everything we do—including our marriages. These are the only tasks we really need to do. The rest is just entertainment, the practice grounds for learning and applying what we know. Relationships are the ultimate place, if not the *only* place, where we can truly grow. They give us feedback. They give us material to work with. They hold up a mirror in which we can see ourselves.

In some cultures people remind each other of their true essence through their greetings. In India, people greet each other by saying "namaste," which (I am told) means, "The divine in me greets the divine in you." In Hawaii we say "aloha," which means more than simply hello or goodbye. Dr. Serge King explains that the word "aloha" comes from the combination of several words: *alo* means to be present to share an experience; *oha* means the joy of greeting someone you love; *ha* is life, breath, spirit. Thus, "aloha" means the joyful (*oha*) sharing (*alo*) of life energy (*ha*) in the present (*alo*). When you greet others, whether total strangers or those you love, remember that the purpose of your interaction is to illuminate the best in each other or, at the very least, to reveal the best in you.

Since our lives are made up of relationships—with our spouses, children, parents, siblings, friends, teachers, students, coworkers, employers, employees, customers, strangers, animals, God, and ourselves—there is no avoiding the importance of learning relationship skills, mastering our ability to get along with others, and learning to love ourselves. Unless you live alone in a cave in the Himalayas, you are going to have to interact with people, depend on people, and affect people. Even in a cave you'd still have to grapple with your relationship with yourself and with God.

♡ *Love Tip:* When you find yourself upset about serving your partner, stop serving your partner and start serving the divine within your partner. Serving egos and personalities will burn you out; serving God will uplift you.

Family as a Spiritual Journey

While it may be preferable that you and your spouse have religious or spiritual beliefs in common, it is more important that you honor and respect each other's beliefs and put them into practice in the way you live. My husband and I were raised in very different religious traditions, but we have in common a deep love of God and an overwhelming gratitude for the blessings in our lives. We can share these things every day, no matter what name each of us chooses to call God, how we honor God, or how we develop our spirituality.

EXERCISE ∾ *Refer to the list of values you generated in Chapter 3, and determine if you can take actions that will help you live in alignment with them. For instance, if "worshipping God" is on your list, what does this value look like to you in the form of a daily action? Does saying grace before meals do the trick, or does worshipping God mean more to you than that? Would meditating or praying every morning fulfill your worship of God? What would? If "being of service" is on your list, what can you do each day to move toward living in alignment with that value? If your spiritual practice is not on your list of values, ask yourself if adding it would be authentic for you.* ∾

Children (and adults) crave a sense of the sacred and the ability to express that aspect of themselves. Children are closer to their true nature than adults because they have lived through fewer experiences that might block the flow of love and authenticity. You can nurture your children's spirituality by fostering their understanding that any time they want to connect with source or with God, they simply need to get silent and listen to their inner voice of wisdom. Your children will undoubtedly be able to nurture your and your spouse's spiritual lives by sharing with you what they hear. Children are much less hesitant or doubtful about what they hear God saying.

Spiritual rituals help kids (and adults) put a form to something that is intangible. Help your children develop a daily ritual that honors their bodies, minds, spirits—and their capacity to love. Perhaps you can do a ritual each day that includes your whole family. Light a candle, say a prayer, offer a flower, pass a feather, share a hug, offer thanks, or watch the sun rise or set. It doesn't have to take long to be meaningful. Provide opportunities for your children so that any time they want to express their spirituality they can tap into their creativity and sing, dance, draw, or color their experience of God.

Getting outside into nature is a wonderful way to nurture your family's and your children's sense of wonder, beauty, awe, and appreciation. Author Richard Louv recently released a book with a subtitle that I love: *Last Child in the Woods: Saving our Children from Nature Deficit Disorder.* The idea that many children and adults suffer from "nature-deficit disorder" rings so true. When you were a child you probably played outside for many hours a day. Perhaps you collected worms, stomped in puddles, gathered flowers and feathers, and made forts and rivers in the yard. When many of today's children grow up, their memories are more likely to be of the computer technology they played with as children, which doubtless will no longer exist by then. They will remember watching television shows and playing computer games rather than building sand castles or playing hide-and-seek with the neighbors. Nature is God's creativity in full bloom, and we humans are so obviously a part of that creation. Experiences in nature give us a sense of awe and of unlimited possibilities. One cannot help but ponder life's mysteries when looking up at a night sky full of stars that were invisible by daylight but were there nonetheless. What else is always there that we simply can't see? Sitting in the presense of absolute beauty evokes a deep feeling of love that is lasting and can be shared. Being in nature also inspires a desire to be silent, to listen. That is when the whispers of God can be heard. Sharing these experiences with your family can create a powerful bond.

When your kids get older, you can serve them by remembering who they really are. You can also help them remember, and you can remind them when they forget. When I worked in a middle school with hormonal adolescents, I used to imagine that each one of them was God in disguise, that it was God's way of playing hide-and-seek with me. It was a fun game because some of them were extremely good camouflages. Once I was able to see through their disguises, it would move me to tears to walk into a classroom. Doing this with your own kids may not outwardly affect them, but it will affect you. When you remember who you are really raising, you will treat your family differently. While you are at it, remember that your spouse is simply God in disguise, too. Your job is to see past the exterior into the heart and to go from there.

Remember that this is also true of you. . . .

I once facilitated a labyrinth walk for a teen church group in Lahaina, Maui. When we arrived to set up the labyrinth, the Tongan community was holding its weekly service inside the church. We were serenaded by their angelic singing as we laid out the canvas labyrinth on the grass. Several local children gathered to watch and asked us what we were doing. As we did our best to explain it to them, we realized that any efforts to save the experience for the older kids was futile. We instructed them to take off their slippers and roller blades, and soon the labyrinth was swarming with running, laughing children. When the youth group was to begin its turn on the labyrinth, we asked the little ones to step aside. They obediently left the circle, only to stand patiently on the side, watching and waiting for their turn again. "Auntie," they cried, "when the big kids are done can we go again? Can we? Can we?"

The teens listened as I explained the nature of the metaphorical pilgrimage. They walked the labyrinth with a seriousness that was a marked contrast to the little ones' playful antics. After the walk, we sat in a circle to discuss our thoughts and feelings. The younger children came and sat with us, quietly soaking up the "adult" experience. When the older kids moved off to the side to have pizza, a few of the younger ones asked if they could now, finally, have their turn again. This time, rather than running around and treating it as a game, the children walked quietly in prayer, as they had seen their older brothers and sisters do. When there were only two little ones left on the labyrinth—a handsome four-year-old boy with a shaved head and a beautiful, sparkly-eyed seven-year-old girl—I decided to take my turn. When the three of us reached the center, we sat down cross-legged and closed our eyes. We all happened to open our eyes to sneak a "peek" at the others at the exact same time, prompting giggles from us all since we were all caught in the act. As I looked at these two beautiful children, I felt as if I were sitting with the young Dalai Lama and a young Mary or Holy Mother. Tears came to my eyes as I sat with them, humbled.

Then Malia, the little girl, said, "Okay, close your eyes, let's listen to God." We followed her instructions. Seconds later she said again, "Listen for God!" After several minutes, when the two children got up to walk out, I whispered, "Did you hear God?" They both smiled and nodded. I asked, "What did he say?" Malia looked thoughtful and then answered sweetly, "He said, 'I am always with you!'" She turned and followed the labyrinth path back out, knowing God was with her.

All kids need is a little guidance and an opportunity to experience and express their spirituality. All adults need is to listen to children to hear what God has to say.

Love Tip: Find a way to experience internal peace daily through meditation, exercise, or breathing deeply (without the use of substances). Return to that peaceful place within whenever you start to feel stress.

➤ HEATHER AND RIK, MARRIED THIRTEEN YEARS

I believe it is essential for each person in the marriage to see both partners as gifts from God rather than as possessions. To see each other as a gift from God and to connect with that Holy Being in marriage is a process that develops honor and respect. When we are able to receive the gift of ourselves from God, we are more able to offer that gift to each other and back to God, with freedom and love.

The lesson is yours

Dear Eve,

I met a guy about six months ago who was totally attracted to my spiritual life and the element of magic in my daily existence. When we first met he wanted to know everything I knew so he could experience the "magic," too. We soon got engaged and moved in together, and everything was going great. Then he started to get freaked out. I have an intense work ethic, and that includes work on my self-improvement. I think I overwhelmed him by expecting the same from him. I was trying to teach him and to share the light with him. Suddenly he began resisting doing anything spiritual or working on himself or our relationship and started playing video games several hours a day. As a single mom, I already have one child. I can't bear to have a partner who wastes time like this. I pushed him to stop, and he left. I really thought that his interest in the light was sincere and that we were going to share a long and happy life together. Now I just don't know. Any suggestions?

Aloha,

It sounds like you have taken on the role of "elder" or "teacher" and what your fiancé wanted was a partner and a lover. He responded to your parental role by turning into the rebellious teenager. My best suggestion, if your goal is to keep this man, is to stop trying to change him and stop trying to teach him. If he is ready, he will learn, whether you teach him or not. Continue growing and learning yourself. He will grow automatically by being in relationship with you; he can't help it. But to be told he needs to change is like saying he isn't okay, which touches all of his self-esteem issues.

There is a saying that goes something like this: "If you behave like Jesus, people will be drawn to you. It you talk about Jesus, people will be repelled from you." Spirituality is an experience of the heart, not of the head. When your boyfriend met you, he felt your love and your connection to spirit and was drawn to that light. When you started teaching him at every opportunity and talking about the light, you were no longer embodying it, and he was no longer able to feel it.

I suggest that you make a list of the qualities that are "spiritual and magical" and then look to see if anywhere on that list are words like "judgmental, controlling, ego, my way, my timeline, driven, full of expectations" — qualities that are implied in your letter. I'm guessing they aren't. If instead you see words like "unconditional love, spontaneity, miracles, magic, trust, acceptance, playfulness, process, God's timeline," take a step back

and consider the possibility that this relationship may
really be a spiritual lesson for you. View this relationship — whether it lasts or not — as the perfect classroom
for putting into practice what you hold dear. Put your
list of spiritual qualities to work in your relationship.
I often hear people claiming to be spiritual, but their
relationships are a mess. If you do nothing but apply
your spirituality to the realm of relationship, you will
quickly ascend. There is no better practice ground, but
your lessons are uniquely for you. Your partner's lessons
may be completely different.

Look for what he is teaching you. Perhaps he is able to
play, and you need someone to balance your intense work
ethic. Perhaps as a single mom you have kept your inner
child or inner teenager under absolute control all these
years, and that's why you go nuts when he plays games.
Stop and ponder which buttons of yours he manages to push,
and then see if you can figure out what it is about you
that you need to learn. Remember, it is all about you!
Pretend that none of what bothers you in him has anything
to do with him, and see what is revealed to you about you.
That is when and where the true spiritual work begins.

With aloha,

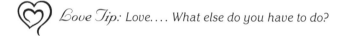
Love Tip: Love.... *What else do you have to do?*

Getting Through the Big Stuff

When big events happen in a marriage—infidelity, serious health issues, financial challenges, broken trust, deaths in the family—big decisions must be made. These are the times when you may question
everything you've ever believed about marriage, God, and divine order, and when your spirituality will be called upon to save your marriage or your sanity. These are the times when you must draw heavily
from your spiritual "bank account" and hope that you have enough
strength, faith, and wisdom saved up to see you through. It is time to

put into practice every skill you have gained and every tool at your disposal to determine what is the most authentic, inspired choice for you. Sometimes the choice will be to get out of the marriage, but often the greatest rewards come when you transcend your ego and find your way back to love and trust *within* the marriage. This is your opportunity to turn your "test" into your "testimony."

Big events serve as wake-up calls. Sometimes the message is "I am in a marriage that is not for the highest good of all involved; it is no longer serving any of us." Sometimes it is "I am not doing my part to make this marriage loving and healthy." Sometimes it is "I am not taking care of myself or loving myself enough to inspire being loved and taken care of." Sometimes it is "Wow, I have been taking everything and everyone for granted, and I need to shift into being more honoring and appreciative and expressive toward those whom I love." Whatever the message, allow the difficult times to reveal to you what you most need to see—in yourself.

> *Love Tip:* By saying a prayer of thanks for even the most devastating circumstances, you will open the door to your ability to see the emergence in the emergency.

A wake-up call affords the oportunity to explore deeper spiritual questions, for example, "Who are you without your ego? Who are you without your spouse? Who are you without your marriage? What is your life purpose? Are you fulfilling it? What can you do to take responsibility for the quality of your marriage and the quality of your life? Are you living appreciatively, vibrantly, kindly, authentically? Do you have integrity? What is really important? What really matters?" The more you enhance your self-esteem and access your authentic self, the stronger you will be and the easier you will find it to tap into that essence when needed.

In remembering who you really are, it is helpful to keep in mind who you are *not*. You are not your ego. You are not your fear. You are not your shame. You are not your body. You are not your finances. Nor is your partner any of these things. You are spirit. When the crap hits the fan, you are not only given the opportunity to "do what Jesus would do" or "do what Buddha would do" or Krishna or Mary or Moses or Mohammed. You are also given the time to figure out what *you* would do if you were not your ego but were instead a spiritual being. Ego comes to the conclusion that love and trust should be withdrawn, while spirit determines to go forth and love with trust more fully, albeit more wisely. This is not to say you have no right to be angry or scared, or to expect more or better. Certainly you may, but remember, these are the reactions of your ego, your small self. While they are very real and important to notice and experience, the key is not to get stuck there. The key is to transform your anger back to love, to move from focusing on your fear to focusing on that which your fear is trying to protect: what you treasure and care about. If you don't move from ego back into a healthy, manageable, and negotiable place, you are missing the true lesson. Even if you decide to get out of the marriage, which may be the best possible choice for you and your partner, you still have to decide from the heart, that is, from understanding and compassion, rather than from judgment and blame. Otherwise you will make the current situation more difficult and will also take the problem with you into whatever comes next.

If divorce becomes the only viable option for you, remember that divorce, too, is a spiritual journey. Divorce provides another opportunity to evoke your most spiritual self. Life is simply a pilgrimage, so *every* encounter provides this opportunity. One of the saddest things is when two people who loved each other, shared lives, grew together, and maybe even created children together begin acting mean, hateful, nasty, and vengeful toward each other. Although forgiveness, respect, and love are a service to others, we forgive others not just for their sake but for our own. We are respectful of others because it makes *us* feel better to be respectful. We transform the anger we hold toward someone so that *our* souls can reside in peace instead of turmoil. If you can't muster the energy to rise to your highest self for the other person's sake, do it for your own. Life is too short to spend it feeling worried, angry, and victimized. In fact, the point is to learn to *love* through life, not to merely *live* through it. Perhaps the question isn't so much what would *you* do if you were God, but what would you do if your *spouse,* or former spouse, were God?

When I was dealing with my mother's death and felt as though my world were imploding, a dear friend said, "Your ego thinks this is the worst experience of your life, but your spirit thinks it is the best." Our greatest spiritual growth comes during the most difficult moments, not the easiest.

➤ DEBRA AND JIM, MARRIED TWENTY-ONE YEARS

What has worked for us? Forgiveness, and I mean the really tough kind. I don't mean forgiveness for not putting the toilet seat down. I mean the kind of forgiveness it takes to mend a relationship when something major arises, the kind of forgiveness that you really have to dig deep for and that challenges you as a person. That's when you see what you are truly made of. That's when you see what your marriage is really worth to you.

Love Tip: We all have immense power to transform our relationships when we transcend our egos and let compassion and understanding do the work.

The following story, written by Karlene McCowan and excerpted from *Chicken Soup for the African American Soul,* beautifully illustrates the struggle between deciding to give up and deciding to take the necessary steps to love your marriage. "Getting out" is always an option, but, unless you are in a dangerous situation, see what happens when you decide to make it your very last option. Use everything at your disposal—including prayer—to give your marriage the nourishment it needs to thrive.

A MIRACLE FOR MY HEART

Imagine a boulder being jarred loose from its solid-rock foundation after a series of earthquakes. Can you see it perched precariously on a crumbling, rocky overhang midway down a steep mountainside, one aftershock away from violent descent and disintegration into millions of tiny fragments? If you have a mental picture of that, then you can visualize my marriage from 1991 to 1996. After nine sometimes challenging but mostly wonderful years, my standard response to any cheerful, "Hi, how are you?" was a flat, "Hey, just trying to stay married." And I wasn't trying to be funny. I was just keeping it real. But when had reality deteriorated to this? I had to dig deep to resurrect our first reality, the happy one, the beginning. . . .

Our first official date at a restaurant ended with us hanging out at his mother's house with his sister and her boyfriend. Lots of talking and laughing, meaningful glances, teasing, testing. But more than anything, I remember feeling incredibly comfortable and connected. Somewhere near the end of the evening, this funny, spiritual, musical, ambitious, solid-rock-steady, bold, beautiful Black man became the brand-new owner of my heart. Gradually, the tart aftertaste from my previous relationship was displaced by the fresh sweetness of our romance. We laughed and played, kissed and cuddled, shared and dreamed. I didn't have to wonder what heaven was like. Being with this man was the closest I'd ever come to being on hallowed ground. Now, don't get me wrong. Naturally, I'd always understood God as holy and Creator, but I'd never experienced Him as friend and companion. I realize now that if there had been a simpler, less painful way for me to learn that my God—not my fiancé—was to be the number-one Man in my life, events would have unfolded differently.

So what was all the talk about "marriage is work"? Marriage was marvelous! I didn't know who all the other women in the world had married, but I had me a prince! That's why I was careful not to rock the boat, not to say or be anything that might jeopardize this miracle on earth. I was determined that nothing would separate us—not careers, or children, or "growing apart," or "irreconcilable differences." I wanted it to be a perfect marriage, but I didn't understand that perfection grows from the seeds of humanness, watered by divine grace. How could I possibly see the turbulent waterfall we were headed for when we were floating in a pristine pool of calm, clear, deeply peaceful waters? I had read that God's strength was made perfect in our weakness, but I had to live it to learn it.

Fast forward to the mid-1990s. I was oblivious to politics, the economy, world events, whatever. I only knew that I had forgotten what it meant to be a vibrant, versatile participant in a meaningful life. Everything that could possibly go wrong in our marriage gradually did. I noticed that I was performing my duties as wife, mother, homemaker, RN, and church deaconess with robotic obligation, completely devoid of joy or purpose. God seemed to be on an extended vacation, and I sure hoped He was having fun, because I definitely wasn't. In fact, if this was to be my life, I was no longer interested. How had my failing marriage come to represent my self-esteem, my accomplishments, my entire world? And when exactly had my emotional whirlwind of anger, resentment, irritability, and depression settled into a static state of numb indifference? It would take a miracle for my heart to live and breathe and thrive again. And that is exactly what God had in mind.

By the time my husband invited me to hear him play with a jazz band one evening, I didn't care enough anymore to have any man in my life, divine or otherwise. God, however, being sweet and faithful, looked beyond my faults to see my need. Even as I refused my husband's invitation and ignored the flicker of hope that faded from his eyes as I claimed to be without a babysitter, angels must have been hastily dispatched to do the Master's bidding. While I returned to my magazine, he finished loading up his instruments and paused at the door.

"If we can't support each other anymore," he said, "there's no reason to stay together. If you really don't want to go tonight, it's okay. But I already packed a bag and I won't be back after the concert."

He couldn't possibly feel the chill that descended on my heart and stilled the flow of blood in my veins. He could only see my brief upward glance, and the casual shrug of my shoulders. He only heard a flippant "Okay, whatever," before turning slowly and walking out.

I remember the crushing silence that followed the closing of the door. Finally, it could all be over. Why wasn't I relieved? What was that strange stirring in my heart that in some mystical way made me struggle to catch my breath and order my thoughts? Fear? Indecision? Desperation? Or was it simply the unmistakable fluttering of angels on assignment? I tried to refocus on my ridiculous magazine, but the words blurred into a haze of gray and it fell from my hands.

A silent prayer exploded in my mind. "God, you said you'd handle this and you didn't! I talked to you over and over again about this and trusted you to work it out, but it's falling apart. What about my children? My family? I did my part and you didn't do yours!"

My body slid off the couch and collapsed face down on the carpet, knees drawn up under my belly, arms outstretched in abject surrender.

"God, please. . . ." For the first time in my life I felt truly connected to the Savior as my lifeline. "God, please. . . ." My humanness was swallowed up in His divinity; His peace was mine.

An intense restlessness suddenly dispelled my calm and compelled me to my feet, willing me to the phone. Three attempts. Three failures. No babysitter. A jumble of disconnected thoughts: *Maybe my marriage wasn't meant to work. Why can't I just read my magazine? I don't want him to leave!! But it's too hard; I already tried. It's too soon to give up; it could work. Swallow your pride. You know you still love him, and you saw his eyes; he loves you back. But I'm so tired.*

The shrill ringing of the phone vaporized my thoughts.

"Hello?"

It was a very close family friend, "Is there something you'd like to do tonight? I can babysit for you if you want."

"What??" I was incredulous. How was this possible? (Obviously my faith was quite a bit smaller than a mustard seed.) "I thought you were at a program tonight," I whispered.

"Well, for some reason I think it's more important that I babysit for you. Do you want me to come?"

A surge of excitement. Crazy hope. "Yes!"

He didn't see me slip into an empty seat in an unlit corner, but his eyes periodically swept the room, purposeful, persistent—things I'd always loved about him. When he found me his face lit up like the sun. He grabbed the mike and announced to 150 people that "a very special person has just arrived and I'd like to ask my beautiful wife to please stand."

Even as my tears threaten to spill over as I recall that moment, I would be lying if I said it was easy after that. We returned to the brink of collapse more than once. But that night we both knew that God had engineered a miracle to keep us together. And today, two weeks from our twentieth anniversary, I am still amazed at the shift in my chest when I see him across a crowded room, at the ache in my gut when I miss him and hear his voice on the telephone across the miles, at the way I bask contentedly in the warmth of his eyes and the sweetness of his kiss. And I never cease to wonder that my own personal God loves me enough to send angels on a mission to transform hurt into healing, and to grant me a miracle for my heart.

Love Tip: Quiet time is essential for hearing the voice of wisdom within. It must be provided for in relationships. God's whisper is heard when we stop the constant noise. Honor the need for silence—both yours and your partner's—as a means to reconnect, rejuvenate, and access your inner resources of intuition, wisdom, strength, and calm.

The Irony of the Cosmic Riddle

I have found the paradox that if I love until it hurts, then there is no hurt, but only more love.

MOTHER TERESA

There is a great story about a man whose hometown was flooded. The man climbed up on the roof to escape the rising waters and prayed to God to save him. Before long a fire truck came and the firemen offered the man safe passage. He replied, "No thank you, God is going to save me." The fire truck left, the waters rose higher, and the man again prayed to God to save him. Before long a boat came along and the boatman offered the man safe passage. The man said, "No thank you, God is going to save me." The boat departed and the water rose further until it nearly reached the man on the roof. Again, he prayed to God to save him. Before long a helicopter came and dropped a ladder. The man waved it away and yelled, "No thank you, God is going to save me." The helicopter left, the waters rose, and the man drowned. When he found himself face to face with his maker he asked, "God, I am a good man and I prayed and prayed for you to save me. Why did you let me die?" God sighed and said, "I sent you a truck, a boat, and a helicopter. What more did you want?"

I imagine that God must feel exasperated with us all the time. We have everything we need to be happy and to experience loving, fulfilling lives, and yet we somehow seem to keep missing the boat, so to speak.

Here are some of life's great ironies that, once grasped, can help us master the spiritual journey of marriage:

The only love we get to keep is the love we give away.

When you give up on love it is with the thought that doing so will allow you to avoid pain. But giving up on love causes pain. That is like committing suicide to avoid death.

The more we overcome, the more we are able to handle.

In order to be happy, we have to choose to be happy.

To stop being bored, we have to stop being boring.

In order to raise our self-esteem, we have to do the very things that having more self-esteem would permit us to do.

We can experience loneliness even when we are not alone. It is not a matter of who we are with; it is a matter of how we are with them.

It is often not until we lose something that we know we want it.

Hiding under fear is something we want to protect.

Ego, in an effort to guide and protect us, is the very thing that blocks our path.

We seek outside of ourselves that which we need to see inside of ourselves.

A light in a well-lit room would not be seen, but in darkness would illuminate.

In order to see the point, we have to close our eyes—and look within.

In order to help others, we have to help ourselves.

In order to hear, we have to be silent.

A sense of humor is one the of the most important and wonderful ingredients of both our spiritual journey and our journey through relationships. It is part of the core of who we are. When we are living in alignment with who we really are, instead of getting caught up in our egos, we are able to laugh at life, laugh at ourselves, see the cosmic joke, and take things lightly instead of making every little thing so serious.

Love Tip: The secret to finding love is being loving. The secret to fixing the world's problems is to start by fixing your own.

Unconditional Love and Forgiveness

I once had the honor of sitting across a table from a holy man in India. In that moment, I knew that he knew everything about me, everything I'd ever done, said, or thought. As I sat there, he said nothing. He simply looked at me like he was watching the movie of my life. All I felt from him was unconditional love. He knew everything about me, yet still he accepted me and loved me as is. One might imagine that it was a beautiful experience, and indeed it was—on one hand. On the other hand, it may have been the most uncomfortable moment of my life. I had to sit with the same knowledge he had about me, and although he wasn't judging me, I was. I squirmed in the presence of God and unconditional love because I didn't believe I deserved it. I vowed silently that when I again come face to face with God and have to judge myself in the presence of unconditional love, I would deserve it. I am quite certain that "Judgment Day" is not the day when God judges us, as most of us have been mistakenly taught. Rather, it is the day when we face God's love and judge ourselves. The goal is to be able to sit in the presence of God's pure love and *not* judge ourselves but simply be free to receive, knowing that we deserve this love merely by virtue of living our lives authentically. The more we align ourselves every day with our authentic self, the better prepared we will be. The more we unconditionally love ourselves, the better prepared we will be. The more we pay attention to, appreciate, and allow ourselves to receive the love and blessings already bestowed upon us, the better prepared we will be. The more we treat our spouses and families with unconditional love and respect, the better prepared we will be.

Here is another cosmic irony: You need to live each day as if it is the day when you will sit in the waterfall of God's unconditional love, because, of course, it is . . . and you already are!

EXERCISE ～ *Now, what if you were to shower your spouse with unconditional love? Not love when he or she does what you want, not love withheld or controlled, but simply all the time, knowing all that you know and loving him or her anyway. How would this change your relationship? How would this change you?* ～

This is what we are here to master. All it requires is getting your ego out of the way. God bless you on your journey.

Bibliography

Berkowitz, Bob, and Roger Gittines. *What Men Won't Tell You but Women Need to Know.* New York: Avon Books, 1990.

Berkowitz, Bob. *His Secret Life: Male Sexual Fantasies.* New York: Simon and Schuster, 1997.

Britt, Jim, and Eve Eschner Hogan. *Rings of Truth.* Deerfield Beach, FL: Health Communications, Inc., 1999.

Canfield, Jack, Mark Victor Hansen, Lisa Nichols, and Tom Joyner. *Chicken Soup for the African American Soul.* Deerfield Beach, FL: Health Communications, Inc., 2004.

Canfield, Jack. *Self-Esteem in the Classroom Curriculum Guide.* Culver City, CA: Self-Esteem Seminars, 1988.

Canfield, Jack. *The Success Principles: How to Get from Where You Are to Where You Want to Be.* New York: HarperCollins, 2005.

Capacchione, Lucia. *The Power of Your Other Hand: A Course in Channeling the Inner Wisdom of the Right Brain.* Franklin Lakes, NJ: New Page Books, 2001.

Hogan, Eve Eschner. *Intellectual Foreplay: Questions for Lovers and Lovers-to-Be.* Alameda, CA: Hunter House Publishers, 2000.

Hogan, Eve Eschner. *Virtual Foreplay: Making Your Online Relationship a Real-Life Success.* Alameda, CA: Hunter House Publishers, 2001.

Hogan, Eve Eschner. *Way of the Winding Path: A Map for the Labyrinth of Life.* Ashland, OR: White Cloud Press, 2003.

Katie, Byron. *Loving What Is: Four Questions that Can Change Your Life.* New York: Three Rivers Press, 2002.

Louv, Richard. *Last Child in the Woods: Saving Our Children from Nature-Deficit Disorder.* New York: Algonquin Books, 2005.

Severe, Sal. *How to Behave So Your Children Will, Too!* New York: Penguin Books, 2003.

Waite, Linda, and Maggie Gallagher. *The Case for Marriage.* New York: Broadway Books, 2000.

online Resources

www.EveHogan.com
Author's website. Features articles, advice column, schedule of workshops, books.

www.Gottman.com
Website for the Gottman Institute, which describes its mission as "researching and restoring relationships." Drs. John and Julie Gottman offer seminars for couples, as well as books, audiocassettes, and DVDs. They also certify therapists in the Gottman Method.

http://marriage.rutgers.edu
Website for the National Marriage Project, sponsored by Rutgers University. Features links to publications with titles like "Ten Important Research Findings on Marriage and Choosing a Marriage Partner: Helpful Facts for Young Adults."

www.sexualhealth.com
Includes an advice column on sexuality and disability, by Mitchell Tepper, Ph.D.; and the article "Orgasms: Good for Body, Mind, and Soul," by Kathleen VanKirk, DHS.

Eve Hogan's advice columns and articles are also featured on the following websites:

www.Consciousloving.com
www.Dreammates.com
www.Free-dating-service.info
www.MauiWeekly.com
www.Pregnancy.org
www.Relationship-Talk.com
www.SingleMe.com

index

delity, 55–58; for relationship experiences, 26, 290
risk-taking, 207–208
rituals, spiritual, 315–316
romance, 234–250; after children arrive, 310–311; defined, 240–241; re-creating love, 243–247; romantic gestures, 240–242, 247–250; thoughts affecting intimacy, 238–240; ways of giving and receiving love, 236–238

S

sacred, sense of the, 315
sandwich theory (of self-esteem), 105
self-concept, 98–105
self-esteem, 1, 6, 61; blockages to, 107–108; and body image, 255, 256; defined, 114; false, 120; in families, 295–299; and gaps in self-image, 106–108; impact on relationships, 106–108; misconceptions about, 95–97; role of, 95–113; and the sandwich theory, 105; self-assessment for children, 299–300; self-assessment of, 114–126
self-image, 98–105
self-inquiry, 27, 150
self-observation: and communication, 223–224; and evaluation of motives, 42, 105; as key to change, 26, 148–150, 290–291; during sex, 278; and transcending ego, 159
self-talk, 103, 151–154
self, true: identifying, 97–98; and self-esteem, 137–145

sense of humor, 311, 328–329
separation, physical. *See* long-distance marriage
September 11th terrorist attack, 67–68
Serenity Prayer, 125
service, importance of, 147
sex, frequency of, 254–255
sexuality, 251–284; and body image, 256; and communication, 268–273; experimentation, 266–268; fantasy exchange, 281; and fitness level, 256; foreplay, 252–254; frequency after marriage, 252, 254–257; issues of respect, 264–265; oral sex, 281; reasons for sexual shutdown, 255–256; setting sex dates, 277; sexual aversion, 262–264; tips for improving sex life for men, 280–283; tips for improving sex life for women, 275–280; use of sex toys, 282; virtual fantasies, 281
soul essence, 25–26, 95, 102
spirituality: and defining values, 72; marriage as spiritual journey, 27–28, 291–292, 313–330; and self-assessment, 118
spouse: and accepting differences, 52; and changes in core values, 168–169; complaining about, 78; emotional availability of, 214–215; guidelines for receiving emotions from, 215–219; marriage assessment for, 134–135; self-esteem assessment for, 128–129; telling the painful truth, 209–213; and the true self, 141–142
Springer, Jerry, 66

subpersonalities, 240
substance abuse, 211
success, defining, 172–173
Success Principles, The (Canfield), 6

T

Tepper, Mitchell, 278
therapy, 42
thoughts: impact on intimacy,
　238–240; as response to event,
　59–61
touch, power of, 260–261, 276, 277
trust, 206, 217
truth, microscopic, 85–86
truth, real: receiving from partner,
　218; sharing, 199–200, 202–204

U

unfaithfulness: and the EROS
　equation, 55–58; suspicions of,
　186–188
USA Today, 67–68

V

values: complementary, 69; defin-
　ing, 66–72; family, 294; as
　guideposts to behavior, 24–25,

288–289; prioritizing, 67;
　putting into practice, 72
VanKirk, Kathleen, 261
violence, and fair fighting, 84
vision, creating, 79
vision statement, 79
visualization, 181–183
vows, marriage, 86–90

W

wait time, 224
Waite, Linda, 89
wants, 196
war, and long-distance marriage,
　227–232
Way of the Winding Path (Hogan),
　174
*What Men Won't Tell You but
　Women Need to Know*
　(Berkowitz), 280
With Aloha (advice column), 16
words, empowering, 151–154

Y

yelling during disagreements, 84

Eve Eschner Hogan is available for keynote presentations, workshops, private coaching, weddings, and personalized retreats on Maui.

For more information see:
www.EveHogan.com

or contact:
Wings to Wisdom, LLC
PO Box 943
Puunene HI 96784
Eve@HeartPath.com
(808) 573-6521

WAY OF THE WINDING PATH: A MAP FOR THE SPIRITUAL JOURNEY OF LIFE

The Way of the Winding Path provides the set of instructions, map, and tool kit needed to navigate the labyrinth of life. Life is a sacred journey, which we must see, rather than seek. The light for illuminating the path already burns within you. Reading this book will make your inner light glow more brightly so that you may more easily see your way. The lessons contained within provide the simple steps for living a spiritual, joyful, and blessed life filled with love, gratitude, and wisdom.

$14.95, White Cloud Press

RINGS OF TRUTH

by Jim Britt with Eve Eschner Hogan

Rings of Truth is a novel in the genre of visionary fiction in which an ethereal woman, Alea, guides both the main character and the readers to discover the keys for transcending their egos and to gaining a deep sense of resourcefulness in their lives. Universal wisdom and life-changing truths are shared throughout this fun-to-read novel. *Rings of Truth* will both transform and entertain you.

$12.95, Health Communications Inc.

CHICKEN SOUP FOR THE AFRICAN AMERICAN SOUL, 2004 CHICKEN SOUP FOR THE AFRICAN AMERICAN WOMAN'S SOUL, 2006

by Jack Canfield, Mark Victor Hansen, Lisa Nichols, and Tom Joyner
Senior Editor, Eve Eschner Hogan

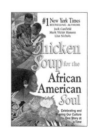

Both books offer an inspiring collection of stories about the African American experience. If you are an African American, the stories will honor your spirit and uplift you in a celebration of your culture. If you are not, the stories will educate you, inspire you, and fill you with admiration and compassion for a culture that emanates strength and endurance, while maintaining a rich spiritual life and deep love of family.

$12.95, Health Communications Inc.

More Hunter House Books

INTELLECTUAL FOREPLAY: Questions for Lovers and Lovers-to-Be

by Eve Eschner Hogan with Steven Hogan

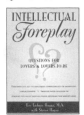

Do you want to find out whether a romantic partner is "the one"? Practice intellectual foreplay! This book of open-ended questions is arranged in thirty-four chapters ranging from Romance and Sex to Values and Beliefs, from Sports and Hobbies to Money, Home, and Children. It can help you get to know a partner—and yourself—in a deep, practical way, and improve your chances of finding the right partner while avoiding the wrong one.

Unlike other "question books," which serve as getting-acquainted exercises or parlor games, *Intellectual Foreplay* offers guidelines for working with a partner's responses and jointly creating a decision-making process, making it an exciting tool for discovery and growth.

288 pages ... Paperback $15.95

VIRTUAL FOREPLAY: Making Your Online Relationship a Real-Life Success

by Eve Eschner Hogan

The world of online dating can be intimidating. What do you want? What should you say about yourself? How do you transition from the virtual world to real meetings? These are just a few of the questions that are addressed in *Virtual Foreplay*. This book will help you define your values and goals, improve your online presentation skills, and build confidence and self-esteem.

Also included are real-life tales of cyber-romances that did and didn't work, important dos and don'ts, and other practical advice on topics like

- choosing and using online dating services
- how to handle online rejection
- where and when to meet

240 pages ... Paperback $13.95

LOVING YOUR PARTNER WITHOUT LOSING YOUR SELF

by Martha Beveridge, MSSW

The crucial role that boundaries—or "personal space"—play in healthy, lasting relationships is not always understood. This book fills an important need by explaining the importance of maintaining a sense of self that is distinct from your partner. Beveridge, an experienced therapist, explains why loving relationships deteriorate if couples don't respect boundaries. Her book gives couples practical, creative, and unique strategies for transforming struggles into explorations and hostility into deeper intimacy. These include

- getting past the ABCs (Attacking, Blaming, Criticizing)
- recognizing the symptoms of poor boundaries (clinging, jealousy, running away)
- dealing with the smokescreen issues: time, money, sex
- Safe Dialogue: a specific, positive way to communicate during disagreements

256 pages ... Paperback $14.95

To order, or for a FREE catalog of books, please see last page.
All prices subject to change.

More Hunter House Books

THE PLEASURE PRESCRIPTION:
To Love, to Work, to Play—Life in the Balance

by Paul Pearsall, Ph.D.

This *New York Times* bestseller is a prescription for stressed-out lives. Dr. Pearsall is an expert on the relationship between pleasure, stress, and the immune system. According to him, it isn't too much stress but too little joy that is killing people, and he maintains that contentment, wellness, and long life can be found by devoting time to family, helping others, and slowing down.

Pearsall's unique vision also draws on traditional Polynesian culture, which offers an alternative to Western and Eastern lifestyles. He offers inspiration for readers who want to discover a new enjoyment of life and to connect deeply with others.

288 pages ... Paperback $13.95

PARTNERS IN PLEASURE:
Sharing Success, Creating Joy, Fulfilling Dreams—Together

by Paul Pearsall, Ph.D.

Dr. Pearsall introduces the concept of *"naupaka* love"—profound companionship, surrendering to a relationship and embracing it as a journey of discovery and mutual pleasure. A unique combination of oral wisdom and psychological research, *Partners in Pleasure* is nothing less than a re-visioning of marriage. Woven throughout are life and relationship lessons from Hawaiian *kupuna* (elders) and *kahuna* (healers or priests).

Pearsall returns couples to the task of becoming the right partners for each other, a lifelong adventure that strengthens and sustains each partner even as it brings harmony and peace to those around them.

288 pages ... Paperback $14.95

PEACE IN EVERYDAY RELATIONSHIPS:
Resolving Conflicts in Your Personal and Work Life

by Sheila Alson and Gayle Burnett, Ph.D.

Resolving conflicts peacefully is a choice—and it requires commitment, insight, and skills. This practical guide outlines how we can successfully negotiate both the big conflicts and the smaller disagreements that we encounter in our daily lives—with neither side feeling like a loser.

The authors draw on psychology and teambuilding practices, martial arts, and spirituality to provide maps of pathways to peace. Using exercises and real-life examples they cover

- strategies for dealing with difficult people
- communication techniques that unite
- cultural differences in communication styles

Whether the conflict is divorce, incompatibility between housemates, adolescent rebellion, workplace squabbles, or a disagreeable boss, this book offers practical, workable, and peaceful solutions.

240 pages ... 1 illus. ... 10 tables ... Paperback $14.95